Lean And Green Cookbook For Beginners

1200-Days Fueling Hacks & Lean and Green Recipes to Burn Fat, Lose Weight, and Achieve a Healthy Lifestyle With 5&1 and 4&2&1 Meal Plan

By
Daisy Kisner

TABLE OF CONTENTS

Introduction

The Lean and Green diet is a great diet to try. It can help you lose weight and eat healthy foods in the process. The diet practically makes the body burn fats much faster than carbohydrates.

If you did not change your way of living altogether and added good fats to your diet, it could take carbohydrates. In that case, you might be waiting for at least a year before you will start losing weight with this diet. For you, it is still worth doing this diet. Even if it is yearlong, you will see a great improvement in your overall health. Therefore, when you ingest fats, instead of your body storing them as fat, they are more likely to be converted into a source of energy.

As fat reserves continue to be burned, the body will tend not to gain weight. This is excellent news because fat reserves are not very easy to get rid of completely.

If you ask a nutritionist about this diet, they will recommend it without a doubt. So, if you feel like cleansing your body and starting a diet that will keep you healthy, well-fed, and slender, this diet should be your primary choice.

Engaging into lean and green diet is a good idea to improve not only our health, but also our environment. One should eat less meat products and consume more of fresh fruits and vegetables to lower the risk for heart disease and cancer. The latter are mostly linked with meat consumption because of the nitrates located in processed meats. Fruits and vegetables are very low-calorie foods, but they are high in fiber content and rich in vitamins.

The vegetables and fruits that deserve to be consumed are the ones that are grown organically. It is very important to avoid processed foods since they contain a high percentage of fat. Green and lean diet is also linked with the environment preservation. By cutting down meat consumption by at least 50%, we save a lot from greenhouse gas emissions. Considering that meat production requires more energy, it causes more carbon dioxide emissions compared to vegetable production. Another advantage of green and lean diet is improved health care system and lower health problems cost.

1200~Day Fueling Hacks Recipes

1. Peanut Butter Energy Bites

Servings: 1
Prep time: 5 minutes
Cooking Time: 0 minutes

Ingredients

- 1 tablespoon of water
- 1 bar of Optavia essential creamy double peanut butter crisp bar
- 2 tablespoon of powdered peanut butter

Preparation

- Form a smooth paste in a small bowl by mixing the water and powdered peanut butter.
- Microwave the creamy double peanut butter for 15 seconds or until it's soft.
- Mix the peanut butter with warm pieces of the bar to create a dough.
- Form 4 bite-sized balls, using a cookie scoop or your finger. Afterwards, refrigerate until it's ready to eat.

2. Grilled Chicken with Eggplant Parmesan

Servings: 4
Prep time: 15 minutes
Cooking Time: 30mins

Ingredients

- ¼ cup of chopped fresh basil
- ¼ teaspoon of salt and pepper (or less)
- 2 cloves of minced garlic
- 1 ½ lbs. Of pre-grilled chicken breast slices
- 2 trimmed and chopped scallions
- Cooking spray
- 6 tablespoon of almond flour
- 1, 14.5-oz can diced tomatoes
- 8 teaspoon of large flake nutritional yeast
- 1 lb. Of eggplant cut into 8 rounds of ½ inch think

Preparation

- Preheat the oven to 400 degrees Fahrenheit.
- In a medium bowl, mix the nutritional yeast, pepper, salt, and almond flour.
- After rinsing the eggplant slices, coat all sides using the almond flour mixture. Put the eggplant slices on a lightly greased baking sheet and bake for 20mins, and flip when you are halfway through.
- In a saucepan, mix the scallions, garlic and tomatoes, and allow it simmer for 15-20mins.
- After eggplant is done, serve with grilled chicken and tomato sauce.

3. Noodles Eggplant & Zucchini Lasagna

Servings: 4

Prep time: 20 minutes

Cooking Time: 45-60 mins

Ingredients

- Cooking spray

- 2 medium zucchini with ends removed

- 1 egg

- 1 ½ cups of Italian tomato sauce

- ½ pound of 94% lean ground turkey

- 1 large eggplant with ends removed (use only the widest section)

- 1 1/3 cups of shredded reduced fat mozzarella cheese

- 1 ½ cups of part skim ricotta

- 1/3 cup of grated parmesan cheese

Preparation

- Preheat the oven to 375 degrees Fahrenheit.

- Slice zucchini into ¼ inch thick slices (vertically) using a knife or mandolin slicer. Slice the eggplant's broadest section into ¼ inch thick rounds (horizontally).

- Place the vegetable slices on the baking sheet and add salt. Allow it to rest for 15mins.

- Using a medium-sized skillet, brown meat. Turn off the heat, add the tomato sauce, and stir to mix. Put it aside.

- Mix one cup of mozzarella, egg, ricotta, and egg in a medium-sized mixing bowl.

- Use paper towels to blot the vegetable slice to eliminate excess salt and moisture as you can.

- To gather lasagna: On the bottom of the lightly greased square glass baking dish, spread 1/3 of the tomato meat mixture. Top the mixture with a layer of zucchini slice with a layer of eggplant rounds. Again, top with 1 ½ of the ricotta mixture. Duplicate the layers twice, and alternate the zucchini slice's direction, ending on the last layer of the exposed eggplant rounds (don't top with ricotta as you should be done with the mixture by now). Sprinkle the rest of the mozzarella on top and bake for 45mins.

- Allow it rest for 15mins (at least) before serving.

4. Chicken Enchilada Rollups

Servings: 4

Prep time: 15 minutes

Cooking Time: 20-35mins

Ingredients

- 3 cups of grated cauliflower

- 1 teaspoon of cumin

- 1, 4 ½ oz. Cubed avocado

- ¼ cup of chopped cilantro (optional)

- 1 teaspoon of chili powder

- 1 teaspoon of garlic powder

- 1, 4-oz can mild green chilies

- 4, 6-oz. Raw boneless skinless butterflied chicken breast

- 1, 10-oz can of mild red enchilada sauce

- 1 cup of reduced fat shredded divided Mexican cheese blend

- ½ cup of diced tomatoes

- 1 teaspoon of dried oregano

Preparation

- Preheat the oven to 375 degrees Fahrenheit.

- Mix the garlic powder, chili powder, and cumin in a small bowl and rub the mixture on each side of every chicken piece.

- Grease a baking dish lightly and pour a thin layer of the enchilada sauce on the baking dish bottom.

- Cut the side of the chicken up on a work surface, at the center of each piece, top with 1 tablespoon of chopped tomatoes, 2 teaspoons of chilies, and 2 tablespoons of cheese. In the baking dish, roll them up and set them side down. Top with the rest of the cheese, chilies, tomatoes, and sauce.

- Cover the lid with foil and bake for 20mins. Detach the foil and bake for 10-15mins more, or till the chicken is done.

- Using 1 tablespoon of water, microwave the grated cauliflower for 6-8mins or till it's very tender.

- Put each chicken roll up on a cauliflower rice bed and top with fresh cilantro and avocado.

5. Caprese Chicken

Servings: 4
Cooking Time: 15-20 mins
Ingredients

- 2 cups of reduced fat shredded mozzarella

- 3 tablespoon of balsamic vinegar

- 2 teaspoon of olive oil

- 4, 4-oz of boneless skinless butterflied and pounded (very thin) chicken breasts (1/8 – ¼ inch thick)

- ½ cup of fresh basil leaves, torn into little pieces

- 2 minced garlic cloves

- 2 halved cups of grape tomatoes

- 2 teaspoon of olive oil

Preparation

- Over medium-high heat, warm olive oil in a large skillet, add garlic, and stir for a minute. Put pepper, tomatoes, balsamic vinegar, and salt, then replace the lid. Cook for 8-10mins or till tomatoes soften.

- Expel from heat and add in fresh basil.

- Over medium-high heat again, Sauté or grill the chicken breasts on each side for a few minutes till it thoroughly cooks. Move it to a baking sheet and top with mozzarella cheese and the tomato mixture like a pizza.

- Broil for 2-5 minutes or till the whole cheese melts.

Note: Serve with either asparagus or broccoli (1 cup of either) for a complete Lean and Green meal.

6. Personal Portobello Mushrooms

Servings: 1
Cooking Time: 10-15mins
Ingredients

- 2 tablespoons of shredded basil (optional)

- Cooking spray

- ¼ cup of no sugar added Italian tomato sauce (e.g. Rao's homemade)

- 2, 2-oz Portobello mushroom caps with gills scraped out and stems removed

- 4 Oz reduced fat shredded mozzarella cheese

Preparation

- Preheat the broiler.

- On a lightly greased baking sheet which has been lined with foil, place the mushroom caps. Apply the cooking spray on the tops and broil for 3-4mins on each side till tender.

- Spread the tomato sauce equally on each cap and top with basil and cheese. Broil it again for 2-3mins till cheese melts.

7. Zucchini Spinach Manicotti

Servings: 4

Cooking time: 25-30 mins

Ingredients

- 1 cup of low sugar tomato sauce
- 2 large zucchini
- 1 egg
- 1/8 teaspoon of salt
- 1 ½ cups of divided reduced fat, shredded mozzarella
- Pinch nutmeg
- ¼ cup of grated parmesan
- 1 cup of thawed and patted dry frozen spinach
- 1 ½ cups of part skim ricotta

Preparation

- Preheat the oven to 375 degrees Fahrenheit.
- Slice the zucchini lengthwise to 1/8-inch-thick slices using a mandolin slicer and set it aside.
- Mix the egg, ½ cup of mozzarella, nutmeg, ricotta, spinach, parmesan, and salt in a medium-sized bowl.
- Place three zucchini slices parallel to each other in a way that they slightly overlap. On one end of the zucchini slices, place a large spoonful of the ricotta mixture and roll it up. Put all the stuffed zucchini beside each other in a lightly greased 9x9 inch baking dish.
- Apply the tomato sauce on top of the zucchini and sprinkle with cheese. Then bake for 25mins.

8. Zucchini Pizza Casserole

Servings: 4

Cooking time: 45-50mins

Ingredients

- 1 chopped small green bell pepper
- 3 ½ cups of shredded unpeeled zucchini (approximately 2 zucchinis)
- 2 eggs
- ¼ Teaspoon of salt
- 4 oz. Divided reduced fat shredded mozzarella cheese
- ½ Lb. 90-94% of lean ground beef
- 1 14.5oz. Can of petite deiced italian tomatoes
- Cooking spray
- ¼ Cup of grated parmesan cheese
- ¼ Cup of chopped onion
- 4 oz. Of divided reduced fat of shredded cheddar cheese

Preparation

- Preheat the oven to 400 degree Fahrenheit
- Sprinkle the zucchini with salt and put it in a strainer. Allow it stay for 10mins, then squeeze to release moisture
- Mix the zucchini with parmesan, cheddar cheese, half of the mozzarella and eggs.
- Press the mixture in a lightly greased baking dish and bake it for 20mins while leaving it uncovered.
- In a medium skillet, cook the onion and beef until it's done. Then clear out any liquid and mix in the tomatoes.
- Sprinkle the zucchini with the remains of the mozzarella cheese and cheddar and pour the beef mix on top. Top using green pepper.
- Bake for 20mins more or till heated through

9. Pumpkin Spiced Latte

Servings: 1

Prep time: 5 minutes

Cooking Time: 1 minute

Ingredients

- 1 sachet of spiced gingerbread
- 2 tablespoons of pumpkin puree
- ½ Cup of unsweetened cashew
- ½ Cup of strong brewed coffee

Preparation

- Place the cashew milk and pumpkin puree in a microwave safe mug and heat for 1 minute.
- Withdraw from the microwave and stir in gingerbread and coffee immediately until smooth.
- Serve.

Nutritional information:

Protein: 11.4g ; Carbohydrates: 17g ; Sugar: 6g ; Sat fat: 20g ; Fat: 3.5g ; Fiber: 5g ; Calories: 134

10. Hot Chocolate

Servings: 1

Prep time: 2 minutes

Cooking Time: 2 minutes

Ingredients

- 1 tablespoon of whipped cream
- 6 ounces of unsweetened almond milk
- 1 sachet of velvety hot chocolate
- Pinch of cayenne pepper
- ½ Teaspoon of ground cinnamon

Preparation

- Beat all the Ingredients in a serving mug except the whipped cream until they blend well.
- Set the microwave to the highest setting and heat for about 2mins
- Top with the whipped cream.
- Serve.

Nutritional information:

Protein: 14.1g; Carbohydrate: 15.9g; Fat: 8.1g; Sat fat: 3.1g; Sugar: 9.1g; Fiber: 5.4g; Calories: 185

11. Eggnog

Servings: 1

Prep time: 5mins

Ingredients

- ¼ Teaspoon of rum extract
- 1 sachet of vanilla shake
- 1 egg (white and yolk separated)
- Pinch of ground nutmeg
- 8 ounces of unsweetened almond milk

Preparation

- Blend the almond milk, vanilla shake sachet, and egg yolk. Blend until smooth.
- Beat the egg white on medium speed in a stand mixer bowl until stiff peak forms.
- Put the egg whites in a serving glass and top with the shake (mixture).
- Sprinkle with nutmeg and stir.
- Serve.

Nutritional information

Protein: 21.5g; Carbohydrates: 15.6g; Fat: 8.7g; Sat fat: 1.7g; Sugar: 7.4g; Fiber: 5g; Calories: 103

12. Chocolate Frappe

Servings: 1

Prep time: 5mins

Ingredients

- ½ Cup of ice
- 4 ounces of unsweetened almond milk
- 1 sachet of frosty mint chocolate soft serve treat
- 1 tablespoon of whipped topping
- ¼ Teaspoon of peppermint extract
- 1 ½ tablespoon of divided sugar free chocolate syrup
- 4 ounces of strong brewed coffee

Preparation

- Blend the coffee, ice, one tablespoon of chocolate syrup, peppermint extract, and chocolate sachet until smooth.
- Turn the mixture over in a glass and top it with the whipping topping.
- Drizzle the chocolate syrup that remains on it and serve.

Nutritional information

Protein: 11.7g; Carbohydrate: 16.4g; Fat: 4.8g; Sat fat: 0.6g; Sugar: 7.4g; Fiber: 4.9g; Calories: 147

13. Shamrock Shake

Servings: 1

Prep time: 5mins

Ingredients

- 1 cup of ice cubes

- 6 ounces of unsweetened almond milk

- 1 packet of vanilla shake

- 1-2 drops of green food coloring

- ¼ Teaspoon of peppermint extract

Preparation

- Place all the Ingredients in a small blender and blend till smooth.

- Pour the shake over in a serving glass and enjoy.

Nutritional information:

Protein: 14.7g; Carbohydrate: 14.5g; Fat: 2.9g; Sat fat: 0.2g; Sugar: 9.1g; Fiber: 3.7g; Calories: 140

14. Pumpkin Frappe

Servings: 1

Prep time: 5mins

Ingredients

- 1 tablespoon of whipped topping

- 4 ounces of strong brewed coffee

- 1 sachet of spiced gingerbread

- 1/8 teaspoon of pumpkin pie spice

- 4 ounces of unsweetened almond milk

- ½ Cup of ice

Preparation

- Blend the pumpkin pie spice, coffee, spiced gingerbread sachet, ice, and almond milk until smooth.

- Pour the mixture in a glass and top it with the whipped topping.

- Serve.

Nutritional information:

Protein: 11.7g; Carbohydrate: 15.4g; Fat: 4.8g; Sat fat: 0.6g; Sugar: 5g; Fiber: 4.5g; Calories: 138

15. Peppermint Mocha

Servings: 1

Preparation Time: 5mins

Ingredients

- ¼ Cup of warm unsweetened almond milk
- 1 tablespoon of whipped topping
- 1 sachet of velvety hot chocolate
- 6 ounces of freshly brewed coffee
- Pinch of ground cinnamon
- ¼ Teaspoon of peppermint extract

Preparation

- Put the peppermint extract, hot chocolate sachet, almond milk, and coffee in a serving mug and stir till well blended
- Use the whipped topping to top the hot chocolate and sprinkle it with cinnamonn. Serve.

Nutritional information:

Protein: 14.6g; Carbohydrate: 16.2g; Fat: 2.1g; Sat fat: 0.5g; Sugar: 10g; Fiber: 4.4g; Calories: 133

16. Coconut Smoothie

Servings: 1

Preparation Time: 5mins

Ingredients

- ¼ Teaspoon of rum extract
- 6 ounces of diet ginger ale
- 2 tablespoons of shredded unsweetened coconut
- ½ Cup of ice
- 6 ounces of unsweetened almond milk

Preparation

- Blend all Ingredients in a small blender until smooth.
- Pour smoothie over in a serving glass. Serve

Nutritional information:

Protein: 1g; Carbohydrate: 2.9g; Fat: 5.7g; Sat fat: 3.2g; Sugar: 0.6g; Fiber: 1.6g; Calories: 65

17. Berry Mojito

Servings: 2

Prep time: 10mins

Ingredients

- 16 ounces of seltzer water

- 2 tablespoons of fresh lime juice

- 1 packet of mixed berry flavor infuser

- 6 fresh mint leaves

- Ice cubes as required

Preparation

- Divide the mint leaves and lime juice in 2 cocktail glasses

- Gently muddle the mint leaves using the end of a spoon

- Add equal amounts of seltzer water and berry infuser to each glass and stir to mix.

- Add ice cubes and serve.

Nutritional information

Protein: 0.1g; Carbohydrate: 2.4g; Fat: 0g; Sat fat: 0g; Fiber: 1.2g; Sugar: 0g; Calories: 8

18. Buffalo Cauliflower Wings

Cooking Time: 25 minutes

Prep Time: 10 minutes

Servings: 2

Ingredients

- ½ Cup of water

- Cooking spray

- 1 teaspoon dry ranch dressing mix

- ¼ cup of low-fat plain Greek yogurt

- ¼ cup of hot Buffalo sauce

- 2 sachets of crumbled Buttermilk cheddar herb biscuit

- ½ Melted tablespoon butter

- 3 cups of cauliflower florets

Preparation

- Grease a lined baking sheet lightly and preheat oven to 400 degrees Fahrenheit

- Mix the water and biscuits in a bowl. Include the cauliflower and toss until florets are evenly coated.

- Take the baking sheet and put the coated florets on it. Bake for 20 minutes.

- Mix the butter and hot buffalo sauce in a medium bowl. Include the cauliflower and shake the sauce well. Put the mix on the baking sheet again. Bake for 5 minutes more.

- Join the ranch dressing mix and yogurt in another bowl for dipping.

Nutritional information

Protein: 2g; Carbohydrate: 13g; Fat: 5g;; Sat fat: 6g; Fiber: 1g; Sugar: 2g; Calories: 116g

19. Red Velvet Cream Pies

Servings: 4

Cooking Time: 15 minutes

Prep Time: 10 minutes

Ingredients

- ½ Cup of low fat cream cheese
- 1 teaspoon of apple cider vinegar
- ½ Cup of unsweetened almond milk
- ½ Tablespoon of unsweetened cocoa powder
- 2 sachets of essential golden chip pancakes mix
- 1 – 2 packets of zero calories sugar substitute
- ½ Teaspoon of baking powder
- 6 tablespoon of liquid egg substitute
- Cooking spray

Preparation

- Set oven to 350 degrees Fahrenheit and preheat.
- In a bowl, combine the baking powder, chocolate chip cookies mix, pancake mix, and cocoa powder.
- Bring in the apple cider vinegar, eggs and milk and mix till there is batter-like consistency.
- Evenly divide the batter gotten among 8 muffins tins. Then, bake for 15 – 20 minutes
- Combine the sugar substitute and cream cheese and mix till they blend well.
- When the pies are cooled, slice them horizontally in half. Apply the cream filling on each half and join them back together.
- Serve

Nutritional information

Protein: 4.4g; Carbohydrate: 82gfat: 14.5g; Calories: 472

20. Mashed Potato And Grilled Cheese Waffles

Servings: 2

Cooking Time: 10 minutes prep Time: 5 minutes

Ingredients

- 1 cup of low fat cheese (mozzarella, cheddar)
- 2 sachets of essential roasted garlic creamy smashed potatoes
- 1 cup of water

Preparation

- Thoroughly combine water and the smashed potatoes mix in a microwave safe, medium bowl. Use the high settings on the microwave and set the time for 30 seconds. Stir well.
- Lightly grease a waffle iron and pour the mix above on it. Allow the mix cook in the waffle iron for 10 minutes.
- On ½ of the waffles, sprinkle cheese and fold the rest. Close waffle iron.
- Let the waffles cook for an additional 2 – 3 minutes till it is either done or cheese melted.

Nutritional information

Protein: 4g; Carbohydrate: 24g; Fat: 5g; Calories: 150

21. Pecan And Sweet Potato Muffins

Servings:4

Cooking Tme: 20 minutes

Prep time 10 minutes

Ingredients

- 1 1/3 cups of chopped pecans
- ½ Teaspoon of baking powder
- ½ Teaspoon pumpkin pie spice
- 6 tablespoons of liquid egg substitute
- 1 cup of cold water
- 2 sachets of select honey sweet potatoes
- 2 sachets of essential spiced gingerbread
- ¼ Cups of unsweetened vanilla almond milk
- ½ Teaspoon of vanilla extract
- Cooking spray

Preparation

- Set the oven to 350 degrees Fahrenheit and preheat
- Follow the Directions accordingly to prepare the potatoes. Allow the mix cool a little.
- Except for the pecans, combine the remaining Ingredients and the cooked potatoes in a medium-sized bowl.
- On a lightly greased standard sized muffin pan, equally divide the mix into 8 slots.
- Top with the chopped pecans and bake for 20 minutes.

Nutritional information

Protein: 2.9g; Carbohydrate: 30.6g; Fat: 9.8g; Calories: 472

22. Greek Yogurt Sticks

Servings: 2

Cooking Time: 8 minutes

Prep Time: 2 minutes

Ingredients

- 1 sachet of crushed essential red berry crunchy o's cereal
- 1 – 2 packets of zero calorie sugar substitute
- 12 ounces of plain low fat Greek yogurt

Preparation

- Combine the sugar substitute and Greek yogurt in a medium-sized bowl.
- Arrange an 8 by 8 inch baking dish with non-stick foil. Lay the Greek yogurt/sugar mix out evenly on the foil.
- Top the mixture by sprinkling the crushed cereal
- Refrigerate for 4 – 5 hours or till the bar is hard. You can also refrigerate overnight.

Nutritional information

Protein: 6g; Carbohydrate: 0g; Fat: 9g; Calories: 100

23. Berry Mojito

Preparation Time: 10 minutes

Servings: 1

Ingredients:

- 1 cup water
- ½ sachet Essential 1 Mixed Berry Flavor Infuser
- 3 fresh mint leaves
- 1 tablespoon fresh lime juice
- Ice cubes, as required

Preparation:

- Take a cocktail glass and put the lime juice and mint leaves in the bottom.
- With the bottom end of a spoon, gently muddle the mint leaves.
- Add the Berry Infuser and water to the glass and stir to combine.
- Add ice cubes.
- Serve and enjoy!
- Serving Suggestion: Garnish it with a wedge of lime and some mint leaves.

Variation Tip: You can use frozen berries instead of fresh ones.

Nutritional information:

Calories: 26 | Fat: 0.3g | Sat Fat: 0.1g | Carbohydrates: 6.6g | Fiber: 2.5g | Sugar: 0.7g | Protein: 1.3g

24. Vanilla Shake

Preparation Time: 5 minutes

Servings: 1

Ingredients:

- 1 cup water
- ½ sachet Essential Creamy Vanilla Shake
- 1 cup unsweetened almond milk
- 1 teaspoon Essential Spiced Gingerbread
- 8 ice cubes

Preparation:

- Place all the Ingredients in a blender and pulse until smooth.
- Pour the drink into serving glasses and serve.
- Serving Suggestion: Garnish with whipped cream, a morello cherry, and a sprinkling of chocolate shavings.

Variation Tip: You can use vanilla ice cream to prepare a thicker milkshake.

Nutritional information:

Calories: 130 | Fat: 3.3g | Sat Fat: 0.2g | Carbohydrates: 15g | Fiber: 4.5g | Sugar: 6g | Protein: 13g

25. Creamy Avocado Banana Green Smoothie

Preparation Time: 5 minutes

Serving: 2

Ingredients:

- One frozen banana – ripe, peeled, sliced
- ¼ – ½ Ripe avocados
- One scoop plain or vanilla protein powder
- One handful greens – spinach, kale, rainbow chard
- ¾ – 1 cup unsweetened plain almond milk
- Optional:
- One tablespoon seed – hemp, flax, sesame, sunflower, chia seeds
- Half teaspoon maca and ashwagandha
- Half cup cucumber or berries – sliced, frozen or fresh

Preparation:

- First, add frozen banana, protein powder, unsweetened plain almond milk, greens, and avocado into the blender and blend at high speed.
- Add in seed, adaptogens, and cucumber or berries to the blender.
- Blend on high speed until smooth and creamy.
- Add more unsweetened plain almond milk to thin the smooth.
- If the smoothie is too thin, add more frozen banana or avocado.
- Add avocado for creaminess, add more banana for sweetness, and add greens for vibrant color.
- Add into serving glass. Add more protein powder for more sweetness.
- Leftover can put into the freezer for up to two weeks or one day into the refrigerator.

- Variation tip: You can add mango fruits in this smoothie.
- Serving Suggestion: Garnish with parsley leaves. Serve with stews.

Nutritional information:

Calories 146 | fat 6g | sodium 138mg | Carbohydrates 18.2g | fiber 5.3g | sugar 7.4g | protein 6.9g

26. Tiramisu Shake

Preparation Time: 5 minutes

Servings: 2

Ingredients:

- 1 cup water
- 1 cup ice, crushed
- 2 tablespoons sugar-free chocolate syrup
- 2 sachets Essential Frothy Cappuccino Boost

Preparation:

- Place all the Ingredients into a blender and pulse until smooth and creamy.
- Pour the shake into a serving glass.
- Serve and enjoy!
- Serving Suggestion: You can serve with chocolate syrup, ladyfinger cookies, and whipped cream on top.

Variation Tip: You can add some vanilla extract to the shake.

Nutritional information:

Calories: 106 | Fat: 3g | Sat Fat: 1g | Carbohydrates: 17g | Fiber: 0g | Sugar: 10g | Protein: 1g

27. Healthy Spinach Smoothie

Preparation Time: 10 minutes

Cooking time: 0 minutes

Servings: 5

Ingredients:

- One cup ice cube

- Two cups frozen pineapple chunks

- Half cup frozen banana slices

- One cup diced apple – Fuji, red, or green apple, cut into 1-inch pieces

- Two cups baby spinach

- Half cup nonfat plain Greek yogurt, or dairy-free

- One cup unsweetened almond milk

Preparation:

- Add almond milk, yogurt, baby spinach, diced apple, banana slices, pineapple, and ice cubes into the blender.

- Cover with lid and blend on medium speed for half-minute.

- Increase the speed of the blender and blend for fifteen to thirty seconds until smooth.

- Add more almond milk if required.

- Add more maple syrup or honey until the sweetness level is set.

- Substitute Greek yogurt for plant-based yogurt, for example, cashew or coconut, soy, and almond.

Variation tip: Substitute Greek yogurt for plant-based yogurt, for example, cashew or coconut, soy, and almond.

Serving Suggestion: Garnish with sliced spinach leaves. Serve with stews.

Nutritional information:

Calories 105 | Fat 1g | Sodium 85mg | Carbohydrates 23g | Fiber 3g | Sugar 19g | Protein 3g

28. Mint Cookies

Preparation Time: 10 minutes

Cooking time: 15 minutes

Servings: 4

Ingredients:

- 1 tablespoon liquid egg substitute

- 2 tablespoons unsweetened almond milk

- 2 essential chocolate mint cookie crisp bars

- 2 sachets Essential Decadent Double Chocolate Brownies

Preparation:

- Preheat the oven to 350°F. Line a cookie sheet with parchment paper.

- Place the cookie bars in a food processor and pulse until fully crushed.

- Transfer the crushed bars to a bowl with the other Ingredients and mix until well blended.

- Using a spoon, form 8 cookie dough balls from the mixture and place them onto the prepared cookie sheet. Press each ball slightly with your fingers.

- Bake for 13 to 15 minutes.

- Remove the cookie sheet from the oven and let it cool for 5 minutes on a wire rack.

- Turn out the cookies onto the wire rack to cool before serving.

Serving Suggestion: These cookies are perfect as they are!

Variation Tip: Add some mint extract for an extra punch of flavor.

Nutritional information:

Calories: 175 | Fat: 6.1g | Sat Fat: 2.5g | Carbohydrates: 20.7g | Fiber: 1.3g | Sugar: 14.1g | Protein: 9.8g

29. Mocha Cake

Preparation Time: 5 minutes

Cooking time: 2 minutes

Servings: 2

Ingredients:

- ¼ Cup water

- ¼ Teaspoon baking powder

- 1 tablespoon Egg Beaters

- 1 sachet stevia

- 1 sachet Essential Golden Chocolate Chip Pancakes

- 1 sachet Essential Frothy Cappuccino Boost

Preparation:

- Add all of the Ingredients to a microwave-safe bowl and stir until they are well combined.

- Place the mixture into the microwave for 1 to 2 minutes.

- Take the cake out from the microwave and cut it in half horizontally.

- Serve warm.

Serving Suggestion: Layer with sugar-free frosting and top with a few cacao nibs for some crunch.

Variation Tip: This cake is perfect as it is!

Nutritional information:

Calories: 195 | Fat: 4.5g | Sat Fat: 1g | Carbohydrates: 28.9g | Fiber: 2.5g | Sugar: 11g | Protein: 11g

30. Pumpkin Waffles

Preparation Time: 10 minutes

Cooking time: 8 minutes

Servings: 4

Ingredients:

- 1 cup water

- Pinch of ground cinnamon

- 1 teaspoon pumpkin pie spice

- 4 tablespoons canned pumpkin

- 4 sachets Essential Golden Pancake mixture

- 8 tablespoons sugar-free pancake syrup

Preparation:

- Lightly grease and heat the waffle iron.

- In a bowl, add all the Ingredients apart from the syrup and blend until well combined.

- Place half the mixture into the preheated waffle iron and cook for 3 to 4 minutes or until golden brown.

- Repeat with the remaining mixture.

- Serve the waffles warm and drizzled with the pancake syrup. Enjoy!

Serving Suggestion: Serve with some toasted pumpkin seeds.

Variation Tip: You can use honey instead of pancake syrup.

Nutritional information:

Calories: 148 | Fat: 3.1g | Sat Fat: 0.3g | Carbohydrates: 27.5g | Fiber: 3.2g | Sugar: 11.4g | Protein: 3.6g

31. Chocolate Donuts

Preparation Time: 5 minutes

Cooking time: 15 minutes

Servings: 4

Ingredients:

- ½ Teaspoon vanilla extract
- ½ Teaspoon baking powder
- ¼ Cup unsweetened almond milk
- 6 tablespoons liquid egg substitute
- 2 sachets Essential Golden Chocolate Chip Pancakes
- 2 sachets Essential Decadent Chocolate Brownie

Preparation:

- Prehcat the oven to 350°F. Lightly grease 4 holes of a donut pan.
- Take a bowl, add all the Ingredients, and mix until well blended.
- Evenly place the mixture into the prepared donut pan.
- Bake for 12 to 15 minutes or until the donuts are set completely.
- Remove from the oven and set aside to cool slightly before eating.

Serving Suggestion: Serve with chocolate chips or crushed Oreos on top.

Variation Tip: You can use any other kind of milk.

Nutritional information:

Calories: 212 | Fat: 7.2g | Sat Fat: 1.5g | Carbohydrates: 31.1g | Fiber: 1.6g | Sugar: 11.2g | Protein: 6.4g

32. Chicken Nuggets

Preparation Time: 10 minutes

Cooking time: 20 minutes

Servings: 4

Ingredients:

- 2 tablespoons olive oil
- 1 egg
- 4 tablespoons Essential Honey Mustard & Onion Sticks, finely crushed
- ¾ Pound boneless, skinless chicken breast, cubed
- 3 tablespoons lemon juice

Preparation:

- Preheat the oven to 400°F. Line a baking sheet with a lightly greased piece of foil.
- Crack the egg into a bowl and beat it well.
- Place the crushed sticks into another bowl.
- Dip the chicken cubes in the beaten egg mixture and then coat with the crushed sticks.
- Arrange the coated chicken cubes onto the prepared baking sheet in a single layer and spray with cooking spray.
- Bake for 18 to 20 minutes, flipping once halfway through.
- Remove the baking sheet from the oven and set the nuggets aside to cool slightly.

Serving Suggestion: Serve with ketchup (or any of your favorite sauces!).

Variation Tip: You can add any kind of seasonings according to your taste.

Nutritional information:

Calories: 134 | Fat: 3.4g | Sat Fat: 0.4g | Carbohydrates: 4.6g | Fiber: 0.8g | Sugar: 2.3g | Protein: 19.9g

33. Vanilla Frappé

Preparation Time: 5 minutes

Servings: 1

Ingredients:

- ½ Cup ice
- 1 tablespoon whipped topping
- 1 cup unsweetened almond milk
- 1 sachet Essential Creamy Vanilla Shake

Preparation:

- Put the shake mixture, almond milk, and ice into a blender.
- Blend until smooth.
- Pour the mixture into a glass.
- Top it with the whipped topping.
- Serve and enjoy!

Serving Suggestion: You can add cherries or berries as a pretty garnish.

Variation Tip: Use coconut syrup for a tropical flavor.

Nutritional information:

Calories: 308 | Fat: 11.2g | Sat Fat: 1.5g | Carbohydrates: 10.4g | Fiber: 9g | Sugar: 2.2g | Protein: 41.1g

34. Chocolate Popsicles

Preparation Time: 5 minutes

Servings: 6

Ingredients:

- 1 teaspoon vanilla extract
- 4 teaspoons zero-calorie sugar substitute
- 1 sachet Select Dark Chocolate Covered Cherry Shake
- 2 cups plain low-fat Greek yogurt
- 1 tablespoon instant espresso powder
- 1 cup unsweetened almond milk

Preparation:

- Pour the almond milk into a large mug and microwave on high for 45 seconds.
- Remove the mug from the microwave and immediately stir in the espresso powder until it dissolves completely.
- Set aside to cool completely.
- In a blender, add the cooled espresso milk mixture and the remaining Ingredients. Pulse until smooth.
- Divide the mixture into 6 large popsicle molds and freeze overnight before serving.

Serving Suggestion: Sprinkle chocolate chips on top.

Variation Tip: Coconut milk can be used instead of almond milk.

Nutritional information:

Calories: 51 | Fat: 1.7g | Sat Fat: 0.8g | Carbohydrates: 4.2g | Fiber: 0.3g | Sugar: 3.4g | Protein: 4.4g

35. Tropical Smoothie Bowl

Preparation Time: 10 minutes

Servings: 2

Ingredients:

- 2 tablespoons unsweetened coconut, shredded

- 1 teaspoon chia seeds

- 1 teaspoon lime zest, grated

- 2 tablespoons cashews

- 1 cup ice cubes

- 1 cup unsweetened coconut milk

- 1 sachet Essential Tropical Fruit Smoothie

Preparation:

- Put the smoothie mixture, coconut milk, and ice cubes into a blender and pulse until smooth.

- Take a serving bowl and add the mixture to it.

- Top with the remaining Ingredients.

- Serve and enjoy!

Serving Suggestion: Add a variety of toppings such as berries, toasted coconut, or seeds.

Variation Tip: You can also add chocolate syrup to sweeten the bowl further.

Nutritional information:

Calories: 944 | Fat: 41.2g|Sat Fat: 28.6g|Carbohydrates: 142.1g|Fiber: 12.5g|Sugar: 103.1g|Protein: 8.5g

36. Chia Seed Pudding

Preparation Time: 10 minutes

Cooking time: 11 minutes

Servings: 1

Ingredients:

- 1 cup unsweetened almond milk

- ¼ Cup chia seeds

- 1 sachet Chia Bliss Smoothie

Preparation:

- In a serving bowl, add all the Ingredients and mix until well blended.

- Refrigerate overnight before serving.

Serving Suggestion: Mix the pudding mixture with honey and vanilla extract for extra sweetness. Top with sliced strawberries and blueberries.

Variation Tip: You can also use coconut milk.

Nutritional information:

Calories: 414 | Fat: 13.7g|Sat Fat: 1.5g|Carbohydrates: 67g|Fiber: 15.4g|Sugar: 48g|Protein: 8.2g

37. Brownie Pudding Cups

Preparation Time: 10 minutes

Cooking time: 1 minute

Servings: 2

Ingredients:

- 2 sachets Essential Chocolate Fudge Pudding

- 2 tablespoons sugar-free caramel syrup

- 1 cup water, divided

- 2 sachets Essential Decadent Chocolate Brownie

Preparation:

- In a bowl, add the brownie mix and 3 tablespoons of water and combine well.

- Divide the mixture equally into ramekins and microwave each for 1 minute.

- Chill the mixtures completely.

- In a bowl, add the pudding mix to the remaining water, and mix well.

- Divide the pudding mixture over the brownie mixture equally.

- Drizzle each mixture with the caramel syrup, and with a knife, swirl the caramel into pudding.

- Refrigerate until set completely.

Serving Suggestion: Top with crushed Oreos before serving.

Variation Tip: You can use sugar-free chocolate syrup if you prefer.

Nutritional information:

Calories: 106 | Fat: 2.1g | Sat Fat: 0.4g | Carbohydrates: 21.8g | Fiber: 0.5g | Sugar: 0g | Protein: 0.6g

38. Potato Bagels

Preparation Time: 15 minutes

Cooking time: 12 minutes

Servings: 2

Ingredients:

- 4 egg whites

- 2 teaspoons baking powder

- 2 sachets Essential Roasted Garlic Creamy Smashed Potatoes

Preparation:

- Preheat the oven to 350˚F.

- Lightly grease the holes of a donut pan.

- Take a bowl, add the egg whites and beat until foamy.

- Add the baking powder and mashed potatoes mixture and beat until well blended.

- Place the mixture into the prepared donut holes.

- Bake for 10 to 12 minutes (or until completely baked through).

- Serve warm.

Serving Suggestion: Serve warm with some cream cheese.

Variation Tip: You can sprinkle on seeds or seasoning of your choice before baking and broil the bagels after cooking for extra crispiness.

Nutritional information:

Calories: 106 | Fat: 1.1g | Sat Fat: 0.4g | Carbohydrates: 15.7g | Fiber: 0.1g | Sugar: 0.5g | Protein: 9.1g

39. Peanut Butter Cookies

Preparation Time: 10 minutes
Cooking time: 15 minutes
Servings: 4

Ingredients:

- ¼ Teaspoon vanilla extract
- ⅛ Teaspoon sea salt
- 1 tablespoon margarine, softened
- ¼ Cup unsweetened almond milk
- ¼ Teaspoon baking powder
- 4 sachets Essential Silky Peanut Butter Shake

Preparation:

- Heat the oven to 350°F.
- Take a bowl and add the shake mixture and baking powder and blend well.
- Add the almond milk, margarine, and vanilla and combine well.
- Mold the cookie dough into balls and place them onto a lined cookie sheet in a single layer.
- Using a fork, lightly press each ball and sprinkle with some salt.
- Place the cookie sheet into the oven and cook for 15 minutes.
- Take the cookie sheet out of the oven and allow it to cool for 5 minutes. Turn out the cookies onto a wire rack and allow them to cool.

Serving Suggestion: Serve with chocolate chip toppings.

Variation Tip: You can use natural peanut butter instead of the shake mixture.

Nutritional information:

Calories: 589 | Fat: 34.6g|Sat Fat: 11.5g|Carbohydrates: 64.4g|Fiber: 0.1g|Sugar: 53.5g|Protein: 9.1g

40. Maple Pancakes

Preparation Time: 10 minutes
Cooking time: 6 minutes
Servings: 1

Ingredients:

- ¼ Cup water
- ¼ Teaspoon ground cinnamon
- 1 sachet stevia
- 1 tablespoon Egg Beaters
- ¼ Teaspoon baking powder
- 1 sachet Essential Old-Fashioned Maple & Brown Sugar Oatmeal
- 2 tablespoons sugar-free pancake syrup

Preparation:

- Add all the Ingredients (except for the syrup) to a large bowl.
- Combine them until well mixed.
- Gently grease a skillet and warm it on medium-high.
- Add a few tablespoons of the mixture to the skillet and cook on both sides until golden brown. Repeat until all the mixture is used.
- Drizzle with the pancake syrup before serving.

Serving Suggestion: Serve with a topping of pomegranate seeds or blueberries.

Variation Tip: You can also add some vanilla extract to enhance the flavor.

Nutritional information:

Calories: 11 | Fat: 2.5g|Sat Fat: 0.5g|Carbohydrates: 33.2g|Fiber: 3.3g|Sugar: 9.1g|Protein: 5.9g

41. Little Fudge Balls

Preparation Time: 10 minutes

Servings: 2

Ingredients:

- 4 tablespoons powdered peanut butter
- ¼ Cup unsweetened almond milk
- 2 tablespoons water
- 1 sachet Essential Creamy Chocolate shake
- 1 sachet Essential Chocolate Fudge Pudding

Preparation:

- Add all the Ingredients to a small bowl and blend until well combined.
- Make eight little equal-sized balls from the mixture.
- Place the balls onto a parchment paper-lined baking sheet and refrigerate until set.

Serving Suggestion: Serve with chocolate sprinkles on top.

Variation Tip: You can use coconut milk instead of almond.

Nutritional information:

Calories: 538 | Fat: 14.3g | Sat Fat: 7.2g | Carbohydrates: 81.8g | Fiber: 5.8g | Sugar: 57.5g | Protein: 24.5g

42. Brownie Cookies

Preparation Time: 10 minutes

Cooking time: 2 minutes 20 seconds

Servings: 2

Ingredients:

- ⅓ Cup water
- 2 sachets Essential Decadent Chocolate Brownie
- 1 essential silky peanut butter & chocolate chip bar

Preparation:

- In a bowl, add the brownie mix and water and mix well. Set aside.
- Put the peanut butter and chocolate bar in a microwave-safe bowl and microwave on high for 20 seconds or until slightly melted.
- Add the crunch bar to the brownie mixture and mix until well combined.
- Divide the mixture into 2 small microwave-safe ramekins and microwave on high for 2 minutes.
- Remove from the microwave and set aside to cool for 5 minutes before serving.
- Enjoy!

Serving Suggestion: Top with your favorite type of nuts or chocolate chips.

Variation Tip: You can also add milk chocolate or white chocolate chunks to the mixture.

Nutritional information:

Calories: 186 | Fat: 6.1g | Sat Fat: 2.1g | Carbohydrates: 25.8g | Fiber: 2g | Sugar: 6g | Protein: 8.6g

43. Mini Chocolate Cakes

Preparation Time: 10 minutes

Cooking time: 15 minutes

Servings: 2

Ingredients:

- ¼ Cup water

- ¼ Teaspoon baking powder

- 1 sachet Essential Decadent Chocolate Brownie

- 1 sachet Essential Golden Chocolate Chip Pancakes

Preparation:

- Preheat the oven to 350˚F.

- Place all the Ingredients in a large bowl and mix thoroughly.

- Divide the mixture equally in a greased muffin tray.

- Bake for 15 minutes.

- Take the tray out and let it cool.

- Refrigerate the muffins for a better taste.

- Serve and enjoy!

Serving Suggestion: Serve with chocolate syrup and sprinkles on top.

Variation Tip: You can use gluten-free flour instead of the pancake mix if needed.

Nutritional information:

Calories: 197 | Fat: 6.6g|Sat Fat: 1.4g|Carbohydrates: 32.1g|Fiber: 0.5g|Sugar: 6g|Protein: 3.6g

44. Flavorsome Waffles

Preparation Time: 18 minutes

Cooking time: 8 minutes

Servings: 2

Ingredients:

- ½ Cup water

- 2 tablespoons canned pumpkin

- ½ Teaspoon pumpkin pie spice

- 2 sachets Essential Golden Chocolate Chip Pancakes

- 4 tablespoons sugar-free pancake syrup

Preparation:

- Grease and preheat the waffle iron.

- Place all the Ingredients in a bowl, except for the pancake syrup, and blend until well combined.

- Place half of the mixture into the preheated waffle iron and cook for 3 to 4 minutes or until golden brown.

- Repeat with the remaining mixture.

- Serve warm!

Serving Suggestion: Drizzle the waffle with pancake syrup.

Variation Tip: Add chopped strawberries or cherries on top for an even yummier taste.

Nutritional information:

Calories: 139 | Fat: 4.6g|Sat Fat: 1g|Carbohydrates: 21.8g|Fiber: 0.8g|Sugar: 6.3g|Protein: 3.1g

45. Richly Tasty Crepe

Preparation Time: 10 minutes

Cooking time: 4 minutes

Servings: 1

Ingredients:

- ⅛ Teaspoon vanilla extract

- 1 tablespoon sugar-free chocolate syrup

- 1 teaspoon stevia

- ¼ Cup part-skim ricotta cheese

- ¼ Cup water

- 1 sachet Essential Golden Chocolate Chip Pancakes

Preparation:

- Put the pancake mix and water in a bowl and blend well.

- Heat a lightly greased frying pan over medium heat.

- Pour the mixture into the pan and swirl it around to create a thin, round crepe.

- Cook for 1 to 2 minutes on each side or until golden brown.

- Place the crepe on a plate and carefully cut a slit in the middle.

- Put the cheese, stevia, and vanilla extract in a small bowl and blend until well combined.

- Place the mixture inside the crepe.

- Serve and enjoy!

Serving Suggestion: Drizzle with chocolate syrup.

Variation Tip: Add chopped hazelnuts to the cheese mixture to enhance the flavor of the crepe.

Nutritional information:

Calories: 365 | Fat: 13.9g | Sat Fat: 5.1g | Carbohydrates: 47.3g | Fiber: 1.1g | Sugar: 13.9g | Protein: 13.1g

46. Pumpkin Frappé

Preparation Time: 5 minutes

Servings: 1

Ingredients:

- ½ Cup ice

- 1 tablespoon whipped topping

- ⅛ Teaspoon pumpkin pie spice

- ½ Cup unsweetened almond milk

- ½ Cup strong brewed coffee

- 1 sachet Essential Spiced Gingerbread

Preparation:

- Put the gingerbread, coffee, almond milk, pumpkin pie spice, and ice in a blender and pulse until smooth.

- Transfer the mixture into a glass and top with the whipped topping.

- Serve immediately.

Serving Suggestion: Serve with a dusting of cocoa powder on top.

Variation Tip: Pour in an extra shot of espresso according to taste.

Nutritional information:

Calories: 28 | Fat: 7.3g | Sat Fat: 0.6g | Carbohydrates: 21.4g | Fiber: 1.5g | Sugar: 9.3g | Protein: 1.7g

47. Crunchy Cookies

Preparation Time: 10 minutes

Cooking time: 15 minutes

Servings: 2

Ingredients:

- 1 sachet stevia

- ½ Teaspoon vanilla extract

- ⅛ Teaspoon baking powder

- ⅓ Cup water

- ⅛ Teaspoon ground cinnamon

- 1 sachet Essential Old-Fashioned Maple & Brown Sugar Oatmeal

- 1 essential raisin oat cinnamon crisp bar

Preparation:

- Preheat the oven to 350°F. Line a cookie sheet with parchment paper.

- Put the crisp bar in a microwave-safe bowl and microwave on high for 15 seconds or until it has melted slightly.

- Gradually add the remaining Ingredients to the bowl and mix until well combined. Set the mixture aside for 5 minutes.

- Using a spoon, place four cookies onto the cookie sheet and lightly press down on each with your fingers.

- Bake for 12 to 15 minutes or until golden brown.

- Remove the cookie sheet from the oven and place it onto a wire rack to cool for 5 minutes.

- Turn out the cookies onto the wire rack to cool before serving.

Serving Suggestion: Serve with chocolate chips on top.

Variation Tip: You can use brown sugar for extra sweetness.

Nutritional information:

Calories: 110 | Fat: 2.1g | Sat Fat: 0.9g | Carbohydrates: 16g | Fiber: 3.4g | Sugar: 2.8g | Protein: 7.3g

48. Delish French Toast Sticks

Preparation Time: 15 minutes

Cooking time: 4 minutes

Servings: 2

Ingredients:

- 2 tablespoons low-fat cream cheese, softened

- Cooking spray

- 6 tablespoons liquid egg substitute

- 2 sachets Essential Cinnamon Crunchy O's Cereal

Preparation:

- Put the cereal in a food processor and pulse to a fine breadcrumb-like consistency.

- Add the liquid egg substitute and cheese and pulse until a dough is formed.

- Divide the dough into six parts and form these into toast stick shapes.

- Heat a lightly greased pan over medium-high heat and cook the toast sticks for 2 minutes on each side or until golden brown.

- Serve warm.

Serving Suggestion: Top with icing sugar before serving.

Variation Tip: You can add some honey to enhance the flavor.

Nutritional information:

Calories: 120 | Fat: 3g | Sat Fat: 1.5g | Carbohydrates: 17.7g | Fiber: 1.3g | Sugar: 5.6g | Protein: 6.4g

49. Peppermint Mocha

Preparation Time: 5 minutes

Servings: 1

Ingredients:

- ¼ Teaspoon peppermint extract
- 1 tablespoon whipped topping
- Pinch of ground cinnamon
- ¼ Cup warm unsweetened almond milk
- 1 cup freshly brewed coffee
- 1 sachet Essential Velvety Hot Chocolate

Preparation:

- Place the hot chocolate, coffee, almond milk, and peppermint extract in a serving mug and stir until well blended.
- Top the hot chocolate with whipped topping and sprinkle with cinnamon.
- Serve immediately.

Serving Suggestion: Garnish with crushed candy cranes.

Variation Tip: You can use any coffee of your choice.

Nutritional information:

Calories: 61 | Fat: 3.7g | Sat Fat: 1.9g | Carbohydrates: 5.4g | Fiber: 0.6g | Sugar: 4g | Protein: 1.1g

50. No-Bake Chocolate Haystacks

Preparation Time: 10 minutes

Servings: 2

Ingredients:

- 1 sach`et stevia
- 1 packet Essential Cinnamon Sugar Sticks, crushed
- 2 tablespoons powdered peanut butter
- 3 tablespoons water
- 1 sachet Essential Decadent Chocolate Brownie

Preparation:

- Put the brownie mix and water in a bowl and combine into a paste.
- Add the powdered peanut butter and stevia and mix until well combined.
- Add the crushed sugar sticks and mix until well combined.
- With a spoon, place 6 "haystacks" of the mixture onto a piece of foil. Freeze for 1 hour or until the haystacks are set.
- Serve and enjoy!

Serving Suggestion: Garnish with your favorite sprinkles.

Variation Tip: Mini marshmallows and crushed nuts are possible add-ins to the mixture.

Nutritional information:

Calories: 137 | Fat: 3g | Sat Fat: 3.6g | Carbohydrates: 15.5g | Fiber: 5.1g | Sugar: 4.5g | Protein: 15g

51. Marshmallow Cereal Treat

Preparation Time: 5 minutes

Cooking time: 1 minute

Servings: 1

Ingredients:

- 2 tablespoons marshmallow spread

- 1 sachet Essential Red Berry Crunchy O's Cereal

Preparation:

- Put the cereal and marshmallow spread into a small bowl and blend well.

- Place the mixture into a microwave-safe mini loaf pan. Press down lightly on the mixture with the back of a spoon.

- Microwave for 1 minute.

- Set aside to completely cool before serving.

Serving Suggestion: Serve with toppings of your choice.

Variation Tip: Use different varieties of cereal.

Nutritional information:

Calories: 170 | Fat: 4g | Sat Fat: 2g | Carbohydrates: 32g | Fiber: 0g | Sugar: 14g | Protein: 2g

52. Giant Cookie Sandwich

Preparation Time: 15 minutes

Cooking time: 12 minutes

Servings: 1

Ingredients:

- 1 tablespoon whipped cream

- 3 tablespoons water

- ⅛ Teaspoon baking powder

- 1 sachet Chocolate Chip Soft Bake

Preparation:

- Preheat the oven to 375°F. Line a cookie sheet with parchment paper.

- Blend the baking powder and soft bake mix in a bowl.

- Slowly add the water and mix until thoroughly combined.

- Divide the dough into two and place the pieces onto the cookie sheet.

- Lightly press down on each of the pieces.

- Bake for 12 minutes.

- Place the cookie sheet onto a wire rack and leave to cool for 5 minutes.

- Turn out the cookies onto the wire rack and leave to cool completely.

- Spread the whipped cream over the top of one cookie and then place the other on top.

- Serve and enjoy!

Serving Suggestion: Add crushed Oreos to the whipped cream.

Variation Tip: Add some malted milk powder for a hint of butterscotch flavoring.

Nutritional information:

Calories: 44 | Fat: 8.6g | Sat Fat: 3.9g | Carbohydrates: 15.7g | Fiber: 1g | Sugar: 8g | Protein: 2.3g

53. Vanilla Shake

Serving: 1

Difficulty: 1

Preparation Time: 5 minutes

Cooking Time: 0 minutes

Optavia Counts: 0 lean/ 0 green/ 1 healthy fat/ 1 condiments

Ingredients:

- 10 oz. Water
- ½ sachet Essential Creamy Vanilla Shake
- ½ Cup unsweetened almond milk
- 1 tsp. Essential spiced gingerbread
- 12 ice cubes

Preparation:

- Place all the Ingredients in a blender and pulse until smooth.
- Pour the drink into serving glasses and serve.

Serving Suggestion: Garnish with whipped cream, a morello cherry, and a sprinkling of chocolate shavings.

Variation Tip: You can use vanilla ice cream to prepare a thicker milkshake.

Nutritional information: Calories: 130; Fat: 3.3 g; Sat Fat: 0.2 g; Carbs: 15 g; Fiber: 4.5 g; Sugar: 6 g; Protein: 13 g.

54. Maple Pancakes

Serving: 1

Difficulty: 1

Preparation Time: 10 minutes

Cooking Time: 6 minutes

Optavia Counts: 1 lean/ 1 green/ 1 healthy fat/ 2 condiments

Ingredients:

- ¼ Cup water
- ¼ Tsp. Ground cinnamon
- 1 sachet stevia
- 1 tbsp. Egg beaters
- ¼ Tsp. Baking powder
- 1 sachet Essential Old-Fashioned Maple & Brown Sugar Oatmeal
- 1 tbsp. Sugar-free pancake syrup

Preparation:

- Add all the Ingredients (except for the syrup) to a large bowl.
- Combine them until well mixed.
- Gently grease a skillet and warm it on medium-high.
- Add a few tablespoons of the mixture to the skillet and cook on both sides until golden brown. Repeat until all the mixture is used.
- Drizzle with the pancake syrup before serving.

Serving Suggestion: Serve with a topping of pomegranate seeds or blueberries.

Variation Tip: You can also add some vanilla extract to enhance the flavor.

Nutritional information: Calories: 11; Fat: 2.5 g; Sat Fat: 0.5 g; Carbs: 33.2 g; Fiber: 3.3 g; Sugar: 9.1 g; Protein: 5.9 g.

55. Brownie Pudding Cups

Serving: 1

Difficulty: 1

Preparation Time: 10 minutes

Cooking Time: 1 minute

Servings: 2

Optavia Counts: 0 lean/ 0 green/ 0 healthy fat/ 1 condiments

Ingredients:

- 2 sachets essential chocolate fudge pudding

- 1 tbsp. Sugar-free caramel syrup

- 1 cup water, divided

- 2 sachets Essential Decadent Chocolate Brownie

Preparation:

- In a bowl, add the brownie mix and 3 tablespoons of water and combine well.

- Divide the mixture equally into ramekins and microwave each for 1 minute.

- Chill the mixtures completely.

- In a bowl, add the pudding mix to the remaining water, and mix well.

- Divide the pudding mixture over the brownie mixture equally.

- Drizzle each mixture with the caramel syrup, and with a knife, swirl the caramel into pudding.

- Refrigerate until set completely.

Serving Suggestion: Top with crushed Oreos before serving.

Variation Tip: You can use sugar-free chocolate syrup if you prefer.

Nutritional information: Calories: 106; Fat: 2.1 g; Sat Fat: 0.4 g; Carbs: 21.8 g; Fiber: 0.5 g; Sugar: 0 g; Protein: 0.6 g.

56. Tiramisu Shake

Serving: 2

Difficulty: 1

Preparation Time: 5 minutes

Cooking Time: 0 minutes

Optavia Counts: 0 lean/ 0 green/ 0 healthy fat/ 1 condiments

Ingredients:

- 1 cup water

- 1 cup ice, crushed

- 2 tbsp. Sugar-free chocolate syrup

- 2 sachets Essential Frothy Cappuccino Boost

Preparation:

- Place all the Ingredients into a blender and pulse until smooth and creamy.

- Pour the shake into a serving glass.

- Serve and enjoy!

Serving Suggestion: You can serve with chocolate syrup, ladyfinger cookies, and whipped cream on top.

Variation Tip: You can add some vanilla extract to the shake.

Nutritional information: Calories: 106; Fat: 3 g; Sat Fat: 1 g; Carbs: 17 g; Fiber: 0 g; Sugar: 10 g; Protein: 1 g.

57. Potato Bagels

Serving: 2

Difficulty: 1

Preparation Time: 15 minutes

Cooking Time: 12 minutes

Optavia Counts: 1 lean/ 1 green/ 1 healthy fat/ 0 condiments

Ingredients:

- 2 egg whites

- 2 tbsp. Baking powder

- 2 sachets essential roasted garlic creamy smashed potatoes

Preparation:

- Preheat the oven to 350°F.

- Lightly grease the holes of a donut pan.

- Take a bowl, add the egg whites and beat until foamy.

- Add the baking powder and mashed potatoes mixture and beat until well blended.

- Place the mixture into the prepared donut holes.

- Bake for 10 to 12 minutes (or until completely baked through).

- Serve warm.

Serving Suggestion: Serve warm with some cream cheese.

Variation Tip: You can sprinkle on seeds or seasoning of your choice before baking and broil the bagels after cooking for extra crispiness.

Nutritional information: Calories: 106; Fat: 1.1 g; Sat Fat: 0.4 g; Carbs: 15.7 g; Fiber: 0.1 g; Sugar: 0.5 g; Protein: 9.1 g.

58. Tropical Smoothie Bowl

Serving: 2

Difficulty: 1

Preparation Time: 10 minutes

Cooking Time: 0 minutes

Optavia Counts: 0 lean/ 0 green/ 1 healthy fat/ 3 condiments

Ingredients:

- 2 tbsp. Unsweetened coconut, shredded

- 1 tsp. Chia seeds

- 1 tsp. Lime zest, grated

- 2 tbsp. Cashews

- 1 cup ice cubes

- 1 cup unsweetened coconut milk

- 1 sachet Essential Tropical Fruit Smoothie

Preparation:

- Put the smoothie mixture, coconut milk, and ice cubes into a blender and pulse until smooth.

- Take a serving bowl and add the mixture to it.

- Top with the remaining Ingredients.

- Serve and enjoy!

Serving Suggestion: Add a variety of toppings such as berries, toasted coconut, or seeds.

Variation Tip: You can also add chocolate syrup to sweeten the bowl further.

Nutritional information: Calories: 944; Fat: 41.2 g; Sat Fat: 28.6 g; Carbs: 142.1 g; Fiber: 12.5 g; Sugar: 103.1 g; Protein: 8.5 g.

59. Mocha Cake

Serving: 2

Difficulty: 1

Preparation Time: 5 minutes

Cooking Time: 2 minutes

Optavia Counts: 1 lean/ 1 green/ 1 healthy fat/ 0 condiments

Ingredients:

- ¼ Cup water

- ¼ Tsp. Baking powder

- 1 tbsp. Egg beaters

- 1 sachet stevia

- 1 sachet Essential Golden Chocolate Chip Pancakes

- 1 sachet Essential Frothy Cappuccino Boost

Preparation:

- Add all of the Ingredients to a microwave-safe bowl and stir until they are well combined.

- Place the mixture into the microwave for 1 to 2 minutes.

- Take the cake out from the microwave and cut it in half horizontally.

- Serve warm.

Serving Suggestion: Layer with sugar-free frosting and top with a few cacao nibs for some crunch.

Variation Tip: This cake is perfect as it is!

Nutritional information: Calories: 195; Fat: 4.5 g; Sat Fat: 1 g; Carbs: 28.9 g; Fiber: 2.5 g; Sugar: 11 g; Protein: 11 g.

60. Little Fudge Balls

Serving: 2

Difficulty: 1

Preparation Time: 10 minutes

Cooking Time: 0 minutes

Optavia Counts: 0 lean/ 0 green/ 2 healthy fat/ 0 condiments

Ingredients:

- 1 tbsp. Powdered peanut butter

- ¼ Cup unsweetened almond milk

- 1 tbsp. Water

- 1 Sachet Essential Creamy Chocolate shake

- 1 sachet essential chocolate fudge pudding

Preparation:

- Add all the Ingredients to a small bowl and blend until well combined.

- Make eight little equal-sized balls from the mixture.

- Place the balls onto a parchment paper-lined baking sheet and refrigerate until set.

Serving Suggestion: Serve with chocolate sprinkles on top.

Variation Tip: You can use coconut milk instead of almond.

Nutritional information: Calories: 538; Fat: 14.3 g; Sat Fat: 7.2 g; Carbs: 81.8 g; Fiber: 5.8 g; Sugar: 57.5 g; Protein: 24.5 g.

61. Brownie Cookies

Serving: 2

Difficulty: 1

Preparation Time: 10 minutes

Cooking Time: 2 minutes 20 seconds

Optavia Counts: 0 lean/ 0 green/ 0 healthy fat/ 0 condiments

Ingredients:

- ⅓ Cup water
- 2 sachets essential decadent chocolate brownie
- 1 essential silky peanut butter & chocolate chip bar

Preparation:

- In a bowl, add the brownie mix and water; mix well. Set aside.
- Put the peanut butter and chocolate bar in a microwave-safe bowl and microwave on High for 20 seconds or until slightly melted.
- Add the crunch bar to the brownie mixture and mix until well combined.
- Divide the mixture into 2 small microwave-safe ramekins and microwave on high for 2 minutes.
- Remove from the microwave and set aside to cook for 5 minutes before serving.
- Enjoy!

Serving Suggestion: Top with your favorite type of nuts or chocolate chips.

Variation Tip: You can also add milk chocolate or white chocolate chunks to the mixture.

Nutritional information: Calories: 186; Fat: 6.1 g; Sat Fat: 2.1 g; Carbs: 25.8 g; Fiber: 2 g; Sugar: 6 g; Protein: 8.6 g.

62. Zucchini Spaghetti

Serving: 2

Difficulty: 1

Preparation Time: 20 minutes

Cooking Time: 15 minutes

Optavia Counts: 0 lean/ 2 green/ 2 healthy fat/ 3 condiments

Ingredients:

- 1-pound zucchinis, cut with a spiralizer
- 1 cup Parmesan, grated
- ¼ Cup parsley, chopped.
- ¼ Cup olive oil
- 1 garlic cloves; minced
- ½ Tsp. Red pepper flakes
- Salt and black pepper to taste.

Preparation:

- In a pan that fits into your Air Fryer, mix all the Ingredients, toss, put into the fryer and cook at 370°F for 15 minutes.
- Divide between plates and serve as a side dish.

Nutrition: Calories: 200; Fat: 6 g; Carbs: 4 g; Protein: 5 g.

63. Cabbage And Radishes Mix

Serving: 3

Difficulty: 1

Preparation Time: 20 minutes

Cooking Time: 15 minutes

Optavia Counts: 0 lean/ 3 green/ 1 healthy fat/ 4 condiments

Ingredients:

- ½ Small head green cabbage; shredded
- ½ Cup celery leaves; chopped.
- ¼ Cup green onions; chopped.
- bunch radishes; sliced
- 1 tbsp. Olive oil
- tbsps. Balsamic vinegar
- ½ Tsp. Hot paprika
- 1 tsp. Lemon juice

Preparation:

- In your Air Fryer pan, combine all the ingredients and toss well.
- Place the pan in the fryer and cook at 380°F for 15 minutes. Divide between plates and serve as a side dish.

Nutritional information: Calories: 130; Fat: 4 g; Carbs: 4 g; Protein: 7 g.

64. Flavorsome Waffles

Serving: 3

Difficulty: 1

Preparation Time: 18 minutes

Cooking Time: 8 minutes

Optavia Counts: 0 lean/ 0 green/ 0 healthy fat/ 3 condiments

Ingredients:

- ½ Cup water
- 1 tbsp. Canned pumpkin
- ½ Tsp. Pumpkin pie spice
- 2 sachets essential golden chocolate chip pancakes
- 1 tbsp. Sugar-free pancake syrup

Preparation:

- Grease and preheat the waffle iron.
- Place all the Ingredients in a bowl, except for the pancake syrup, and blend until well combined.
- Place half of the mixture into the preheated waffle iron and cook for 3 to 4 minutes or until golden brown.
- Repeat with the remaining mixture.
- Serve warm!

Serving Suggestion: Drizzle the waffle with pancake syrup.

Variation Tip: Add chopped strawberries or cherries on top for an even yummier taste.

Nutritional information: Calories: 139; Fat: 4.6 g; Sat Fat: 1 g; Carbs: 21.8 g; Fiber: 0.8 g; Sugar: 6.3 g; Protein: 3.1 g.

65. Richly Tasty Crepe

Serving: 3

Difficulty: 1

Preparation Time: 10 minutes

Cooking Time: 4 minutes

Optavia Counts: 0 lean/ 1 green/ 1 healthy fat/ 2 condiments

Ingredients:

- ⅛ Tsp. Vanilla extract
- 1 tbsp. Sugar-free chocolate syrup
- 1 tsp. Stevia
- ¼ Cup part-skim ricotta cheese
- ¼ Cup water
- 1 sachet Essential Golden Chocolate Chip Pancakes

Preparation:

- Put the pancake mix and water in a bowl and blend well.
- Heat a lightly greased frying pan over medium fire.
- Pour the mixture into the pan and swirl it around to create a thin, round crepe.
- Cook for 1 to 2 minutes on each side or until golden brown.
- Place the crepe on a plate and carefully cut a slit in the middle.
- Put the cheese, stevia, and vanilla extract in a small bowl and blend until well combined.
- Place the mixture inside the crepe.
- Serve and enjoy!

Serving Suggestion: Drizzle with chocolate syrup.

Variation Tip: Add chopped hazelnuts to the cheese mixture to enhance the flavor of the crepe.

Nutritional information: Calories: 365; Fat: 13.9 g; Sat Fat: 5.1 g; Carbs: 47.3 g; Fiber: 1.1 g; Sugar: 13.9 g; Protein: 13.1 g.

66. Crunchy Cookies

Serving: 3

Difficulty: 1

Preparation Time: 10 minutes

Cooking Time: 15 minutes

Optavia Counts: 0 lean/ 1 green/ 1 healthy fat/ 2 condiments

Ingredients:

- 1 sachet stevia
- ½ Tsp. Vanilla extract
- ⅛ Tsp. Baking powder
- ⅓ Cup water
- ⅛ Tsp. Ground cinnamon
- 1 sachet essential old-fashioned maple & brown sugar oatmeal
- 1 essential raisin oat cinnamon crisp bar

Preparation:

- Preheat the oven to 350°F. Line a cookie sheet with parchment paper.
- Put the crisp bar in a microwave-safe bowl and microwave on High for 15 seconds or until it has melted slightly.
- Gradually add the remaining Ingredients to the bowl and mix until well combined. Set the mixture aside for 5 minutes.
- Using a spoon, place four cookies onto the cookie sheet and lightly press down on each with your fingers.
- Bake for 12 to 15 minutes or until golden brown.
- Remove the cookie sheet from the oven and place it onto a wire rack to cool for 5 minutes.
- Turn out the cookies onto the wire rack to cool before serving.

Serving Suggestion: Serve with chocolate chips on top.

Variation Tip: You can use brown sugar for extra sweetness.

Nutritional information: Calories: 110; Fat: 2.1 g; Sat Fat: 0.9 g; Carbs: 16 g; Fiber: 3.4 g; Sugar: 2.8 g; Protein: 7.3 g.

67. Delicious French Toast Sticks

Serving: 3

Difficulty: 1

Preparation Time: 15 minutes

Cooking Time: 4 minutes

Optavia Counts: 1 lean/ 0 green/ 1 healthy fat/ 1 condiments

Ingredients:

- 2 tbsp. Low-fat cream cheese, softened

- Cooking spray

- 6 tbsp. Liquid egg substitute

- 2 sachets Essential Cinnamon Crunchy O's Cereal

Preparation:

- Put the cereal in a food processor and pulse to a fine breadcrumb-like consistency.

- Add the liquid egg substitute and cheese and pulse until a dough is formed.

- Divide the dough into six parts and form these into toast stick shapes.

- Heat a lightly greased pan over medium-high fire and cook the toast sticks for 2 minutes on each side or until golden brown.

- Serve warm.

Serving Suggestion: Top with icing sugar before serving.

Variation Tip: You can add some honey to enhance the flavor.

Nutritional information: Calories: 120; Fat: 3 g; Sat Fat: 1.5 g; Carbs: 17.7 g; Fiber: 1.3 g; Sugar: 5.6 g; Protein: 6.4 g

68. Shamrock Shake

Serving: 3

Difficulty: 1

Preparation Time: 5 minutes

Cooking Time: 0 minutes

Optavia Counts: 0 lean/ 0 green/ 2 healthy fat/ 2 condiments

Ingredients:

- ¼ Tsp. Peppermint extract

- 10 drops green food coloring

- 1 cup ice cube, crushed

- ¾ Cup unsweetened almond milk

- 1 sachet Essential Creamy Vanilla Shake

Preparation:

- Place all the Ingredients in a blender and pulse until smooth.

- Transfer the shake into a serving glass and serve immediately.

- Serving Suggestion: Top the shake with whipped cream, green sprinkles, and morello cherry.

- Variation Tip: Add an extra hint of vanilla extract to the shake for an enhanced taste.

Nutritional information: Calories: 250; Fat: 10.9 g; Sat Fat: 1.2 g; Carbs: 30.5 g; Fiber: 3.7 g; Sugar: 7.1 g; Protein: 10.7 g.

69. Pumpkin Waffles

Serving: 4

Difficulty: 1

Preparation Time: 10 minutes

Cooking Time: 8 minutes

Optavia Counts: 0 lean/ 0 green/ 0 healthy fat/ 4 condiments

Ingredients:

- 1 cup water

- Pinch of ground cinnamon

- 1 tsp. Pumpkin pie spice

- 1 tbsp. Canned pumpkin

- 2 sachets Essential Golden Pancake mixture

- 1 tbsp. Sugar-free pancake syrup

Preparation:

- Lightly grease and heat the waffle iron.

- In a bowl, add all the ingredients except the syrup and blend until well combined.

- Place half the mixture into the preheated waffle iron and cook for 3 to 4 minutes or until golden brown.

- Repeat with the remaining mixture.

- Serve the waffles warm and drizzled with the pancake syrup. Enjoy!

Serving Suggestion: Serve with some toasted pumpkin seeds.

Variation Tip: You can use honey instead of pancake syrup.

Nutritional information: Calories: 148; Fat: 3.1 g; Sat Fat: 0.3 g; Carbs: 27.5 g; Fiber: 3.2 g; Sugar: 11.4 g; Protein: 3.6 g.

70. Chocolate Donuts

Serving: 4

Difficulty: 1

Preparation Time: 5 minutes

Cooking Time: 15 minutes

Optavia Counts: 1 lean/ 0 green/ 2 healthy fat/ 1 condiments

Ingredients:

- ½ Tsp. Vanilla extract

- ½ Tsp. Baking powder

- ¼ Cup unsweetened almond milk

- 1 tbsp. Liquid egg substitute

- 2 sachets essential golden chocolate chip pancakes

- 2 sachets essential decadent chocolate brownie

Preparation:

- Preheat the oven to 350°F. Lightly grease 4 holes of a donut pan.

- Take a bowl, add all the ingredients, and mix until well blended.

- Evenly place the mixture into the prepared donut pan.

- Bake for 12 to 15 minutes or until the donuts are set completely.

- Remove from the oven and set aside to cool slightly before eating.

Serving Suggestion: Serve with chocolate chips or crushed Oreos on top.

Variation Tip: You can use any other kind of milk.

Nutritional information: Calories: 212; Fat: 7.2 g; Sat Fat: 1.5 g; Carbs: 31.1 g; Fiber: 1.6 g; Sugar: 11.2 g; Protein: 6.4 g.

71. Chicken Nuggets

Serving: 4

Difficulty: 1

Preparation Time: 10 minutes

Cooking Time: 20 minutes

Optavia Counts: 2 lean/ 0 green/ 1 healthy fat/ 2 condiments

Ingredients:

- 1 tbsp. Olive oil
- 1 large egg
- 1 tbsp. Essential honey mustard & onion sticks, finely crushed
- ¾ Pound boneless, skinless chicken breast, cubed
- 1 tbsp. Lemon juice

Preparation:

- Preheat the oven to 400°F. Line a baking sheet with a lightly greased piece of foil.
- Crack the egg into a bowl and beat it well.
- Place the crushed sticks into another bowl.
- Dip the chicken cubes in the beaten egg mixture and then coat with the crushed sticks.
- Arrange the coated chicken cubes onto the prepared baking sheet in a single layer and coat with cooking spray.
- Bake for 18 to 20 minutes, flipping once halfway through.
- Remove the baking sheet from the oven and set the nuggets aside to cool slightly.

Serving Suggestion: Serve with ketchup (or any of your favorite sauces!).

Variation Tip: You can add any kind of seasonings according to your taste.

Nutritional information: Calories: 134; Fat: 3.4 g; Sat Fat: 0.4 g; Carbs: 4.6 g; Fiber: 0.8 g; Sugar: 2.3 g; Protein: 19.9 g.

72. Peanut Butter Cookies

Serving: 4

Difficulty: 1

Preparation Time: 10 minutes

Cooking Time: 15 minutes

Optavia Counts: 0 lean/ 0 green/ 3 healthy fat/ 2 condiments

Ingredients:

- ¼ Tsp. Vanilla extract
- ⅛ Tsp. Sea salt
- 1 tbsp. Margarine, softened
- ¼ Cup unsweetened almond milk
- ¼ Tsp. Baking powder
- 2 sachets essential silky peanut butter shake

Preparation:

- Heat the oven to 350°F.
- Take a bowl and add the shake mixture and baking powder and blend well.
- Add the almond milk, margarine, and vanilla and combine well.
- Mold the cookie dough into balls and place them onto a lined cookie sheet in a single layer.
- Using a fork, lightly press each ball and sprinkle with some salt.
- Place the cookie sheet into the oven and cook for 15 minutes.
- Take the cookie sheet out of the oven and allow it to cool for 5 minutes. Turn out the cookies onto a wire rack and allow them to cool.

Serving Suggestion: Serve with chocolate chip toppings.

Variation Tip: You can use natural peanut butter instead of the shake mixture.

Nutritional information: Calories: 589; Fat: 34.6 g; Sat Fat: 11.5 g; Carbs: 64.4 g; Fiber: 0.1 g; Sugar: 53.5 g; Protein: 9.1 g.

73. Mint Cookies

Serving: 4

Difficulty: 1

Preparation Time: 10 minutes

Cooking Time: 15 minutes

Optavia Counts: 1 lean/ 0 green/ 1 healthy fat/ 0 condiments

Ingredients:

- 1 tbsp. Liquid egg substitute
- 2 tbsp. Unsweetened almond milk
- 2 essential chocolate mint cookie crisp bars
- 2 sachets Essential Decadent Double Chocolate Brownies

Preparation:

- Preheat the oven to 350°F. Line a cookie sheet with parchment paper.
- Place the cookie bars in a food processor and pulse until fully crushed.
- Transfer the crushed bars to a bowl with the other Ingredients and mix until well blended.
- Using a spoon, form 8 cookie dough balls from the mixture and place them onto the prepared cookie sheet. Press each ball slightly with your fingers.
- Bake for 13 to 15 minutes.
- Remove the cookie sheet from the oven and let it cool for 5 minutes on a wire rack.
- Turn out the cookies onto the wire rack to cool before serving.

Serving Suggestion: These cookies are perfect as they are!

Variation Tip: Add some mint extract for an extra punch of flavor.

Nutritional information: Calories: 175; Fat: 6.1 g; Sat Fat: 2.5 g; Carbs: 20.7 g; Fiber: 1.3 g; Sugar: 14.1 g; Protein: 9.8 g.

74. Parmesan Zucchini Rounds

Serving: 4

Difficulty: 1

Preparation Time: 25 minutes

Cooking Time: 20 minutes

Optavia Counts: 2 lean/ 2 green/ 1 healthy fat/ 2 condiments

Ingredients:

- 4 zucchinis; sliced
- 1 ½ cups Parmesan; grated
- ¼ Cup parsley; chopped.
- 1 egg; whisked
- 1 egg white; whisked
- ½ Tsp. Garlic powder
- Cooking spray

Preparation:

- Take a bowl and mix the egg with egg whites, Parmesan, parsley, and garlic powder. Then whisk.
- Dredge each zucchini slice in this mix, place them all in your Air Fryer's basket. Grease them with cooking spray and cook at 370°F for 20 minutes.
- Divide between plates and serve as a side dish.

Nutritional information: Calories: 183; Fat: 6 g; Fiber: 2 g; Carbs: 3 g; Protein: 8 g.

75. Green Bean Casserole

Serving: 4

Difficulty: 2

Preparation Time: 25 minutes

Cooking Time: 20 minutes

Optavia Counts: 1 lean/ 1 green/ 2 healthy fat/ 5 condiments

Ingredients:

- 1 pound fresh green beans, edges trimmed
- ½ Oz. Pork rinds, finely ground
- 1 oz. Full-fat cream cheese
- ½ Cup heavy whipping cream.
- ¼ Cup yellow onion, diced
- ½ Cup white mushrooms, chopped
- ½ Cup chicken broth
- 1 tbsp. Unsalted butter
- ¼ Tsp. Xanthan gum

Preparation:

- Melt the butter in a preheated skillet.
- Sauté the onion and mushrooms until soft and fragrant, for 3–5 minutes.
- Add the heavy cream, cream cheese, and broth to the skillet. Lightly beat until smooth. Boil and then simmer. Put the xanthan gum in the pan and remove it from heat.
- Cut green beans into 2-inch pieces and place in a 4-cup round pan. Pour sauce mixture over them and stir until covered. Fill the plate with ground pork rinds. Place in the fryer basket.
- Set the temperature to 320°f and set the timer for 15 minutes. The top will be a golden and green bean fork when fully cooked. Serve hot.

Nutritional information: Calories: 267; Protein: 3.6 g; Fat: 23.4 g; Carbs: 9.7 g.

76. Red velvet cream pies

Prep Time: 10 minutes

Cook Time: 15 minutes

Serves: 4

Ingredients:

- 2 sachets Essential Golden Chip Pancakes mix
- 2 sachets Essential Chewy Chocolate Chip Cookie Mix
- ½ Tablespoon unsweetened cocoa powder
- ½ Teaspoon baking powder
- ½ Cup unsweetened almond milk
- 6 tablespoons liquid egg substitute
- 1 teaspoon apple cider vinegar
- Cooking spray
- ½ Cup low-fat cream cheese
- 1-2 packets zero calories sugar substitute

Preparation:

- Preheat the oven to 350°F.
- Combine the pancake mix, chocolate chip cookies mix, cocoa powder, and baking powder in a bowl.
- Add the milk, eggs, and apple cider vinegar and mix until it has a batter-like consistency.
- Divide the batter among eight muffins tins and bake for 15 to 20 minutes.
- Mix the cream cheese and sugar substitute until they are well combined.
- Once the pies have cooled, slice each in half horizontally, spread the cream filling, and sandwich the halves back together.

Serving Suggestion: Serve the pies topped with whipped cream.

Variation Tip: Add red color to the batter for a red velvet pie.

Nutritional information:

Calories 472 | Carbohydrates 82g | Protein 4.4g | Fat 14.5g | Sodium 505mg| Fiber 1.7g

77. Pecan And Sweet Potato Muffins

Prep Time: 10 minutes

Cook Time: 20 minutes

Serves: 4

Ingredients:

- 2 sachets Select Honey Sweet Potatoes
- 1 cup cold water
- 2 sachets Essential Spiced Gingerbread
- 6 tablespoons liquid egg substitute
- ¼ Cup unsweetened vanilla almond milk
- ½ Teaspoon pumpkin pie spice
- ½ Teaspoon vanilla extract
- ½ Teaspoon baking powder
- Cooking spray
- 1 1/3 cups pecans, chopped

Preparation:

- Preheat the oven to 350°F.

- Prepare the potatoes according to the Directions. Let the mix cool slightly.

- In a medium-sized bowl, combine the cooked potatoes and the remaining Ingredients (except for the pecans).

- Divide the mixture amongst eight slots on a lightly-greased standard-sized muffin pan. Sprinkle the tops with chopped pecans. Bake for 20 minutes.

Serving Suggestion: Serve with hot tea.

Variation Tip: Add chopped almonds instead of pecans.

Nutritional information:

Calories 472 | Carbohydrates 30.6g | Protein 2.9g | Fat 9.8g | Sodium 205mg| Fiber 1.5g

78. Sweet Potato And Goat's Cheese Quiche

Prep Time: 15 minutes

Cook Time: 30 minutes

Serves: 4

Ingredients:

- 4 sachets Select Honey Sweet Potatoes
- 1 cup unsweetened almond milk
- 4 eggs
- 2/3 cup part-skim ricotta cheese
- 1 ounce crumbled goat's cheese
- ¼ Cup yellow onion, diced
- 1 tablespoon fresh rosemary, chopped
- ⅛ Teaspoon nutmeg
- Cooking spray

Preparation:

- Preheat the oven to 375°F.

- In a large, microwave-safe bowl, stir together the potatoes mix and the milk until well combined.

- Microwave on high for 1½ minutes. When done, stir, and let the mixture sit until thickened and cooled.

- Add the remaining Ingredients and mix until well combined.

- Divide the mixture evenly among 12 slots of a standard-sized, lightly-greased muffin tin.

- Baked for 25 to 30 minutes, until the mixture is set and the edges are brown.

Serving Suggestion: Serve the quiche topped with rosemary.

Variation Tip: Add dill for freshness.

Nutritional information:

Calories 403 | Carbohydrates 47g | Protein 15g | Fat 17g | Sodium 351mg| Fiber 7g

79. Cheesy Mashed Potatoes With Spinach

Prep Time: 10 minutes

Cook Time: 25 minutes

Serves: 1

Ingredients:

• 1 sachet Essential Roasted Garlic Creamy Smashed Potatoes

• 1 cup baby spinach

• 1 teaspoon water

• ½ Cup reduced-fat mozzarella cheese, shredded

• 1 tablespoon parmesan cheese, grated

Preparation:

• Prepare the potatoes as per the box instructions.

• Steam the spinach with water in the microwave for 1 minute or until wilted.

• Combine the cooked potatoes, spinach, mozzarella, and parmesan cheese.

Serving Suggestion: Serve hot.

Variation Tip: Add chopped chive to the mix for color.

Nutritional information:

Calories 275.2 | Carbohydrates 48.1g | Protein 6.5g | Fat 7g | Sodium 346.5mg | Fiber 6.1g

80. Honey cinnamon baked oatmeal

Prep Time: 10 minutes.

Cook Time: 25 minutes.

Serves: 4

Ingredients:

• 4 sachets Essential Cinnamon and Honey Hot Cereal

• ½ Teaspoon baking powder

• 3 tablespoons liquid egg substitute

• 1 cup almond milk

• 1/4 teaspoon cinnamon

• Cooking spray

Preparation:

• Preheat the oven to 350°F.

• In a large bowl, combine the cereal and baking powder.

• Add the liquid egg white and almond milk; stir until the milk is fully absorbed.

• Divide the mixture evenly between four lightly greased mason jars, leaving about half an inch at the top. Sprinkle the tops with cinnamon.

• Bake for 20 to 25 minutes on a small baking sheet, until slightly firm and golden on top. Allow the mixture to cool completely.

Serving Suggestion: Serve topped with cream cheese.

Variation Tip: Add pecan and walnuts for crunch.

Nutritional information:

Calories 214.7 | Carbohydrates 39.2g | Protein 5.5g | Fat 5.4g | Sodium 28.5mg | Fiber 4.6g

81. Yogurt Berry Bagel With Cream Cheese

Prep Time: 10 minutes

Cook Time: 10 minutes

Serves: 2

Ingredients:

- 1 sachet Essential Yogurt Berry Blast Smoothie
- ½ Cup unsweetened original almond milk
- 2 tablespoons liquid egg substitute
- ½ Teaspoon baking powder
- 1-ounce light cream cheese

Preparation:

- Preheat the oven to 350°F.

- In a medium-sized bowl, combine the smoothie mix, milk, egg substitute, and baking powder.

- Divide the mixture among four lightly greased slots of a donut pan.

- Bake until the mixture is set, about 12 to 15 minutes.

- Let cool slightly before serving with cream cheese.

Serving Suggestion: Serve the bagel warm.

Variation Tip: Add ham and vegetables.

Nutritional information:

Calories 263 | Carbohydrates 46.4g | Protein 8.9g | Fat 4.3g | Sodium 412mg | Fiber 2.3g

82. Chocolate coconut cream pie

Prep Time: 10 minutes

Cook Time: 30 minutes

Serves: 2

Ingredients:

- 1 essential chocolate fudge crisp bar
- 1 serving Essential Chocolate Fudge Pudding
- Cooking spray
- ½ Cup unsweetened, original coconut milk
- 2 tablespoons pressurized whipped topping
- 1½ unsweetened coconut, shredded

Preparation:

- Place the bar on a small, microwave-safe plate and microwave for 15 to 20 seconds.

- Press the microwaved bar into the bottom of a small, lightly greased ramekin.

- In a small bowl, combine the pudding and milk.

- Pour the mixture over the top of the bar in the ramekin. Refrigerate until set, about 30 minutes.

- Top with the whipped topping and sprinkle with coconut flakes before serving.

Serving Suggestion: Top with whipped topping and sprinkle with coconut flakes before serving.

Variation Tip: To toast the shredded coconut, spread the flakes onto a baking sheet in an even layer. Bake at 325°F for 5 to 7 minutes, until lightly browned.

Nutritional information:

Calories 320 | Carbohydrates 46g | Protein 4g | Fat 14g | Sodium 320mg | Fiber 1g

83. Mocha Cherry Pops

Prep Time: 5 minutes

Cook Time: 5 minutes

Serves: 6

Ingredients:

- 1 cup unsweetened vanilla almond milk
- 1 tablespoon instant espresso powder
- 3 packets Select Dark Chocolate Covered Cherry Shake
- 2 cups plain, low-fat Greek yogurt
- 1-2 packets zero-calorie sugar substitute
- 1 teaspoon vanilla extract

Preparation:

- Microwave the milk in a microwave-safe mug or bowl for 45 seconds.
- Immediately add the espresso powder and stir until completely dissolved.
- Once cooled, add the espresso milk and remaining **Ingredients** to a blender or food processor. Blend until well combined and smooth.
- Distribute the mixture evenly among six large popsicle molds and freeze overnight.

Serving Suggestion: Serve chilled instantly after unmolding.

Variation Tip: You can use unsweetened plain almond milk or cashew milk.

Nutritional information:

Calories 21 | Carbohydrates 4g | Protein 2g | Fat 10g | Sodium 28mg| Fiber 0g

84. Coconut colada shake

Prep Time: 2 minutes

Cook Time: 3 minutes

Serves: 1

Ingredients:

- 1 sachet Essential Creamy Vanilla Shake
- 6 ounces unsweetened, original coconut milk
- 6 ounces diet ginger ale
- 2 tablespoons unsweetened coconut, shredded
- ¼ Teaspoon rum extract
- ½ Cup ice

Preparation:

- Set aside ½ tablespoon of the shredded coconut.
- Combine all of the remaining **Ingredients** in a blender, and blend until smooth and icy.
- Divide the mixture among two piña colada glasses, and top with the remaining shredded coconut.

Serving Suggestion: Serve chilled.

Variation Tip: Add coconut shavings for a crunchy texture.

Nutritional information:

Calories 158.7 | Carbohydrates 23.1g | Protein 2.7g | Fat 6.6g | Sodium 39.1mg| Fiber 1.4g

85. Chocolaty Peanut Butter Donuts

Prep Time: 10 minutes

Cook Time: 10 minutes

Serves: 4

Ingredients:

For the Donuts

- 2 sachets Essential Golden Chocolate Chip Pancakes
- 2 sachets Essential Decadent Double Chocolate Brownies
- 6 tablespoons liquid egg substitute
- ¼ Cup unsweetened vanilla almond milk
- ½ Teaspoon vanilla extract
- ½ Teaspoon baking powder
- Cooking spray

For the Glaze

- ¼ Cup powdered peanut butter
- 3-4 tablespoons unsweetened vanilla almond milk,

To thin

Preparation:

- Preheat the oven to 350°F.
- Sift out the chocolate chips from the pancake mix and set them aside.
- In a medium-sized bowl, combine the sifted pancake mix, brownie mix, egg substitute, milk, vanilla extract, and baking powder.
- Divide the mixture evenly amongst four slots of a donut pan. Bake until the mixture is set, about 12 to 15 minutes. Let cool before glazing.
- Meanwhile, prepare the peanut butter glaze. In a small shallow bowl, combine the powdered peanut butter and milk until smooth and slightly runny. Dip each donut into the glaze.

Serving Suggestion: Serve the glazed donuts topped with chocolate chips.

Variation Tip: Add butterscotch cream for taste.

Nutritional information :
Calories 360 | Carbohydrates 43g | Protein 3g | Fat 19g | Sodium 360mg| Fiber 1g

86. Mashed Potato And Grilled Cheese Waffles

Prep Time: 5 minutes

Cook Time: 10 minutes

Serves: 2

Ingredients:

- 2 sachets Essential Roasted Garlic Creamy Smashed Potatoes
- 1 cup water
- 1 cup low-fat cheese (cheddar, mozzarella)

Preparation:

- In a microwave-safe, medium bowl, thoroughly combine the smashed potatoes mix and water. Microwave on high for 30 seconds and stir well.
- Pour this mixture onto a hot, lightly greased waffle iron and cook for about 10 minutes.
- Sprinkle cheese on one-half of the waffles and fold the other half. Close the waffle iron and cook the waffles for another 2 to 3 minutes until done or the cheese has melted.

Serving Suggestion: Serve with dill garnishing or enjoy as it is.

Variation Tip: Use chopped dill for garnish.

Nutritional information:
Calories 150 | Carbohydrates 24g | Protein 4g | Fat 5g | Sodium 680mg| Fiber 1g

87. Taco salad

Prep Time: 5 minutes

Cook Time: 7 minutes

Serves: 2

Ingredients:

- 4 ounces lean ground beef
- ½ Teaspoon taco seasoning mix
- 1/3 cup tomatoes, chopped
- 13/4 cup romaine lettuce, shredded
- 1 packet tortilla taco chips

Preparation:

- In a medium-sized skillet, brown the lean ground beef. Drain the meat and return to the skillet.
- Stir in the taco seasoning and heat for approximately 2 to 3 minutes. Set aside and let cool.
- Shred the lettuce and add the chopped tomatoes to the bowl. Mix in the seasoned ground beef.
- Top the beef salad with the taco chips.

Serving Suggestion: Serve the salad topped with shredded low-fat cheese.

Variation Tip: Add chili flakes to the beef for spiciness.

Nutritional information:
Calories 321.5 | Carbohydrates 25.5g | Protein 17.8g | Fat 16.5g | Sodium 404.9mg| Fiber 5.7g

88. Greek Yogurt Sticks

Prep Time: 2 minutes

Cook Time: 8 minutes

Serves: 2

Ingredients:

- •2 ounces plain low-fat Greek yogurt
- 1-2 packets zero-calorie sugar substitute
- 1 sachet Essential Red Berry Crunchy O's Cereal, crushed

Preparation:

- In a medium-sized bowl, combine the Greek yogurt and sugar substitute.
- Line an 8x8 inch baking dish with non-stick foil. Spread the Greek yogurt/sugar mix in an even layer onto the foil.
- Sprinkle the crushed cereal on top of the mix.
- Freeze for 4 to 5 hours or overnight until the bar is hard.

Serving Suggestion: Break the bar into smaller pieces with a sharp knife. Store leftovers in freezer-safe bags or containers in the freezer.

Variation Tip: Add chopped nuts for extra crunch.

Nutritional information:
Calories 100 | Carbohydrates 0g | Protein 6g | Fat 9g | Sodium 120mg| Fiber 0g

89. Peanut butter energy bites

Prep Time: 2 minutes

Cook Time: 3 minutes

Serves: 1

Ingredients:

- 1 essential creamy double peanut butter crisp bar

- 2 tablespoons powdered peanut butter

- 1 tablespoon water

Preparation:

- Mix the powdered peanut butter and water in a small bowl to form a smooth paste.

- Place the peanut butter bar on a microwave-safe plate and microwave for 15 seconds or until soft.

- Combine the warm pieces of the bar with the peanut butter to form a dough.

- Use a cookie scoop or your fingers to form four bite-sized balls. Refrigerate until ready to serve.

Serving Suggestion: Serve as chilled energy bars.

Variation Tip: Add fresh nuts and unsweetened maple syrup.

Nutritional information:

Calories 189| Carbohydrates 17.5g | Protein 5.4g | Fat 11.8g | Sodium 65.3mg| Fiber 2.9g

90. Guacamole With Zesty Tortilla Chips

Prep Time: 10 minutes

Cook Time: 10 minutes

Serves: 2

Ingredients:

Chips

- 2 packets Essential Hearty Red Bean & Vegetable Chili

- ¼ Cup water

- Cooking spray

Guacamole

- 3 ounces avocado, peeled, pitted, and mashed

- 1 tablespoon pico de gallo

- ½ Teaspoon lemon or lime juice

- ⅛ Teaspoon salt

Preparation:

- Preheat the oven to 350°F.

- Empty the contents of the chili mix packets into a food processor. Pulverize into a fine powder.

- Transfer the powder into a small mixing bowl. Add water, and whisk until smooth and a dough-like consistency.

- Place the mixture onto a piece of lightly greased parchment paper. Use your fingers to press the dough into a ¼-inch thick circle. Use a pizza cutter to cut tortilla-shaped pieces.

- Place the parchment paper with the tortilla-like pieces onto a baking sheet. Bake for 10 minutes, flip, and bake an additional 10 to 15 minutes or until the chips are crispy.

- Meanwhile, prepare the guacamole. Place the mashed avocado in a small mixing bowl, stir in the remaining Ingredients, and refrigerate until ready to serve.

Serving Suggestion: Serve chilled.

Variation Tip: Alternatively, you can eat tortilla chips made from cauliflower with this guacamole.

Nutritional information:

Calories 130 | Carbohydrates 16g | Protein 2g | Fat 7g | Sodium 140mg| Fiber 1g

91. Honey Chicken Nuggets With Mustard Dip

Prep Time: 10 minutes

Cook Time: 15 minutes

Serves: 2

Ingredients:

- 12 ounces boneless, skinless chicken breast, cubed
- 1 egg, beaten
- 2 sachets Essential Honey Mustard & Onion Sticks, Crumbled
- ¼ cup plain low-fat Greek yogurt
- 2 teaspoons spicy brown mustard
- ¼ Teaspoon garlic powder
- Cooking spray

Preparation:

- Preheat the oven to 400°F.
- Place the egg and crumbled mustard and onion sticks into two separate small, shallow bowls.
- Dip each chicken piece into the egg, and then roll in the crumbs until completely coated.
- Place the coated chicken pieces onto a lightly greased, foil-lined baking sheet. Lightly spray the tops with cooking spray.
- Bake until the coating turns golden, and the internal temperature of the chicken pieces reaches 165°F (about 18 to 20 minutes), flipping halfway through.
- Meanwhile, combine the Greek yogurt, mustard, and garlic powder in a small bowl.

Serving Suggestion: Serve the nuggets with the yogurt dip.

Variation Tip: Add chili flakes for spice.

Nutritional information:

Calories 211 | Carbohydrates 13.6g | Protein 21.9g | Fat 7.7g | Sodium 5.7mg| Fiber 1.4g

92. Chocolate cake fries

Preparation Time: 10 minutes

Cooking Time: 4 minutes

Servings: 2

Ingredients:

- 2 sachets Golden Chocolate Chip Pancakes
- ¼ Cup liquid egg substitute
- 2 teaspoons vegetable oil

Preparation:

- In a bowl, add pancake sachets and egg substitute and mix until well-combined.
- Place the mixture into a resealable plastic bag.
- Cut off a small hole on tip of the bag.
- In a wok, heat oil over medium heat.
- In the wok, pipe mixture in long, straight lines and cook for about two minutes per side.
- Serve warm.

Serving Suggestions: Serve with sugar-free chocolate syrup on the top.

Variation Tip: Don't overcook the fries.

Nutritional information:

Calories: 167 | Fat: 6g | Sat Fat: 1.9g | Carbohydrates: 16.2g | Fiber: 4g | Sugar: 6.2g | Protein: 14.8g

93. Oatmeal Breakfast Cookies

Prep Time: 10 minutes

Cook Time: 25 minutes

Serves: 2

Ingredients:

- 1 sachet Essential Old-Fashioned Maple & Brown
- Sugar Oatmeal
- 1 essential raisin oat cinnamon crisp bar
- ⅛ Teaspoon cinnamon
- 1 packet Stevia
- 1/3 cup water
- ⅛ Teaspoon baking powder
- ½ Teaspoon vanilla
- 2 tablespoons PB2

Preparation:

- Preheat the oven to 350°F.
- Microwave the raisin bar for 15 seconds until slightly melted.
- Mix the bar with all the other Ingredients and let sit for 5 minutes.
- Line a cookie sheet with parchment paper or spray with cooking spray.
- Drop spoonfuls of the mixture onto the sheet to make four cookies. Bake for 12-15 minutes.

Serving Suggestion: Serve warm with cold almond milk.

Variation Tip: Add fresh raisins to the mixture for chewiness.

Nutritional information:
Calories 123 | Carbohydrates 24.7g | Protein 3.9g | Fat 1.5g | Sodium 5.7mg | Fiber 2.6g

94. Cheesy Savory Waffles

Prep Time: 5 minutes

Cook Time: 10 minutes

Serves: 4

Ingredients:

- 4 packets Essential Roasted Garlic Creamy Smashed Potatoes
- ½ Cup unsweetened almond or cashew milk
- ½ Cup reduced-fat cheddar cheese, shredded
- ½ Cup liquid egg substitute
- 2 slices turkey bacon, cooked
- ¼ Cup scallions, chopped
- Cooking spray

Preparation:

- Mix the contents of the potato-mix packets, milk, cheese, and egg substitute in a medium-sized bowl until well combined.
- Fold in the remaining Ingredients.
- Pour the mixture into a hot, lightly greased waffle iron. Close the lid and bake for 5 to 7 minutes, until golden brown. Carefully remove the waffle and serve.

Serving Suggestion: Serve hot.

Variation Tip: Add some low-fat Greek yogurt as a topping.

Nutritional information:
Calories 115.4 | Carbohydrates 13.6g | Protein 6.0g | Fat 4.3g | Sodium 356.8mg | Fiber 0.5g

95. Lemon Bites

Prep Time: 5 minutes

Cook Time: 10 minutes

Serves: 2

Ingredients:

- 2 essential zesty lemon crisp bars
- 1½ cups low-fat plain Greek yogurt
- 1 (0.3 ounces) sachet sugar-free lemon gelatin
- ½ Teaspoon lime zest

Preparation:

- Line a muffin tin with six cupcake liners.
- Break each lemon bar into thirds and place in a microwave-safe bowl. Microwave for 10 to 15 seconds.
- Press the mix into six cupcake liners to form a thin crust.
- In a microwave-safe bowl, mix the yogurt and gelatin powder. Microwave on high for 2 minutes, stirring after each minute.
- Pour ¼ cup of the yogurt mixture on top of each crust.
- Allow the mixture to chill for at least 1 hour. Garnish with lime zest if desired.

Serving Suggestion: Serve chilled topped with lemon zest.

Variation Tip: Add cream cheese for extra cheesiness.

Nutritional information:
Calories 130| Carbohydrates 19g | Protein 1g | Fat 5g | Sodium 95mg| Fiber 0g

96. Tropical smoothie bowl

Prep Time: 2 minutes

Cook Time: 3 minutes

Serves: 1

Ingredients:

- 1 sachet Essential Tropical Fruit Smoothie
- ½ Cup unsweetened, original coconut milk
- ½ Cup ice
- ½ Ounce macadamias or cashews, chopped
- 1 tablespoon unsweetened coconut, shredded
- ½ Tablespoon chia seeds
- ½ Teaspoon lime zest

Preparation:

- Add the smoothie mix, milk, and ice to a blender and blend until smooth.
- Pour the smoothie mixture into a small, shallow bowl.
- Top with the remaining Ingredients and serve.

Serving Suggestion: Serve chilled.

Variation Tip: Add almond essence or chopped almonds for flavor.

Nutritional information:
Calories 134 | Carbohydrates 17g | Protein 7g | Fat 5.5g | Sodium 25mg| Fiber 2g

97. Gingerbread Trifle

Prep Time: 5 minutes

Cook Time: 10 minutes

Serves: 4

Ingredients:

- 2 sachets Essential Spiced Gingerbread
- 2 sachets Essential Creamy Vanilla Shake
- 12 ounces plain, low-fat Greek yogurt
- ½ Cup pressurized whipped topping
- ¼ Cup sugar-free salted caramel

Preparation:

- Prepare the gingerbread as per the box instructions. Allow it to cool, and then cut it into small cubes.
- In a mixing bowl, beat the vanilla shake mix with the Greek yogurt.
- Evenly divide the yogurt mixture and cake cubes among four small trifle or parfait dishes.

Serving Suggestion: Serve the trifle topped with the whipped topping and drizzle with non-sugar syrup.

Variation Tip: Add fresh fruit if you like.

Nutritional information:
Calories 164 | Carbohydrates 24.7g | Protein 1.8g | Fat 6.3g | Sodium 218.8mg| Fiber 1.9g

98. Buffalo cauliflower wings

Prep Time: 10 minutes

Cook Time: 25 minutes

Serves: 2

Ingredients:

- 2 sachets Buttermilk Cheddar Herb Biscuit, crumbled
- ½ Cup water
- 3 cups cauliflower florets
- Cooking spray
- ¼ cup hot Buffalo sauce
- ½ Tablespoon butter, melted
- ¼ cup low-fat plain Greek yogurt
- 1 teaspoon dry ranch dressing mix

Preparation:

- Preheat the oven to 400°F. Lightly grease a lined baking sheet.
- Mix together the biscuits and water in a bowl. Add the cauliflower and toss well until the florets are thoroughly and evenly coated.
- Place the coated florets on the baking sheet and bake for 20 minutes.
- Meanwhile, in a medium bowl, mix the hot Buffalo sauce and butter.
- Add the baked cauliflower and toss in the sauce well. Place the mixture back onto the baking sheet and bake for 5 more minutes.
- In another bowl, combine the yogurt and ranch dressing mix for dipping.

Serving Suggestion: Serve Buffalo cauliflower wings with the ranch dressing mixture.

Variation Tip: Add chopped chives for garnishing.

Nutritional information:
Calories 116 | Carbohydrates 13g | Protein 2g | Fat 5g | Sodium 1577mg| Fiber 1g

99. Skinny Peppermint Mocha

Prep Time: 2 minutes

Cook Time: 3 minutes

Serves: 1

Ingredients:

- • 1 sachet Essential Velvety Hot Chocolate
- • 6 ounces freshly brewed coffee
- • ¼ Cup unsweetened almond milk
- •¼ Teaspoon peppermint extract
- 2 tablespoons pressurized whipped topping
- A pinch of cinnamon

Preparation:

- Combine the first three Ingredients in a mug or coffee cup and stir until the hot chocolate mixture is fully dissolved.

Serving Suggestion: Serve topped with the whipped topping and sprinkle with cinnamon.

Variation Tip: Add unsweetened cocoa powder for an intense chocolaty flavor.

Nutritional information:
Calories 130 | Carbohydrates 17g | Protein 13g | Fat 1.5g | Sodium 150mg| Fiber 4g

100. Shamrock Shake

Preparation Time: 5 minutes

Serving: 1

Ingredients:

- 1 packet vanilla shake
- 6 ounces unsweetened almond milk
- ¼ Teaspoon peppermint extract
- 1-2 drops green food coloring
- 1 cup ice cubes

Preparation:

- In a small blender, place all Ingredients and pulse until smooth.
- Transfer the shake into a serving glass and serve immediately.

Serving Suggestions: Serve with mint leaves garnishing.

Variation Tip: Try to use high quality food colouring.

Nutritional information:
Calories: 140 | Fat: 2.9g | Sat Fat: 0.2g | Carbohydrates: 14.5g | Fiber: 3.7g | Sugar: 9.1g | Protein: 14.7g

101. Cheddar pancakes

Preparation Time: 10 minutes

Cooking Time: 12 minutes

Servings: 2

Ingredients:

- 1 garlic mashed potatoes
- ¼ Cup low-fat cheddar cheese, shredded
- ¼ Teaspoon baking powder
- ½ Cup water
- 2 tablespoons low-fat sour cream

Preparation:

- In a bowl, add all the ingredients except for sour cream and mix until well-blended.
- Set the bowl of mixture aside for about five minutes.
- Heat a lightly greased cast-iron wok over medium heat.
- Place half of the mixture and with the back of a spoon, spread the mixture into a circle.
- Cook for about 2-3 minutes per side or until golden brown.
- Repeat with the remaining mixture.
- Serve warm with the topping of sour cream.

Serving Suggestions: Serve with scallion greens garnishing.

Variation Tip: Use low-fat sour cream.

Nutritional information:
Calories: 138 | Fat: 7.4g | Sat Fat: 2.1g | Carbohydrates: 8.5g | Fiber: 2g | Sugar: 1.1g | Protein: 9.4g

102. Pumpkin Frappe

Preparation Time: 5 minutes

Serving: 1

Ingredients:

- 1 sachet spiced gingerbread
- 4 ounces strong brewed coffee
- 4 ounces unsweetened almond milk
- ⅛ Teaspoon pumpkin pie spice
- ½ Cup ice
- 1 tablespoon whipped topping

Preparation:

- In a blender, add the spiced gingerbread sachet, coffee, almond milk, pumpkin pie spice, ice and pulse until smooth.
- Transfer the mixture into a glass and top with whipped topping.
- Serve immediately.

Serving Suggestions: Serve with the sprinkling of cinnamon.

Variation Tip: You can adjust the ratio of pumpkin pie spice according to your taste.

Nutritional information:
Calories: 138 | Fat: 4.8g | Sat Fat: 0.6g | Carbohydrates: 15.4g | Fiber: 4.5g | Sugar: 5g | Protein: 11.7g

103. Coconut smoothie

Preparation Time: 5 minutes

Serving: 1

Ingredients:

- 6 ounces unsweetened almond milk

- 6 ounces diet ginger ale

- 2 tablespoons unsweetened coconut, shredded

- ¼ Teaspoon rum extract

- ½ cup ice

Preparation:

- In a small blender, place all Ingredients and pulse until smooth.

- Transfer the smoothie into a serving glass and serve immediately.

Serving Suggestions: Serve with the topping of unsweetened shredded coconut.

Variation Tip: Unsweetened almond milk can be replaced with unsweetened cashew milk.

Nutritional information:
Calories: 65 | Fat: 5.7g | Sat Fat: 3.2g |
Carbohydrates: 2.9g | Fiber: 1.6g | Sugar: 0.6g |
Protein: 1g

104. Hot chocolate

Preparation Time: 10 minutes
Cooking Time: 2 minutes
Serving: 1
Ingredients:

- 1 sachet velvety hot chocolate

- ½ Teaspoon ground cinnamon

- Pinch of cayenne pepper

- 6 ounces unsweetened almond milk

- 1 tablespoon whipped cream

Preparation:
In a serving mug, place all the ingredients except for whipped cream and beat until well-blended.

- Microwave on high for about two minutes.

- Top with whipped cream and serve.

Serving Suggestions: Serve with unsweetened chocolate chips on the top.

Variation Tip: Ground cinnamon can be replaced with ground nutmeg.

Nutritional information:
Calories: 185 | Fat: 8.1g | Sat Fat: 3.1g |
Carbohydrates: 15.9g | Fiber: 5.4g | Sugar: 9.1g |
Protein: 14.1g

105. Blueberry Scones

Preparation Time: 15 minutes

Cooking Time: 20 minutes

Servings: 6

Ingredients:

- 4 sachets Blueberry Almond Hot Cereal

- ¼ Cup ground flaxseed

- 1-2 packets zero-calorie sugar substitute

- ½ Teaspoon baking powder

- 3 tablespoons frozen unsalted butter, cut into ½-inch pieces

- 3 tablespoons low-fat plain Greek yogurt

- ¼ Teaspoon almond extract

- ¼ teaspoon ground cinnamon

Preparation:

- Preheat your oven to 400° F.

- Line a baking sheet with parchment paper.

- In a food processor, add the hot cereal sachet, flaxseed, sugar substitute and baking powder, and pulse until well blended.

- Add the butter and pulse until a coarse meal-like mixture is formed.

- Add the yogurt and almond extract and pulse until just blended.

- Place the dough onto the prepared baking sheet and shape into a six-inch circle.

- Sprinkle the top of the dough circle with cinnamon.

- Bake for approximately 15-20 minutes or until top becomes golden brown.

- Remove the baking sheet from oven and set aside to cool.

- Cut the dough circle into six wedges and serve.

Serving Suggestions: Serve with powdered sugar substitute sprinkling.

Variation Tip: Almond extract can be replaced with vanilla extract.

Nutritional information:
Calories: 155 | Fat: 8.6g | Sat Fat: 3.9g | Carbohydrates: 12.2g | Fiber: 3.9g | Sugar: 1.9g | Protein: 8.7g

106. Gingersnap Cookies

Preparation Time: 10 minutes

Cooking Time: 20 minutes

Serving: 1

Ingredients:

- 1 sachet spiced gingerbread

- 2 tablespoons cold water

- Olive oil cooking spray

- 2 tablespoons low-fat whipped cream cheese spread

- ⅛ Teaspoon vanilla extract

- 3-5 drops liquid stevia

Preparation:

- Preheat your oven to 350° F.

- Lightly grease a cookie sheet.

- In a bowl, add spiced gingerbread sachet and beat until smooth.

- With a small spoon, place about three cookies onto the prepared cookie sheet in a single layer.

- Bake for approximately 18-20 minutes or until golden brown.

- Remove from the oven and place the cookie sheet onto a wire rack to cool for about five minutes.

- Now, invert the cookies onto the wire rack to cool before serving.

- Meanwhile, in a small bowl, place cream cheese, vanilla extract and stevia and beat until smooth.

- Spread frosting over cookies and serve.

Serving Suggestions: Enjoy with a cup of warm non-dairy milk.

Variation Tip: Vanilla extract can be replaced with almond extract.

Nutritional information:
Calories: 142 | Fat: 2.5g | Sat Fat: 0g | Carbohydrates: 16.1g | Fiber: 4g | Sugar: 6.1g | Protein: 15g

107.   Peanut Butter Cookies

Preparation Time: 10 minutes

Cooking Time: 12 minutes

Servings: 4

Ingredients:

- 4 sachets Silky Peanut Butter Shake

- ¼ Teaspoon baking powder

- ¼ Cup unsweetened almond milk

- 1 tablespoon margarine, softened

- ¼ Teaspoon vanilla extract

- ⅛ teaspoon sea salt

Preparation:

- Preheat your oven to 350° F. Line a cookie sheet with parchment paper.

- In a bowl, add the peanut butter shake and baking powder, and mix well.

- Add the almond milk, margarine and vanilla extract and mix until well blended.

- With a spoon, place eight cookies onto the prepared cookie sheet in a single layer and with a fork, press each ball slightly.

- Sprinkle salt on each cookie and bake for approximately 10-12 minutes.

- Remove from the oven and place the cookie sheet onto a wire rack to cool for about five minutes.

- Now, invert the cookies onto the wire rack to cool before serving.

Serving Suggestions: Serve with powdered sugar substitute on the top.

Variation Tip: Use unsalted margarine.

Nutritional information:

Calories: 139 | Fat: 5.6g | Sat Fat: 0.5g | Carbohydrates: 15.3g | Fiber: 4.1g | Sugar: 13g | Protein: 0.8g

108.   Gingerbread Biscotti

Preparation Time: 15 minutes

Cooking Time: 45 minutes

Servings: 2

Ingredients:

- 1 sachet spiced gingerbread

- ¼ Teaspoon baking powder

- 2 tablespoons sugar-free maple syrup

- 2 egg whites

Preparation:

- Preheat your oven to 350° F. Line a baking sheet with parchment paper.

- In a bowl, mix together the gingerbread sachet and baking powder.

- In the bowl, add the maple syrup and egg whites and mix until well-blended.

- With lightly greased hands, place the dough onto the prepared baking sheet.

- With your hands, shape the dough into an 8-inch-long log.

- Bake for approximately 25-30 minutes or until the top is firm.

- Remove the baking sheet from oven and set aside to cool for about 5-10 minutes.

- Cut the log into 8 (1-inch thick) slices.

- Arrange the biscotti slices onto the baking sheet in a single layer, cut side down.

- Now, set the temperature of the oven to 325° F and Bake for approximately 15 minutes.

- Remove the baking sheet from oven and place the baking sheet onto a wire rack to cool for about five minutes.

- Now, invert the biscotti sticks onto the wire rack to cool before serving.

Serving Suggestions: Serve with sugar-free berry jam.

Variation Tip: Make sure to use sugar-free maple syrup.

Nutritional information:

Calories: 83 | Fat: 1.4g | Sat Fat: 0g | Carbohydrates: 10.3g | Fiber: 0g | Sugar: 2.7g | Protein: 9.1g

109.   Sriracha Popcorn

Preparation Time: 5 minutes

Serving: 1

Ingredients:

- 1 teaspoon unsalted butter, melted
- 1 teaspoon Sriracha
- Pinch of stevia powder
- 1 sachet Sharp Cheddar & Sour Cream Popcorn

Preparation:

- In a zip lock bag, place all Ingredients.
- Seal the bag and shake to coat well.
- Serve immediately.
- Serving Suggestions: Serve with the drizzling of extra butter.

Variation Tip: Stevia powder can be replaced with maple syrup.

Nutritional information:
Calories: 109 | Fat: 7.6g | Sat Fat: 2.4g | Carbohydrates: 7g | Fiber: 1g | Sugar: 0g | Protein: 1g

110.   Tortilla Chips

Preparation Time: 10 minutes

Cooking Time: 25 minutes

Servings: 2

Ingredients:

- 2 sachets Hearty Red Bean & Vegetable Chili
- ¼ cup water

Preparation:

- Preheat your oven to 350° F.
- Line a rimmed baking sheet with a lightly greased parchment paper.
- In a food processor, add the vegetable chili sachet and pulse until finely powdered.
- Transfer the vegetable chili powder into a bowl with water and beat until smooth.
- Arrange the dough onto the prepared baking sheet and with your hands, smooth the top surface.
- With a knife, cut the dough into chips-size pieces.
- Bake for approximately ten minutes.
- Carefully flip the dough pieces and bake for approximately 10-15 minutes.
- Remove the baking sheet of chips from the oven and set aside to cool before serving.
- Serving Suggestions: Serve with fresh salsa.

Variation Tip: You can also score the chips with a pizza cutter.

Nutritional information:
Calories: 110 | Fat: 1g | Sat Fat: 0g | Carbohydrates: 15g | Fiber: 4g | Sugar: 4g | Protein: 12g

111. Mac & Cheese Doritos

Preparation Time: 15 minutes

Cooking Time: 15 minutes

Serving: 1

Ingredients:

- 1 packet macaroni & cheese
- ¼ Teaspoon garlic salt
- ¼ Teaspoon red pepper flakes, crushed
- 2 tablespoons water
- Pinch of red chili powder
- Non-stick cooking spray

Preparation:

- Preheat your oven to 350° F.
- In a food processor, add mac & cheese packet, garlic salt and red pepper flakes, and pulse until finely powdered.
- Transfer into a bowl with water and stir to combine.
- Set aside for about 2 minutes.
- Place the dough between two greased pieces of parchment and with your hands, spread into a thin circle.
- Carefully peel off the top layer of parchment.
- Arrange the dough onto a baking sheet alongside the parchment paper.
- Sprinkle the dough with chili powder.
- Bake for approximately ten minutes.
- Remove from the oven and with a pizza cutter, cut into chip-size pieces.
- Flip the chips and bake for approximately 3-5 minutes.
- Remove from the oven and set aside to cool completely before serving.
- Serving Suggestions: Serve with tomato sauce.

Variation Tip: You can use simple salt instead of garlic salt.

Nutritional information: Calories: 115 | Fat: 1.7g | Sat Fat: 0g | Carbohydrates: 15.9g | Fiber: 4.3g | Sugar: 1.2g | Protein: 11.2g

112. Mini Biscuit Pizza

Preparation Time: 10 minutes

Cooking Time: 14 minutes

Servings: 1

Ingredients:

- 1 sachet Buttermilk Cheddar and Herb Biscuit
- 2 tablespoons water
- 1 tablespoon tomato sauce
- 1 tablespoon low-fat cheddar cheese, shredded

Preparation:

- Preheat your oven to 350° F.
- In a small bowl, add the biscuit and water and mix well.
- Place the biscuit mixture onto a parchment paper and with a spoon, spread into a thin circle.
- Bake for approximately ten minutes.
- Remove from the oven and spread the tomato sauce over the biscuit circle.
- Sprinkle with cheddar cheese.
- Bake for approximately 2-4 minutes or until cheese is melted.
- Remove from the oven and set aside for about 3-5 minutes.
- Serve warm.
- Serving Suggestions: Serve with olives on the top.

Variation Tip: Use sugar-free tomato sauce.

Nutritional information: Calories: 142 | Fat: 5.4g | Sat Fat: 2.3g | Carbohydrates: 13.9g | Fiber: 4.2g | Sugar: 2.7g | Protein: 13g

113. Potato Bagels

Preparation Time: 10 minutes

Cooking Time: 12 minutes

Serving: 1

Ingredients:

- 2 egg whites
- 1 sachet mashed potatoes
- 1 teaspoon baking powder

Preparation:

- Preheat your oven to 350° F.
- Lightly grease one hole of a donut pan.
- In a bowl, add the egg whites and beat until foamy.
- Add the baking powder and mashed potatoes and beat until well-blended.
- Place the mixture into the prepared donut hole.
- Bake for approximately 10-12 minutes or until done.
- Serve warm.

Serving Suggestions: Serve with unsalted butter topping.

Variation Tip: Use a wire whisk to whip the egg whites.

Nutritional information:

Calories: 149 | Fat: 0.6g | Sat Fat: 0g | Carbohydrates: 16.8g | Fiber: 4.1g | Sugar: 2.5g | Protein: 18.2g

Breakfast Recipes

1. Alkaline Blueberry Spelt Pancakes

Preparation Time: 6 minutes

Cooking Time: 20 minutes

Servings: 3

Ingredients:

- 2 cups spelt flour

- 1 cup of coconut milk

- 1/2 cup alkaline water

- 2 tablespoons grapeseed oil

- 1/2 cup agave

- 1/2 cup blueberries

- 1/4 teaspoons sea moss

Directions:

- Mix the spelt flour, agave, grapeseed oil, hemp seeds, and sea moss in a bowl. Add in 1 cup of hemp milk and alkaline water to the mixture until you get the consistent mixture you like.

- Crimp the blueberries into the batter. Heat the skillet to moderate heat, then lightly coat it with the grapeseed oil.

- Pour the batter into the skillet, then let them cook for approximately 5 minutes on every side. Serve and enjoy.

Nutritional information: Calories: 203, Fat: 1.4 g, Carbs: 41.6 g, Proteins: 4.8 g

2. Alkaline Blueberry Muffins

Preparation Time: 5 minutes

Cooking Time: 20 minutes

Servings: 3

Ingredients:

- 1 cup of coconut milk

- 3/4 cup spelt flour

- 3/4 teff flour

- 1/2 cup blueberries

- 1/3 cup agave

- 1/4 cup sea moss gel

- 1/2 teaspoons sea salt

- Grapeseed oil

Directions:

- Adjust the temperature of the oven to 365°f. Grease 6 regular-size muffin cups with muffin liners.

- In a bowl, mix sea salt, sea moss, agave, coconut milk, and flour gel until they are properly blended. You then crimp in blueberries.

- Coat the muffin pan lightly with the grapeseed oil. Pour in the muffin batter. Bake for at least 30 minutes until it turns golden brown. Serve.

Nutritional information: Calories: 160, Fat: 5 g, Carbs: 25 g, Proteins: 2 g

3. Crunchy Quinoa Meal

Preparation Time: 5 minutes

Cooking Time: 25 minutes

Servings: 2

Ingredients:

- 3 cups of coconut milk

- 1 cup rinsed quinoa

- 1/8 teaspoons ground cinnamon

- 1 cup raspberry

- 1/2 cup chopped coconuts

Directions:

- In a saucepan, pour milk and bring to a boil over moderate heat. Add the quinoa to the milk, and then bring it to a boil once more.

- You then let it simmer for at least 15 minutes on medium heat until the milk is reduced. Stir in the cinnamon, then mix properly.

- Cover it, then cook for 8 minutes until the milk is completely absorbed. Add the raspberry and cook the meal for 30 seconds. Serve and enjoy.

Nutritional information: Calories: 271, Fat: 3.7 g, Carbs: 54 g, Proteins: 6.5 g

4. Coconut Pancakes

Preparation Time: 5 minutes

Cooking Time: 15 minutes

Servings: 4

Ingredients:

- 1 cup coconut flour

- 2 tablespoons arrowroot powder

- 1 teaspoon baking powder

- 1 cup of coconut milk

- 3 tablespoons coconut oil

Directions:

- In a medium container, mix in all the dry **Ingredients**. Add the coconut milk and 2 tablespoons of coconut oil, then mix properly.

- In a skillet, dissolve 1 teaspoon of coconut oil. Put the batter into the skillet, then swirl the pan to spread the batter evenly into a smooth pancake.

- Cook it for like 3 minutes on medium heat until it becomes firm. Turn the pancake to the other side, then cook it for another 2 minutes until it turns golden brown.

- Cook the remaining pancakes in the same process. Serve.

Nutritional information: Calories: 377, Fat: 14.9 g, Carbs: 60.7 g, Protein: 6.4 g

5. Quinoa Porridge

Preparation Time: 5 minutes

Cooking Time: 25 minutes

Servings: 2

Ingredients:

- 2 cups of coconut milk

- 1 cup rinsed quinoa

- 1/8 teaspoons ground cinnamon

- 1 cup fresh blueberries

Directions:

- In a saucepan, boil the coconut milk over high heat. Add the quinoa to the milk, then bring the mixture to a boil.

- You then let it simmer for 15 minutes on medium heat until the milk is reducing. Add the cinnamon, then mix it properly in the saucepan.

- Cover the saucepan and cook for at least 8 minutes until the milk is completely absorbed. Add in the blueberries, then cook for 30 more seconds. Serve.

Nutritional information: Calories: 271, Fat: 3.7 g, Carbs: 54 g, Protein:6.5 g

6. Amaranth Porridge

Preparation Time: 5 minutes

Cooking Time: 30 minutes

Servings: 2

Ingredients:

- 2 cups of coconut milk

- 2 cups alkaline water

- 1 cup amaranth

- 2 tablespoons coconut oil

- 1 tablespoon ground cinnamon

Directions:

- In a saucepan, mix the milk with water, then boil the mixture. You stir in the amaranth, then reduce the heat to medium.

- Cook on medium heat, then simmers for at least 30 minutes as you stir it occasionally. Turn off the heat. Add in cinnamon and coconut oil, then stir. Serve.

Nutritional information: Calories: 434, Fat: 35 g, Carbs: 27 g, Protein: 6.7 g

7. Banana Barley Porridge

Preparation Time: 15 minutes

Cooking Time: 5 minutes

Servings: 2

Ingredients:

- 1 cup divided unsweetened coconut milk
- 1 small peeled and sliced banana
- 1/2 cup barley
- 3 drops liquid stevia
- 1/4 cup chopped coconuts

Directions:

- In a bowl, properly mix barley with half of the coconut milk and stevia. Cover the mixing bowl, then refrigerate for about 6 hours.
- In a saucepan, mix the barley mixture with coconut milk—Cook for about 5 minutes on moderate heat. Then top it with the chopped coconuts and the banana slices. Serve.

Nutritional information: Calories: 159, Fat: 8.4 g, Carbs: 19.8 g, Proteins: 4.6 g

8. Zucchini Muffins

Preparation Time: 10 minutes

Cooking Time: 25 minutes

Servings: 16

Ingredients:

- 1 tablespoon ground flaxseed
- 3 tablespoons alkaline water
- 1/4 cup walnut butter
- 3 medium over-ripe bananas
- 2 small grated zucchinis
- 1/2 cup coconut milk
- 1 teaspoon vanilla extract
- 2 cups coconut flour
- 1 tablespoon baking powder
- 1 teaspoon cinnamon
- 1/4 teaspoons sea salt

Directions:

- Tune the temperature of your oven to 375°f. Grease the muffin tray with the cooking spray.
- In a bowl, mix the flaxseed with water. In a glass bowl, mash the bananas, then stir in the remaining Ingredients.
- Properly mix and then divide the mixture into the muffin tray. Bake it for 25 minutes. Serve.

Nutrition: Calories: 127, Fat: 6.6 g, Carbs: 13 g, Protein: 0.7 g

9. Millet Porridge

Preparation Time: 10 minutes

Cooking Time: 20 minutes

Servings: 2

Ingredients:

- Sea salt
- 1 tablespoon finely chopped coconuts
- 1/2 cup unsweetened coconut milk
- 1/2 cup rinsed and drained millet
- 1-1/2 cups alkaline water
- 3 drops liquid stevia

Directions:

- Sauté the millet in a non-stick skillet for about 3 minutes. Add salt and water, then stir. Let the meal boil, then reduce the amount of heat.
- Cook for 15 minutes, then add the remaining Ingredients. Stir—Cook the meal for 4 extra minutes. Serve the meal with a topping of the chopped nuts.

Nutritional information: Calories: 219, Fat: 4.5 g, Carbs: 38.2 g, Protein: 6.4 g

10. Jackfruit Vegetable Fry

Preparation Time: 5 minutes

Cooking Time: 5 minutes

Servings: 6

Ingredients:

- 2 finely chopped small onions
- 2 cups finely chopped cherry tomatoes
- 1/8 teaspoons ground turmeric
- 1 tablespoon olive oil
- 2 seeded and chopped red bell peppers
- 3 cups seeded and chopped firm jackfruit - 1/8 teaspoons cayenne pepper - 2 tablespoons chopped fresh basil leaves - Salt

Directions:

- In a greased skillet, sauté the onions and bell peppers for about 5 minutes. Add the tomatoes, then stir. Cook for 2 minutes.
- Then add the jackfruit, cayenne pepper, salt, and turmeric—Cook for about 8 minutes. Garnish the meal with basil leaves. Serve warm.

Nutritional information: Calories: 236, Fat: 1.8 g, Carbs: 48.3 g, Protein: 7 g

11. Zucchini Pancakes

Preparation Time: 15 minutes

Cooking Time: 8 minutes

Servings: 8

Ingredients:

- 12 tablespoons alkaline water

- 6 large grated zucchinis

- Sea salt

- 4 tablespoons ground Flax Seeds

- 2 teaspoons olive oil

- 2 finely chopped jalapeño peppers

- 1/2 cup finely chopped scallions

Directions:

- In a bowl, mix water, and the flax seeds, then set them aside. Pour oil into a large non-stick skillet, then heat it on medium heat. Then add the black pepper, salt, and zucchini.

- Cook for 3 minutes, then transfer the zucchini into a large bowl. Add the flaxseed and the scallion mixture, then mix it.

- Preheat a griddle, then grease it lightly with the cooking spray. Pour 1/4 of the zucchini mixture into the griddle, then cook for 3 minutes.

- Flip the side carefully, then cook for 2 more minutes. Repeat the procedure with the remaining mixture in batches. Serve.

Nutritional information: Calories: 71, Fat: 2.8 g, Carbs: 9.8 g, Protein: 3.7 g

12. Squash Hash

Preparation Time: 2 minutes

Cooking Time: 10 minutes

Servings: 2

Ingredients:

- 1 teaspoon onion powder

- 1/2 cup finely chopped onion

- 2 cups spaghetti squash

- 1/2 teaspoons sea salt

Directions:

- Using paper towels, squeeze extra moisture from spaghetti squash. Place the squash into a bowl, then add the salt, onion, and onion powder.

- Stir properly to mix them. Spray a non-stick cooking skillet with cooking spray, then place it over moderate heat. Add the spaghetti squash to the pan.

- Cook the squash for about 5 minutes. Flip the hash browns using a spatula. Cook for 5 minutes until the desired crispness is reached. Serve.

Nutritional information: Calories: 44, Fat: 0.6 g, Carbs: 9.7 g, Protein: 0.9 g

13. Pumpkin Spice Quinoa

Preparation Time: 10 minutes

Cooking Time: 0 minutes

Servings: 2

Ingredients:

- 1 cup cooked quinoa

- 1 cup unsweetened coconut milk

- 1 large mashed banana

- 1/4 cup pumpkin puree

- 1 teaspoon pumpkin spice

- 2 teaspoons chia seeds

Directions:

- In a container, mix all the **Ingredients**. Seal the lid, then shake the container properly to mix. Refrigerate overnight. Serve.

Nutritional information: Calories: 212, Fat: 11.9 g, Carbs: 31.7 g, Protein: 7.3 g

14. Chocolate Cherry Crunch Granola

Preparation Time: 10 minutes

Cooking Time: 20 minutes

Servings: 6

Ingredients:

- 3 cups rolled oats
- 2 cups assorted seeds, such as sesame, chia, sunflower, and pepitas (hulled pumpkin seeds)
- 1 cup sliced almonds
- 1 cup unsweetened coconut flakes
- 2 teaspoons vanilla extract
- 2 teaspoons ground cinnamon
- 1 teaspoon fine sea salt
- ½ Cup of cocoa powder
- ½ Cup pure maple syrup
- ¼ Cup coconut oil or canola oil
- 1 cup dried cherries (unsweetened, if possible)
- 1 cup of chocolate chips

Directions:

- Warm oven to 350°f. Spread 2 large baking sheets with parchment paper.
- Stir the oats, seeds, almonds, and coconut in a large bowl. Add the vanilla, cinnamon, salt, and cocoa powder. Stir to combine.
- In a frying pan on low, heat the maple syrup and coconut oil. Pour the warm syrup and oil over the oat mixture and stir to coat. On the prepared baking sheets, spread the granola in even layers.
- Bake for 15 to 18 minutes, scraping and mixing occasionally, then remove from the oven.
- Put in the dried cherries and chocolate chips, then return to the oven, now turned off but still warm, and let the granola cool and dry thoroughly.

Nutritional information: Calories: 570, Fat: 31 g, Protein: 12 g

15. Mango Coconut Oatmeal

Preparation Time: 5 minutes

Cooking Time: 5 minutes

Servings: 2

Ingredients:

- 1 ½ cups water
- ½ Cup 5-minute steel cut oats
- ¼ Cup unsweetened canned coconut milk, plus more for serving (optional)
- 1 tablespoon pure maple syrup
- 1 teaspoon sesame seeds
- Dash ground cinnamon
- 1 mango, stripped, pitted, and divide into slices
- 1 tablespoon unsweetened coconut flakes

Directions:

- In a frying pan over high heat, boil water. Put the oats and lower the heat. Cook, occasionally stirring, for 5 minutes.
- Put in the coconut milk, maple syrup, and salt to combine. Get two bowls and sprinkle with the sesame seeds and cinnamon. Top with sliced mango and coconut flakes.

Nutritional information: Calories: 373, Fat: 11 g, Carbs: 0 g, Protein: 12 g

16. Scrambled Eggs With Soy Sauce And Broccoli Slaw

Preparation Time: 5 minutes

Cooking Time: 10 minutes

Servings: 2

Ingredients:

- 1 tablespoon peanut oil, divided
- 4 large eggs
- ½ to 1 tablespoon soy sauce, tamari, or Bragg's liquid aminos
- 1 tablespoon water
- 1 cup shredded broccoli slaw or other shredded vegetables
- Kosher salt
- Chopped fresh cilantro for serving
- Hot sauce, for serving

Directions:

- In a medium non-stick skillet or cast-iron skillet over medium heat, heat 2 teaspoons of peanut oil, swirling to coat the skillet.
- In a small bowl, whip the eggs, soy sauce, and water until smooth. Pour the eggs into the pan and let the bottom set.
- Using a wooden spoon, spread the eggs from one side to the other a couple of times so the uncooked portions on top pool into the bottom. Cook until the eggs are set.
- In a medium container, stir together the broccoli slaw, the remaining 1 teaspoon of peanut oil, and a touch of salt. Divide the slaw between 2 plates.
- Top with the eggs and scatter cilantro on each serving. Serve with hot sauce.

Nutritional information: Calories: 222, Fat: 4 g, Carbs: 2 g, Protein: 12 g

17. Tasty Breakfast Donuts

Preparation Time: 5 minutes

Cooking Time: 5 minutes

Servings: 4

Ingredients:

- 43 grams' cream cheese
- 2 eggs
- 2 tablespoons almond flour
- 2 tablespoons erythritol
- 1 ½ tablespoons coconut flour
- ½ Teaspoon baking powder
- ½ Teaspoon vanilla extract
- 5 drops stevia (liquid form)
- 2 strips bacon, fried until crispy

Directions:

- Rub coconut oil over the donut maker and turn it on. Pulse all **Ingredients** except bacon in a blender or food processor until smooth (it should take around 1 minute).
- Pour batter into donut maker, leaving 1/10 in each round for rising. Leave for 3 minutes before flipping each donut.
- Leave for another 2 minutes or until the fork comes out clean when piercing them. Take donuts out and let cool. Crumble bacon into bits and use it to top donuts.

Nutritional information: Calories: 60, Fat: 5 g, Carbs: 1 g, Protein: 3 g

18. Cheesy Spicy Bacon Bowls

Preparation Time: 10 minutes

Cooking Time: 22 minutes

Servings: 12

Ingredients:

- 6 strips bacon, pan-fried until cooked but still malleable
- 4 eggs
- 60 grams' cheddar cheese
- 40 grams' cream cheese, grated
- 2 Jalapenos, sliced and seeds removed
- 2 tablespoons coconut oil
- ¼ Teaspoon onion powder
- ¼ Teaspoon garlic powder
- Dash of salt and pepper

Directions:

- Preheat oven to 375°f.
- In a bowl, beat together eggs, cream cheese, jalapenos (minus 6 slices), coconut oil, onion powder, garlic powder, and salt and pepper.
- Use the leftover bacon to grease on a muffin tray, rubbing it into each insert. Place bacon-wrapped inside the parameters of each insert.
- Pour the beaten mixture halfway up each bacon bowl. Garnish each bacon bowl with cheese and leftover jalapeno slices (placing one on top of each).

- Leave in the oven for about 22 minutes, or until the egg is thoroughly cooked and cheese is bubbly. Remove from oven and let cool until edible. Enjoy!

Nutritional information: Calories: 259, Fat: 24 g, Carbs: 1 g, Protein: 10 g

19. Goat Cheese Zucchini Kale Quiche

Preparation Time: 35 minutes

Cooking Time: 1 hour 10 minutes

Servings: 4

Ingredients:

- 4 large eggs
- 8 ounces' fresh zucchini, sliced
- 10 ounces' kale
- 3 garlic cloves (minced)
- 1 cup of soy milk
- 1 ounce's goat cheese
- 1cup grated parmesan
- 1cup shredded cheddar cheese
- 2 teaspoons olive oil
- Salt and pepper, to taste

Directions:

- Preheat oven to 350°F. Heat up 1 teaspoon of olive oil in a saucepan over medium-high heat. Sauté garlic for 1 minute until flavored.
- Add the zucchini and cook for another 5-7 minutes until soft. Beat the eggs, and then add a little milk and Parmesan cheese.
- Meanwhile, heat the remaining olive oil in another saucepan and add the cabbage. Cover and cook for 5 minutes until dry.
- Slightly grease a baking dish with cooking spray and spread the kale leaves across the bottom. Add the zucchini and top with goat cheese.
- Pour the egg, milk, and parmesan mixture evenly over the other **Ingredients**. Top with cheddar cheese.
- Bake for 50–60 minutes until golden brown. Check the center of the quiche; it should have a solid consistency. Let chill for a few minutes before serving.

Nutritional information: Calories: 290, Carbohydrates: 15 g, Protein: 19 g, Fat: 18 g

20. Ricotta Ramekins

Preparation Time: 10 minutes

Cooking Time: 1 hour

Servings: 4

Ingredients:

- 6 eggs, whisked
- 1 and ½ pounds ricotta cheese, soft
- ½ Pound stevia
- 1 teaspoon vanilla extract
- ½ Teaspoon baking powder
- Cooking spray

Directions:

- In a bowl, mix the eggs, ricotta, and the other **Ingredients** except for the cooking spray and whisk well.
- Grease 4 ramekins with the cooking spray, pour the ricotta cream in each and bake at 360°f for 1 hour. Serve cold.

Nutritional information: Calories 180, Fat 5.3 g, Carbs 11.5 g, Protein 4 g

21. Chicken Lo Mein

Preparation Time: 15 minutes
Cooking Time: 30 minutes
Servings: 4

Ingredients:

- 2 tablespoons + 2 teaspoons sesame oil, divided - 790 g boneless. Skinless chicken breasts, sliced

- ¼ Teaspoon ground black pepper

- 2 tablespoons soy sauce

- 2 tablespoons oyster sauce

- 1 garlic clove, minced

- 2 teaspoons peeled and minced fresh ginger-root

- 2 spring onions, trimmed and sliced with white and green parts separated

- 110 g fresh mushrooms, divided

- 1 medium red bell pepper, membranes, and seeds removed

- 2 medium zucchinis (400 g), cut, sliced

Directions:

- In a skillet, heat one teaspoon sesame oil over medium-high heat. Put the sliced chicken, season with black pepper, and cook until the chicken is done (internal temperature about 165°F). Dismiss from wok or skillet and set aside. While the chicken cooks, prepare the sauce by combining the oyster sauce, soy sauce, and 2 tablespoons of sesame oil in a bowl and whisking together. Set aside.

- With the same skillet used to cook the chicken, heat 1 teaspoon sesame oil and put the garlic, ginger, and white spring onion pieces; cook until fragrant, about 1 minute.

- Put the mushrooms and bell peppers and continue to cook until just tender, about 3 minutes. Add zucchini noodles and toss to combine.

- Pour in the sauce and put the chicken; cook until zucchini is tender and the mixture is heated for 5 minutes. Garnish with green parts of spring onions.

Nutritional information: Calories: 312, Protein: 9 g, Fat: 10 g, Carbs: 22 g

22. Pancakes With Berries

Preparation Time: 5 minutes
Cooking Time: 20 minutes
Servings: 2

Ingredients:

Pancake:

- 1 egg

- 50 g spelled flour

- 50 g almond flour

- 15 g coconut flour

- 150 ml of water

- Salt

Filling:

- 40 g mixed berries

- 10 g chocolate

- 5 g powdered sugar

- 4 tablespoons yogurt

Directions:

- Put the flour, egg, and some salt in a blender jar. Add 150 ml of water. Mix everything with a whisk. Heat a coated pan.

- Put in half of the batter. Once the pancake is firm, turn it over. Take out the pancake, add the second half of the batter to the pan, and repeat.

- Melt chocolate over a water bath. Let the pancakes cool. Brush the pancakes with the yogurt. Wash the berry and let it drain. Put berries on the yogurt.

- Roll up the pancakes, then sprinkle them with powdered sugar. Decorate the whole thing with the melted chocolate.

Nutritional information: Calories: 298, Carbohydrates: 26 g, Protein: 21 g, Fat: 9 g

23. Omelet À La Margherita

Preparation Time: 10 minutes
Cooking Time: 20 minutes
Servings: 2

Ingredients:

- 3 eggs
- 50 g parmesan cheese
- 2 tablespoons heavy cream
- 1 tablespoon olive oil
- 1 teaspoon oregano
- Nutmeg
- Salt
- Pepper

For covering:

- 3 - 4 stalks of basil
- 1 tomato
- 100 g grated mozzarella

Directions:

- Mix the cream plus eggs in a medium bowl. Add the grated parmesan, nutmeg, oregano, pepper, and salt, and stir everything. Heat the oil in a pan.
- Add 1/2 of the egg and cream to the pan. Let the omelet set over medium heat, turn it, and then remove it.
- Repeat with the second half of the egg mixture. Cut the tomatoes into slices and place them on top of the omelets. Scatter the mozzarella over the tomatoes.
- Place the omelets on a baking sheet—Cook at 180 degrees for 5 to 10 minutes. Then take the omelets out and decorate them with the basil leaves.

Nutritional information: Calories: 402, Carbohydrates: 7 g, Protein: 21 g, Fat: 34 g

24. Omelet With Tomatoes And Spring Onions

Preparation Time: 5 minutes
Cooking Time: 20 minutes
Servings: 3

Ingredients:

- 6 eggs
- 2 tomatoes
- 2 spring onions
- 1 shallot
- 2 tablespoons butter
- 1 tablespoon olive oil
- 1 pinch of nutmeg
- Salt and pepper

Directions:

- Whisk the eggs in a bowl. Mix them and season them with salt and pepper. Peel the shallot and chop it up.
- Clean the onions and cut them into rings. Wash the tomatoes and cut them into pieces—heat butter and oil in a pan.
- Braise half of the shallots in it, then add half the egg mixture. Let everything set over medium heat. Scatter a few tomatoes and onion rings on top. Repeat with the second half of the egg mixture. In the end, spread the grated nutmeg over the whole thing.

Nutritional information: Calories: 263, Carbohydrates: 8 g, Protein: 20.3 g, Fat: 24 g

25. Yogurt With Granola And Persimmon

Preparation Time: 5 minutes
Cooking Time: 5 minutes
Servings: 1

Ingredients:

- 150 g Greek-style yogurt
- 20 g oatmeal
- 60 g fresh persimmons
- 30 ml of tap water

Directions:

- Put the oatmeal in the pan without any fat.
- Toast them, stirring constantly, until golden brown.
- Then put them on a plate and let them cool down briefly.
- Peel the persimmon and put it in a bowl with the water. Mix the whole thing into a fine puree.
- Put the yogurt, the toasted oatmeal, and the puree in layers in a glass and serve.

Nutritional information: kcal: 286, Carbohydrates: 29 g, Protein: 1 g, Fat: 11 g

26. Smoothie Bowl With Spinach, Mango And Muesli

Preparation Time: 10 minutes
Cooking Time: 0 minutes
Servings: 1
Ingredients:

- 150 g yogurt
- 30 g apple
- 30 g mango
- 30 g low carb muesli
- 10 g spinach
- 10 g chia seeds

Directions:

- Soak the spinach leaves and let them drain.
- Peel the mango and cut it into strips.
- Remove apple core and cut it into pieces.
- Put everything except the mango together with the yogurt in a blender and make a fine puree out of it.
- Put the spinach smoothie in a bowl.
- Add the muesli, chia seeds, and mango.
- Serve the whole thing

Nutritional information: kcal: 362, Carbohydrates: 21 g, Protein: 12 g, Fat: 21 g

27. Fried Egg With Bacon

Preparation Time: 5 minutes
Cooking Time: 10 minutes
Servings: 1
Ingredients:

- 2 eggs
- 30 grams of bacon
- 2 tablespoons olive oil
- Salt
- Pepper

Directions:

- Heat oil in the pan and fry the bacon.
- Reduce the heat and beat the eggs in the pan.
- Cook the eggs and season with salt and pepper.
- Serve the fried eggs hot with the bacon.

Nutritional information: kcal: 405, Carbohydrates: 1 g, Protein: 19 g, Fat: 38 g

28. Smoothie Bowl With Berries, Poppy Seeds, Nuts, And Seeds

Preparation Time: 15 minutes
Cooking Time: 0 minutes
Servings: 2
Ingredients:

- 5 chopped almonds
- 2 chopped walnuts
- 1 apple
- ¼ Banana
- 300 g yogurt
- 60 g raspberries
- 20 g blueberries
- 20 g rolled oats, roasted in a pan
- 10 g poppy seeds
- 1 teaspoon pumpkin seeds
- Agave syrup

Directions:

- Clean the fruit and let it drain.
- Take some berries and set them aside.
- Place the remaining berries in a tall mixing vessel.
- Cut the banana into slices. Put a few aside.
- Add the rest of the banana to the berries.
- Remove the core of the apple and cut it into quarters.
- Cut the quarters into thin wedges and set a few aside.
- Add the remaining wedges to the berries.
- Add the yogurt to the fruits and mix everything into a puree.
- Sweeten the smoothie with the agave syrup.
- Divide it into two bowls.
- Serve it with the remaining fruit, poppy seeds, oatmeal, nuts, and seeds.

Nutritional information: kcal: 284, Carbohydrates: 21 g, Protein: 11 g, Fat: 19 g

29. Whole Grain Bread And Avocado

Preparation Time: 5 minutes
Cooking Time: 0 minutes
Servings: 1
Ingredients:

- 2 slices of whole meal bread
- 60 g of cottage cheese
- 1 stick of thyme
- ½ Avocado
- ½ Lime
- Chili flakes
- Salt
- Pepper

Directions:

- Cut the avocado in half.
- Remove the pulp and cut it into slices.
- Pour the lime juice over it.
- Wash the thyme and shake it dry.
- Remove the leaves from the stem.
- Brush the whole wheat bread with the cottage cheese.
- Place the avocado slices on top.
- Top with the chili flakes and thyme.
- Add salt and pepper and serve.

Nutritional information: kcal: 490, Carbohydrates: 31 g, Protein: 19 g, Fat: 21 g

30. Porridge With Walnuts

Preparation Time: 5 minutes
Cooking Time: 10 minutes
Servings: 1
Ingredients:

- 50 g raspberries
- 50 g blueberries
- 25 g of ground walnuts
- 20 g of crushed flaxseed
- 10 g of oatmeal
- 200 ml nut drink
- Agave syrup
- ½ Teaspoon cinnamon
- Salt

Directions:

- Warm the nut drink in a small saucepan.
- Add the walnuts, flaxseed, and oatmeal, stirring constantly.
- Stir in the cinnamon and salt.
- Simmer for 8 minutes.
- Keep stirring everything.
- Sweet the whole thing.
- Put the porridge in a bowl.
- Wash the berries and let them drain.
- Add them to the porridge and serve everything.

Nutritional information: kcal: 378, Carbohydrates: 11 g, Protein: 18 g, Fat: 27 g

31. Hemp Seed Porridge

Preparation Time: 5 minutes
Cooking Time: 5 minutes
Servings: 6
Ingredients:

- 3 cups cooked hemp seed
- 1 packet Stevia
- 1 cup coconut milk

Directions:

- In a saucepan, mix the rice and the coconut milk over moderate heat for about 5 minutes as you stir it constantly.
- Remove the pan from the burner then add the Stevia. Stir.
- Serve in 6 bowls.
- Enjoy.

Nutritional information: Calories: 236, Fat: 1.8 g, Carbs: 48.3 g, Protein: 7 g

32. Mini Mac In A Bowl

Preparation Time: 5 minutes
Cooking Time: 15 minutes
Servings: 1
Ingredients:

- 5 ounces lean ground beef

- 2 tablespoons diced white or yellow onion.

- 1/8 teaspoon onion powder

- 1/8 teaspoon white vinegar

- 1 ounce dill pickle slices

- 1 teaspoon sesame seed

- 3 cups shredded Romaine lettuce

- Cooking spray

- 2 tablespoons reduced-fat shredded cheddar cheese

- 2 tablespoons Wish-Bone light thousand island as dressing

Directions:

- Place a lightly greased small skillet on fire to heat.

- Add your onion to cook for about 2-3 minutes. Next, add the beef and allow cooking until it's brown.

- Next, mix your vinegar and onion powder with the dressing.

- Finally, top the lettuce with the cooked meat and sprinkle cheese on it, add your pickle slices.

- Drizzle the mixture with the sauce and sprinkle the sesame seeds.

- Your mini mac in a bowl is ready for consumption.

Nutritional information: Calories: 150, Protein: 21 g, Carbohydrates: 32 g, Fats: 19 g

33. Shake Cake Fueling

Preparation Time: 5 minutes
Cooking Time: 0 minutes
Servings: 1
Ingredients:

- 1 packet Optavia shakes.

- 1/4 teaspoon baking powder

- 2 tablespoons eggbeaters or egg whites

- 2 tablespoons water

- Other options that are not compulsory include sweetener, reduced-fat cream cheese, etc.

Directions:

- Begin by preheating the oven.

- Mix all the **Ingredients**. Begin with the dry **Ingredients**, and then add the wet **Ingredients**.

- After the mixture/batter is ready, pour gently into muffin cups.

- Inside the oven, place, and bake for about 16-18 minutes or until it is baked and ready. Allow it to cool completely.

- Add additional toppings of your choice and ensure your delicious shake cake is refreshing.

Nutritional information: Calories: 896, Fat: 37 g, Carbohydrates: 115 g, Protein: 34 g

34. Optavia Biscuit Pizza

Preparation Time: 5 minutes
Cooking Time: 15-20 minutes
Servings: 1
Ingredients:

- 1/4 sachet Optavia buttermilk cheddar and herb biscuit

- 1/4 tablespoon tomato sauce

- 1/4 tablespoon low-fat shredded cheese

- ¼ Bottle water

- Parchment paper

Directions:

- Begin by preheating the oven to about 350°F

- Mix the biscuit and water and stir properly.

- In the parchment paper, pour the mixture and spread it into a thin circle. Allow cooking for 10 minutes.

- Take it out and add the tomato sauce and shredded cheese.

- Bake it for a few more minutes.

Nutritional information: Calories: 478, Protein: 30 g, Carbohydrates: 22 g, Fats: 29 g

35. Lean And Green Smoothie

Preparation Time: 5 minutes

Cooking Time: 0 minutes

Servings: 1

Ingredients:

- 2 1/2 cups kale leaves

- 3/4 cup chilled apple juice

- 1 cup cubed pineapple

- 1/2 cup frozen green grapes

- 1/2 cup chopped apple

Directions:

- Place the pineapple, apple juice, apple, frozen seedless grapes, and kale leaves in a blender.

- Cover and blend until it's smooth.

- Smoothie is ready and can be garnished with halved grapes if you wish.

Nutritional information: Calories: 81, Protein: 2 g, Carbohydrates: 19 g, Fats: 1 g

36. Lean And Green Chicken Pesto Pasta

Preparation Time: 5 minutes

Cooking Time: 15 minutes

Servings: 1

Ingredients:

- 3 cups raw kale leaves

- 2 tablespoons olive oil

- 2 cups fresh basil - 1/4 teaspoon salt

- 3 tablespoons lemon juice

- 3 garlic cloves

- 2 cups cooked chicken breast

- 1 cup baby spinach

- 6 ounces uncooked chicken pasta

- 3 ounces diced fresh mozzarella

- Basil leaves red pepper flakes to garnish

Directions:

- Start by making the pesto; add the kale, lemon juice, basil, garlic cloves, olive oil, and salt to a blender and blend until it's smooth.

- Add salt and pepper to taste.

- Cook the pasta and strain off the water. Reserve 1/4 cup of the liquid.

- Get a bowl and mix everything, the cooked pasta,

pesto, diced chicken, spinach, mozzarella, and the reserved pasta liquid.

- Sprinkle the mixture with additional chopped basil or red paper flakes (optional). Now your salad is ready. You may serve it warm or chilled. Also, it can be taken as a salad mix-ins or as a side dish. Leftovers should be stored in the refrigerator inside an air-tight container for 3-5 days.

Nutritional information: Calories: 244, Protein: 20.5 g, Carbohydrates: 22.5 g, Fats: 10 g

37. Open-Face Egg Sandwiches With Cilantro-Jalapeño Spread

Preparation Time: 20 minutes

Cooking Time: 10 minutes

Servings: 2

Ingredients:

For the cilantro and jalapeño spread

- 1 cup filled up fresh cilantro leaves and stems (about a bunch)

- 1 jalapeño pepper, seeded and roughly chopped

- ½ Cup extra-virgin olive oil

- ¼ Cup pepitas (hulled pumpkin seeds), raw or roasted

- 2 garlic cloves, thinly sliced

- 1 tablespoon freshly squeezed lime juice

- 1 teaspoon kosher salt

For the eggs

- 4 large eggs

- ¼ Cup milk

- ¼ To ½ teaspoon kosher salt

- 2 tablespoons butter

For the sandwich

- 2 slices bread

- 1 tablespoon butter

- 1 avocado, halved, pitted, and divided into slices

- Microgreens or sprouts, for garnish

Directions:

- To make the cilantro and jalapeño spread

- In a food processor, combine the cilantro, jalapeño, oil, pepitas, garlic, lime juice, and salt. Whirl until smooth. Refrigerate if making in advance; otherwise set aside.

- To make the eggs

- In a medium bowl, whisk the eggs, milk, and salt.

- Dissolve the butter in a skillet over low heat, swirling to coat the bottom of the pan. Pour in the whisked eggs.

- Cook until they begin to set then, using a heatproof spatula, push them to the sides, allowing the uncooked portions to run into the bottom of the skillet.

- Continue until the eggs are set.

- To assemble the sandwiches

- Toast the bed and spread with butter.

- Spread a spoonful of the cilantro-jalapeño spread on each piece of toast. Top each with scrambled eggs.

- Arrange avocado over each sandwich and garnish with microgreens.

Nutritional information: Calories: 711, Total fat: 4 g, Cholesterol: 54 mg, Fiber: 12 g, Protein: 12 g, Sodium: 327 mg

38. Apple Kale Cucumber Smoothie

Preparation Time: 5 minutes

Cooking Time: 5 minutes

Servings: 1

Ingredients:

- ¾ Cup water

- ½ Green apple, diced

- ¾ Cup kale

- ½ Cucumber

Directions:

- Toss all your Ingredients into your blender then process till smooth and creamy.

- Serve immediately and enjoy.

Nutritional information: Calories: 86, Fat: 0.5 g, Carbs: 21.7 g, Protein: 1.9 g, Fiber: 0 g

39. Refreshing Cucumber Smoothie

Preparation Time: 5 minutes

Cooking Time: 5 minutes

Servings: 2

Ingredients:

- 1 cup ice cubes

- 20 drops liquid stevia

- 2 fresh limes, peeled and halved

- 1 teaspoon lime zest, grated

- 1 cucumber, chopped

- 1 avocado, pitted and peeled

- 2 cups kale

- 1 tablespoon creamed coconut

- ¾ Cup coconut water

Directions:

- Toss all your Ingredients into your blender then process till smooth and creamy.

- Serve immediately and enjoy.

Nutritional information: Calories: 313, Fat: 25.1 g, Carbs: 24.7 g, Protein: 4.9 g, Fiber: 0 g

40. Cauliflower Veggie Smoothie

Preparation Time: 5 minutes

Cooking Time: 5 minutes

Servings: 4

Ingredients:

- 1 zucchini, peeled and chopped

- 1 Seville orange, peeled

- 1 apple, diced

- 1 banana

- 1 cup kale

- ½ Cup cauliflower

Directions:

- Toss all your Ingredients into your blender then process till smooth and creamy.

- Serve immediately and enjoy.

Nutritional information: Calories: 71, Fat: 0.3 g, Carbs: 18.3 g, Protein: 1.3 g, Fiber: 0 g

41. Tofu Omelet

Preparation Time: 10 minutes
Cooking Time: 5 minutes
Servings: 2

Ingredients:

- 1 teaspoon arrowroot starch
- 2 teaspoons water
- 3 eggs, whisked
- 2 teaspoons fish sauce
- Black pepper, to taste
- ¼ Cup fresh spinach, chopped
- ¼ Cup tofu, pressed and sliced
- Olive oil, for greasing

Preparation:

- In a bowl, combine the arrowroot starch and water. Mix well.
- Add the eggs, pepper, and fish sauce. Mix well.
- Add the spinach and combine.
- Take a pan, grease it with the olive oil, and heat it on medium.
- Now add the tofu and the egg mixture to the pan and cook for few minutes until the egg cooks.

When cooked, place it on a plate, let it cool and serve.

Serving Suggestion: Serve with sour cream on top.

Variation Tip: You can skip the fish sauce.

Nutritional information:

Calories: 178 | Fat: 11.2g | Sat Fat: 6.7g | Carbohydrates: 3.9g | Fiber: 0.2g | Sugar: 1.6g | Protein: 15.6g

42. Zucchini Pancakes

Preparation Time: 15 minutes
Cooking Time: 15 minutes
Servings: 4

Ingredients:

- 4 cups zucchini, shredded
- Salt and black pepper, to taste
- ¼ Cup cooked chicken, shredded
- 1 egg, beaten
- ¼ Cup coconut flour
- 2 tablespoons olive oil

Preparation:

- Sauté the zucchini with some salt until tender, about 5 minutes.
- Squeeze and drain the zucchini. Set aside for 10 minutes.
- Put the cooked zucchini in a mixing bowl.
- Add the remaining Ingredients except for the olive oil and mix well.
- Put a skillet on medium heat, add the olive oil, and heat it.
- Put the batter in the skillet a little at a time to make pancakes. Cook for 4 minutes per side.
- Serve warm.
- Serving Suggestion: Serve with shredded cheese on top.
- Variation Tip: You can skip the meat.

Nutritional information:

Calories: 83 | Fat: 5.2g | Sat Fat: 1.1g | Carbohydrates: 4.8g | Fiber: 1.7g | Sugar: 2.2g | Protein: 5.5g

43. Spinach Omelet

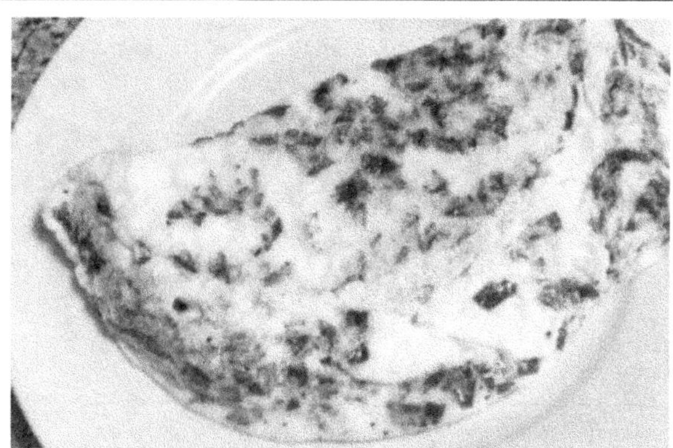

Preparation Time: 5 minutes

Cooking Time: 10 minutes

Servings: 1

Ingredients:

- 2 tablespoons milk

- 2 eggs

- Salt, to taste

- Dash of pepper

- ¼ cup mozzarella cheese, shredded

- ¼ cup fresh spinach, shredded

- Cooking spray

Preparation:

- Whisk the eggs, milk, pepper, and salt.

- Spray a pan with cooking spray and heat it over medium heat.

- Pour the mixture into the pan. When the eggs are cooked, sprinkle with the cheese and add the spinach.

- Cook for 1 minute until the cheese melts.

Serving Suggestion: Serve with berries.

Variation Tip: 2 eggs can be replaced with 4 egg whites.

Nutritional information

Calories: 163 | Fat: 10.7g | Sat Fat: 3.9g | Carbohydrates: 2.8g | Fiber: 0.2g | Sugar: 2.1g | Protein: 14.3g

44. Cheese Egg Muffins

Preparation Time: 11 minutes

Cooking Time: 25 minutes

Servings: 4

Ingredients:

- 9 eggs, beaten

- 1 cup egg whites, beaten

- ¼ cup low-fat Greek yogurt, beaten

- ¼ cup goat's cheese, cubed

- 2 cups cherry tomatoes, chopped

- Cooking spray

Preparation:

- Preheat the oven to 375°F.

- Put the eggs, egg whites, Greek yogurt, and cheese in a bowl and whisk.

- Add the cherry tomatoes and combine well.

- Lightly grease a muffin tin with cooking spray and evenly distribute the mixture.

- Bake for 25 minutes, and then let the muffins cool.

Serving Suggestion: Top with cheese of your choice.

Variation Tip: You can skip the cherry tomatoes.

Nutritional information

Calories: 396 | Fat: 25.4g | Sat Fat: 13.7g | Carbohydrates: 8.5g | Fiber: 1.1g | Sugar: 7.3g | Protein: 33.4g

45. Cinnamon Baked Oatmeal

Preparation Time: 5 minutes

Cooking Time: 25 minutes

Servings: 4

Ingredients:

- ½ Teaspoon baking powder

- 3 tablespoons egg white

- 1 cup unsweetened almond milk

- ¼ Teaspoon ground cinnamon

- Cooking spray

- 4 sachets Lean & Green Cinnamon and Hot Cereal

Preparation:

- Preheat the oven to 350°F.

- In a large bowl, thoroughly mix the cereal, baking powder, eggs, and almond milk.

- Lightly grease four small oven-proof mason jars with cooking spray. Divide the mixture into the jars, leaving ½-inch from the top.

- Sprinkle cinnamon over the top.

- Place the jars on a baking sheet and bake for 20 to 25 minutes. Let them cool completely before serving.

Serving Suggestion: Serve with chopped nuts sprinkled on top.

Variation Tip: You can use cashew milk instead of almond milk.

Nutritional information:

Calories: 145 | Fat: 14.3g | Sat Fat: 12.7g | Carbohydrates: 3.8g | Fiber: 1.4g | Sugar: 2.1g | Protein: 2.6g

46. Mini Omelet Waffle

Preparation Time: 5 minutes

Cooking Time: 4 minutes

Servings: 1

Ingredients:

- 6 tablespoons egg white

- 2 tablespoons red bell peppers, finely chopped

- 1 tablespoon raw spinach, finely chopped

- 2 tablespoons onion, finely chopped

- Cooking spray

- ¼ Avocado, peeled, cored, and cut into small cubes

Preparation:

- In a bowl, thoroughly mix the egg, spinach, bell pepper, and onion.

- Lightly grease a waffle maker with cooking spray.

- Pour half of the mixture into the waffle maker. Cook for 3 to 4 minutes.

- Take out and repeat for the rest of the mixture. Let the waffles cool, and then serve.

Serving Suggestion: Serve with the cubed avocado.

Variation Tip: You can also use jalapeños for more flavor.

Nutritional information: Calories: 234 | Fat: 10.6g | Sat Fat: 2.1g | Carbohydrates: 24.9g | Fiber: 7g | Sugar: 13.8g | Protein: 13.6g

47. Broccoli Bake

Preparation Time: 10 minutes

Cooking Time: 45 minutes

Servings: 4

Ingredients:

- 6 cups small broccoli florets
- 3 tablespoons water
- 9 eggs
- 1 cup unsweetened almond milk
- ¼ Teaspoon black pepper
- Salt, to taste
- ¼ Cup reduced-fat cheddar cheese, shredded
- Cooking spray

Preparation:

- Preheat the oven to 375°F.
- Put the broccoli and water into a microwave-safe dish and microwave on high for 4 minutes. When done, drain off any excess liquid. Set aside.
- In a bowl, mix the eggs, milk, salt, and pepper.
- Lightly grease a baking dish with cooking spray. Add the broccoli, then pour in the egg mixture. Sprinkle the cheese over the top.
- Bake for about 45 minutes. When done, let it cool, and serve.

Serving Suggestion: Serve with cherry tomatoes.

Variation Tip: You can also use jalapeños for extra flavor.

Nutritional information:

Calories: 346 | Fat: 26.1g | Sat Fat: 16.6g | Carbohydrates: 13.2g | Fiber: 4.9g | Sugar: 5.1g | Protein: 19.7g

48. Cheese Waffles

Preparation Time: 15 minutes

Cooking Time: 5 minutes

Servings: 8

Ingredients:

- 2 eggs, beaten
- 2 cups ricotta cheese, shredded
- 2 garlic cloves, minced
- 1 cup frozen spinach
- 1 cup part-skim mozzarella cheese, shredded
- Salt and black pepper, to taste
- ½ Cup low-fat parmesan cheese, grated
- Cooking spray

Preparation:

- Lightly grease a waffle maker with cooking spray; allow it to preheat.
- In a bowl, beat together the eggs, garlic, ricotta, and spinach.
- Add the mozzarella, parmesan, pepper, and salt, and whisk.
- Pour the mixture into the waffle maker in batches, cooking for 5 minutes per batch.

Serving Suggestion: Serve with maple syrup on top.

Variation Tip: You can skip the spinach.

Nutritional information:

Calories: 119 | Fat: 7g | Sat Fat: 4g | Carbohydrates: 3.9g | Fiber: 0.1g | Sugar: 0.3g | Protein: 10.2g

49. Basil Omelet

Preparation Time: 5 minutes
Cooking Time: 4 minutes
Servings: 4

Ingredients:

- 8 eggs
- 2 tablespoons olive oil
- ½ Tablespoon red pepper flakes
- ½ Cup basil, chopped
- 1 cup tomatoes, chopped
- Salt, to taste
- Olive oil

Preparation:

- Beat the eggs in a bowl, then add the red pepper flakes and salt. Mix well.
- Add the tomatoes and basil and mix well.
- Heat some olive oil in a skillet over medium heat. Pour in the egg mixture.
- Cook for about 4 minutes and serve.
- Serving Suggestion: Top with shredded cheese.

Variation Tip: You can replace red pepper flakes with black pepper.

Nutritional information:

Calories: 197 | Fat: 16g | Sat Fat: 3.8g | Carbohydrates: 2.9g | Fiber: 0.8g | Sugar: 1.9g | Protein: 11.6g

50. Eggs In Pepper Rings

Preparation Time: 5 minutes
Cooking Time: 6 minutes
Servings: 4

Ingredients:

- 2 bell peppers, cut into rings
- 8 eggs
- 2 tablespoons fresh chives, chopped
- 2 tablespoons fresh parsley, chopped
- Salt and pepper, to taste

Preparation:

- Take a non-stick pan, grease it, and add the bell pepper rings. Cook for 2 minutes.
- Flip the rings over and pour an egg in the middle of each.
- Add salt and pepper on top and cook for 4 minutes. Remove from the pan and add parsley and chives on top.

Serving Suggestion: Top with some shredded cheese.

Variation Tip: You can also use chili flakes.

Nutritional information:

Calories: 146 | Fat: 8.9g | Sat Fat: 2.7g | Carbohydrates: 5.4g | Fiber: 0.9g | Sugar: 3.7g | Protein: 11.8g

51. Cheddar Broccoli Bread

Preparation Time: 15 minutes

Cooking time: 45 minutes

Servings: 3

Ingredients:

- ¼ Cup shredded reduced-fat cheddar

- 3 cups small broccoli florets

- ⅛ Teaspoon cayenne pepper

- 4 eggs

- ⅛ Teaspoon black pepper

- ½ Cup unsweetened almond milk

- Salt, to taste

Preparation:

- Preheat the oven to 375°F.

- Put 2 tablespoons of water and the broccoli into a microwave-safe bowl and microwave for 4 minutes.

- Take out the bowl and strain the broccoli.

- Meanwhile, add the black pepper, cayenne pepper, salt, eggs, and almond milk to a large bowl. Beat well.

- In a greased baking dish, arrange the broccoli on the bottom and sprinkle it with the cheese.

- Pour the egg mixture onto the broccoli and cheese and bake for 45 minutes.

- Take out, slice, and serve.

Serving Suggestion: Serve with your favorite hot beverage.

Variation Tip: You can also use mozzarella cheese for a fuller flavor.

Nutritional information:

Calories: 653 | Fat: 36.9g | Sat Fat: 2.2g | Carbohydrates: 24g | Fiber: 9.2g | Sugar: 0.5g | Protein: 57.2g

52. Broccoli Waffles

Preparation Time: 10 minutes

Cooking time: 8 minutes

Servings: 4

Ingredients:

- ½ Cup chopped broccoli

- 2 eggs

- ½ Cup low-fat cheddar cheese, shredded

- 1 teaspoon garlic powder

- 1 teaspoon dried onion, minced

- Salt and black pepper, to taste

Preparation:

- Grease and preheat a waffle iron.

- Meanwhile, add the broccoli, cheddar cheese, eggs, dried onion, garlic powder, salt, and pepper to a large bowl. Mix well.

- Pour the batter onto the waffle iron and cook for 4 minutes.

Serving Suggestion: Serve with green chili sauce.

Variation Tip: You can omit the garlic powder if you prefer.

Nutritional information:

Calories: 95 | Fat: 6.9g | Sat Fat: 3.7g | Carbohydrates: 1.7g | Fiber: 0.4g | Sugar: 0.6g | Protein: 6.7g

53. Mushroom & Spinach Egg Muffins

Preparation Time: 10 minutes

Cooking time: 25 minutes

Servings: 2

Ingredients:

- ½ Cup frozen spinach, chopped
- 1 cup mushrooms, chopped
- 4 eggs
- 2 tablespoons low-fat Greek yogurt
- Salt, to taste

Preparation:

- Add the eggs, yogurt, mushrooms, spinach, and salt to a large bowl. Beat well.
- Preheat the baking oven to 375˚F and grease a muffin tin.
- Pour the mushroom batter into the muffin tin and bake for 25 minutes.

Serving Suggestion: Serve with tomato ketchup.

Variation Tip: Use cayenne pepper for a flavor kick.

Nutritional information:

Calories: 150 | Fat: 9.1g | Sat Fat: 2.8g | Carbohydrates: 5g | Fiber: 0.5g | Sugar: 4.2g | Protein: 13g

54. Egg Muffins

Preparation Time: 10 minutes

Cooking time: 20 minutes

Servings: 3

Ingredients:

- 4 eggs
- 6 tablespoons low-fat Greek yogurt
- ½ Cup liquid egg whites
- Salt, to taste

Preparation:

- Warm up the baking oven to 375˚F.
- Meanwhile, add the eggs, yogurt, egg whites, and salt to a bowl. Whisk well.
- Pour the mixture into a greased muffin tin and place it into the oven.
- Bake for 20 minutes.

Serving Suggestion: Serve with honey drizzled on top.

Variation Tip: You can add herbs of your choice to enhance the taste of the muffins.

Nutritional information:

Calories: 136 | Fat: 6.2g | Sat Fat: 2.1g | Carbohydrates: 6.2g | Fiber: 0g | Sugar: 6.2g | Protein: 13g

55. Cheese Waffles

Preparation Time: 15 minutes

Cooking time: 20 minutes

Servings: 8

Ingredients:

- 2 eggs, beaten
- 2 garlic cloves, minced
- 2 cups part-skim ricotta cheese, crumbled
- 1 cup frozen spinach
- 1 cup part-skim mozzarella cheese, shredded
- ½ Cup low-fat parmesan cheese, grated
- Salt and black pepper, to taste

Preparation:

- Grease and preheat a waffle iron.
- Add the eggs, garlic cloves, ricotta cheese, and spinach to a large bowl. Beat well.
- Add the mozzarella cheese, parmesan cheese, salt, and pepper. Whisk thoroughly.
- Pour the batter into the waffle iron and cook for 5 minutes.
- Take out and serve hot.

Serving Suggestion: Serve with a drizzle of maple syrup on top.

Variation Tip: You can omit spinach.

Nutritional information:

Calories: 119 | Fat: 7g | Sat Fat: 4g | Carbohydrates: 3.9g | Fiber: 0.1g | Sugar: 0.3g | Protein: 10.2g

56. Arugula Omelet

Preparation Time: 5 minutes

Cooking time: 7 minutes

Servings: 2

Ingredients:

- 3 eggs
- 2 scallions, finely chopped
- 1 tablespoon unsweetened almond milk
- 1 tablespoon olive oil
- 1 cup fresh arugula, finely chopped
- Salt, to taste
- Black pepper, to taste

Preparation:

- Add the eggs, scallions, almond milk, arugula, salt, and pepper to a large bowl. Beat well.
- Meanwhile, warm up the olive oil in a non-stick pan.
- Add the egg mixture and cook it for 5 minutes on low heat.

Serving Suggestion: Serve with finely chopped cilantro leaves on top and fresh bread on the side.

Variation Tip: You can also add chopped tomatoes to the omelet.

Nutritional information:

Calories: 163 | Fat: 13.8g | Sat Fat: 3.1g | Carbohydrates: 2.1g | Fiber: 0.6g | Sugar: 1.1g | Protein: 8.9g

57. Cauliflower Breakfast Casserole

Preparation Time: 10 minutes.

Cooking time: 55 minutes.

Servings: 8

Ingredients:

- 8 ounces turkey sausage, cooked
- ¼ Cup onion, chopped
- 2 cups cauliflower florets
- ½ teaspoon Jalapeno Seasoning
- ¼ Teaspoon salt
- ¼ Teaspoon black pepper
- 6 turkey bacon slices, cooked and chopped
- 2 cups Mexican cheese, shredded
- 8 large eggs
- 16 ounces egg whites
- ¼ Cup almond milk

Preparation:

- At 350 degrees F, preheat your oven.
- Grease a baking dish with cooking spray.
- Saute turkey sausage in a skillet until golden brown.
- Saute onions and cauliflower in a same skillet until golden.
- Stir in black pepper, salt, jalapeno seasoning then mix well.
- Sread the cauliflower mixture in the prepared baking dish.
- Top this mixture with cheese and bacon.
- Beat egg whites with eggs and almond milk in a bowl.
- Pour this mixture over the turkey mixture.

- Bake for 45 minutes in the oven.
- Garnish with green onions.
- Serve warm.

Serving Suggestion: Enjoy this breakfast casserole with a refreshing smoothie.

Variation Tip: Add some chopped or shredded zucchini to the casserole.

Nutritional information:

Calories 244 | Fat 7.9g | Sodium 704mg | Carbs 19g | Fiber 2g | Sugar 14g | Protein 14g

58. Eggs In Pepper Rings

Preparation Time: 15 minutes

Cooking time: 6 minutes

Servings: 4

Ingredients:

- 2 bell peppers, seeded and cut into rings
- 8 eggs
- 2 tablespoons fresh chives, chopped
- 2 tablespoons fresh parsley, chopped
- Salt and pepper, to taste

Preparation:

- Add the bell pepper rings to a greased, heated, non-stick pan and cook for 2 minutes.
- Flip the rings and crack an egg into the middle of each.
- Top with salt and pepper and cook for 4 minutes.
- Take out and top with the parsley and chives.

Serving Suggestion: Drizzle some Tabasco sauce over the top.

Variation Tip: You can add chili flakes to the eggs when cooking.

Nutritional information:

Calories: 146 | Fat: 8.9g | Sat Fat: 2.7g | Carbohydrates: 5.4g | Fiber: 0.9g | Sugar: 3.7g | Protein: 11.8g

59. Tasty Bell Pepper Muffins

Preparation Time: 30 minutes

Serving: 3

Ingredients:

- ¼ Cup each green pepper, sweet yellow pepper and sweet red pepper – chopped
- Two tablespoons unsalted butter
- Two cups all-purpose flour
- Two tablespoons sugar
- 2-½ teaspoons baking powder
- Half teaspoon salts
- Half teaspoon dried basil
- One egg
- ¼ Cup egg substitute
- One cup fat-free milk

Preparation:

- Cook pepper in butter into a non-stick skillet and keep it aside.
- Mix the basil, salt, baking powder, sugar, and flour into the bowl.
- Whisk the milk, egg substitute, and egg and then add in dry **Ingredients** and fold in the peppers.
- Next, coat muffin cups with cooking spray and fill with batter.
- Place into the oven and bake at 400 degrees Fahrenheit for fifteen to eighteen minutes.
- Let cool it for five minutes.
- Serve!

Variation tip: You can add almond milk instead of simple milk.

Serving Suggestion: Serve with honey or butter.

Nutritional information:

Calories 119 | fat 3g | sodium 228mg | carbohydrate 20g | fiber 1g | sugars 4g | protein 4g.

60. Baby Spinach Omelet

Preparation Time: 6 minutes

Cooking time: 9 minutes

Servings: 1

Ingredients:

- Two eggs
- One cup torn baby spinach leaves
- 1 ½ tablespoons grated part-skim Parmesan cheese
- ¼ Teaspoon onion powder
- ⅛ Teaspoon ground nutmeg
- Salt and pepper – to taste

Preparation:

- First, beat the eggs into the bowl and then add parmesan cheese and baby spinach – season with pepper, salt, nutmeg, and onion powder.
- Next, coat the skillet with cooking spray over medium flame. Add egg mixture to the skillet and cook for three minutes until set.
- Flip over using a spatula and cook for two to three minutes more.
- Decrease the speed of the flame to low and cook for two to three minutes more.
- Serve and enjoy!

Variation tip: You can add kale instead of spinach. Add Swiss cheese instead of parmesan cheese.

Serving Suggestion: Serve with buns or bread. Garnish with black pepper and fresh parsley.

Nutritional information:

Calories 186 | fat 12.3g | sodium 278.7mg | carbohydrates 2.8g | Fiber 0.8g | sugar 1.3g | protein 16.4g

61. Healthy Egg Muffins

Preparation Time: 15 minutes

Cooking time: 25 minutes

Servings: 12

Ingredients:

- One cup baby spinach – chopped

- ¾ Cup red bell pepper – diced

- ¾ Cup green bell pepper – diced

- ¾ Cup cherry tomatoes or grape tomatoes

- Six eggs

- Four egg whites

- ¼ Teaspoon kosher salt

- ¼ Teaspoon dried basil

- ¼ Teaspoon dried oregano

- Pinch ground black pepper or cayenne pepper

- ¼ Cup crumbled non-fat feta cheese

- Optional toppings: avocado salsa, hot sauce, freshly chopped parsley

Preparation:

- Preheat the oven to 350 degrees Fahrenheit.

- Coat the twelve muffins tin with non-stick cooking spray.

- Split tomatoes, green bell pepper, red bell pepper, and spinach between cups.

- Whisk the pepper, oregano, basil, salt, eggs, and egg white into the bowl. Combine well.

- Fill each muffin tin with egg mixture carefully and sprinkle with feta.

- Place into the oven and bake for twenty-four to twenty-eight minutes.

- Let cool for few minutes.

- Remove from the pan and serve!

- Add leftover into the air-tight container or zip-lock bag and place into the refrigerator for up to three days. You can freeze it for up to three minutes. Reheat into the oven for half-minute to one minute.

Serving Suggestion: Serve with dipping sauce.

Nutritional information:

Calories 70 | fat 3g | sodium 148mg | carbohydrates 3g | fiber 1g | sugar 2g | protein 8g.

62. Basil Tomato Omelet

Preparation Time: 7 minutes

Cooking time: 5 minutes

Servings: 4

Ingredients:

- 8 eggs

- 2 tablespoons olive oil

- ½ Tablespoon red pepper flakes, crushed

- ½ Cup basil, chopped

- 1 cup tomatoes, chopped

- Salt, to taste

- Black pepper, to taste

Preparation:

- Add the eggs, red pepper flakes, salt, and pepper to a large bowl. Beat well.

- Add in the tomatoes and basil. Whisk thoroughly.

- Meanwhile, add the olive oil to a non-stick pan and add the egg mixture to it.

- Cook for 5 minutes.

Serving Suggestion: Top with shredded cheese of your choice before serving.

Variation Tip: You can also add cayenne pepper to enhance the taste.

Nutritional information:

Calories: 197 | Fat: 16g | Sat Fat: 3.8g | Carbohydrates: 2.9g | Fiber: 0.8g | Sugar: 1.9g | Protein: 11.6g

63. Delicious Asparagus Frittata

Preparation Time: 10 minutes

Cooking time: 20 minutes

Servings: 4

Ingredients:

- One tablespoon olive oil

- Two teaspoons un-salted butter

- Half pound asparagus – trimmed, cut into 1-inch pieces

- Eight eggs

- Half cup grated reduced-fat Parmesan cheese

- Seven tablespoons milk

- Salt and freshly ground black pepper – to taste

- One tablespoon fresh parsley – chopped

Preparation:

- Add butter and olive oil to a non-stick pan and cook over medium flame.

- Add asparagus and cook for ten to fifteen minutes.

- Next, beat eggs into the bowl until frothy, and then add milk and parmesan cheese – season with pepper and salt.

- Add egg mixture over asparagus and cook for ten to fifteen minutes.

- Put on the serving plate and garnish with parsley.

- You can use another fresh herb instead of dill and parsley.

- You can add cilantro.

Variation tip: Use basil and thyme instead of parsley.

Serving Suggestion: Serve with salad. Garnish with green onions.

Nutritional information:

Calories 242 | fat 17.6g | sodium 341.9mg | carbohydrates 4.6g | fiber 1.2g | sugar 3.1g | protein17.1g

Lunch Recipes

1. Salmon Burgers

Serving: 1

Difficulty: 1

Preparation Time: 10 minutes

Cooking Time: 15 minutes

Optavia Counts: 1 lean/ 1 green/ 3 healthy fat/ 7 condiments

Ingredients:

- Pound salmon fillets
- 1 onion
- ¼ Dill fronds
- 1 tbsp. Honey
- 1 tbsp. Horseradish
- 1 tbsp. Mustard
- 1 tbsp. Mayonnaise
- 1 tbsp. Olive oil
- Toasted split rolls
- 1 avocado
- Salt and pepper, to taste
- Lettuce for serving

Preparation:

- Place salmon fillets in a blender and blend until smooth. Transfer to a bowl, add onion, dill, honey, horseradish and mix well. Add salt and pepper and form 4 patties.
- In a bowl combine mustard, honey, mayonnaise, and dill in a skillet heat oil add salmon patties and cook for 2 to 3 minutes per side. When ready, remove from heat.
- Divide lettuce and onion between the buns. Place salmon patty on top and spoon mustard mixture and avocado slices.

- Serve when ready.

Nutritional information: Calories: 180; Fat: 7 g; Carbs: 6 g; Protein: 12.8 g.

2. Stuffed Mushrooms

Serving: 1

Difficulty: 1

Preparation Time: 6 minutes

Cooking Time: 12 minutes

Optavia Counts: 0 lean/ 0 green/ 0 healthy fat/ 6 condiments

Ingredients:

- 2 tsp. Cumin powder
- 4 garlic cloves, peeled and minced
- 1 small onion, peeled and chopped
- 18 medium-sized white mushrooms
- Fine sea salt and freshly ground black pepper, to your liking
- A pinch ground allspice
- 1 tbsp. Olive oil

Preparation:

- First, clean the mushrooms; remove the middle stalks from the mushrooms to prepare the "shells."
- Grab a mixing dish and thoroughly combine the remaining items.
- Fill the mushrooms with the prepared mixture.
- Cook the mushrooms at 345°F and heat for 12 minutes. Enjoy!

Nutritional information: Calories: 179; Fat: 14 g; Carbs: 8.8 g; Protein: 4.8 g.

3. Mini Mac In A Bowl

Serving: 1
Difficulty: 1
Preparation Time: 5 minutes
Cooking Time: 15 minutes
Optavia Counts: 1 lean/ 2 green/ 1 healthy fat/ 5 condiments

Ingredients:

- 5 oz. Lean ground beef
- 2 tbsp. Onion
- ⅛ Tsp. Onion powder
- ⅛ Tsp. White vinegar
- 1 oz. Dill pickle slices
- 1 tsp. Sesame seed
- 1 cup romaine lettuce
- 1 tbsp. Reduced-fat cheddar cheese
- 2 tbsp. Thousand islands

Preparation:

- Place a lightly greased small pan on the fire and heat.
- Sautee the diced onion for about 2–3 minutes.
- Then, add the beef and let it fry until brown.
- Next, mix the vinegar and onion powder with the dressing.
- Finally, add the cooked meat on top of the shredded lettuce and sprinkle with cheese. Add the cucumber slices.
- Drizzle with sauce and sprinkle the sesame seeds on top.

Nutritional information: Calories: 646 kcal; Protein: 23.3 g; Fat: 55.9 g; Carbs: 12.4 g.

4. Zucchini Frittata

Serving: 1
Difficulty: 2
Preparation Time: 20 minutes
Cooking Time: 20 minutes
Optavia Counts: 0 lean/ 2 green/ 3 healthy fat/ 2 condiments

Ingredients:

- 2 tbsp. Oil
- 2 zucchinis
- 2 eggs
- 1 cup flour
- 1 tsp. Baking powder
- ½ Cup scallions
- Salt
- Black pepper

Preparation:

- Wash the zucchinis. Cut the ends off the zucchinis and grate them into a mixing bowl.
- Stir in 1 teaspoon of salt and set aside for about 10 minutes.
- Squeeze the grated zucchini dry to remove as much water as possible.
- Add the two whole eggs and the chopped green onions.
- In a bowl, combine 1 cup of flour, ½ teaspoon of salt, ½ teaspoon of black pepper, and 1 teaspoon of baking powder.
- Then add the contents of the smaller bowl to the larger bowl with the grated zucchini.
- Stir everything together; until it's well mixed.
- Preheat a saucepan to medium heat and add two tablespoons of oil.
- Add the zucchini mixture, a heaping tablespoon at a time.
- Fry the mixture for about 4 minutes on each side until the mixture turns a golden-brown color.
- Add more oil to the pan if needed.

Nutritional information: Calories: 1082 kcal; Protein: 39.17 g; Fat: 50.01 g; Carbs: 122.85 g.

5. Chicken Omelet

Serving: 1
Difficulty: 1
Preparation Time: 5 minutes
Cooking Time: 15 minutes
Optavia Counts: 3 lean/ 1 green/ 2 healthy fat/ 3 condiments

Ingredients:

- 1 oz. Rotisserie chicken; shredded
- 1 tsp. Mustard
- 4 eggs
- 1 tbsp. Mayonnaise
- 1 tomato
- 6 bacon slices
- 1 small avocado
- Sea salt
- Black pepper

Preparation:

- In a bowl, mix the eggs with a little salt and pepper and whisk.
- Heat a skillet over medium fire; spray it with a little cooking oil, add the eggs, and fry your omelet for 5 minutes.
- Add chicken, avocado, chopped tomato, cooked and crumbled bacon, mayo, and mustard to one-half of the omelet.
- Fold the omelet, cover the pan and cook for another 5 minutes.
- Transfer to a plate and serve.

Nutritional information: Calories: 400 kcal; Protein: 25.6 g; Fat: 32.4 g; Carbs: 4.4 g.

6. Chicken Pesto Pasta

Serving: 1
Difficulty: 2
Preparation Time: 5 minutes
Cooking Time: 15 minutes
Optavia Counts: 2 lean/ 3 green/ 2 healthy fat/ 4 condiments

Ingredients:

- 3 cups raw kale leaves
- 2 tbsp. Olive oil
- 2 cups basil
- Salt
- 3 tbsp. Lemon juice
- 3 garlic cloves
- 2 cups cooked chicken breast
- 1 cup baby spinach
- 6 oz. Uncooked chicken pasta
- 1/8 oz. Ball of fresh mozzarella
- Basil leaves
- Red pepper flakes

Preparation:

- Pesto: Put the kale, lemon juice, basil, garlic cloves, olive oil, and salt in a blender and puree until smooth. Season to taste with pepper.
- Pasta: Boil the pasta and drain the water. Reserve ¼ cup of the liquid.
- Take a bowl and mix everything, the cooked pasta, the pesto, the chicken cubes, the spinach, the mozzarella, and the reserved pasta liquid.
- Sprinkle with chopped basil or red paper flakes.
- Serve warm or chilled.

Nutritional information: Calories: 1206 kcal; Protein: 128.22 g; Fat: 50.2 g; Carbs: 61.8 g.

7. Crab Cakes

Serving: 2

Difficulty: 1

Preparation Time: 20 minutes

Cooking Time: 10 minutes

Optavia Counts: 2 lean/ 1 green/ 2 healthy fat/ 4 condiments

Ingredients:

- ½ Pound lump crabmeat, drained
- 2 tbsp. Coconut flour
- 1 tbsp. Mayonnaise
- ¼ Tsp. Green tabasco sauce
- 1 tbsp. Butter
- 1 small egg, beaten
- ¾ Tbsp. Fresh parsley, chopped
- ½ Tsp. Yellow mustard
- Salt and black pepper, to taste

Preparation:

- Mix together all the Ingredients in a bowl except butter.
- Make patties from this mixture and set them aside.
- Heat butter in a skillet over medium fire and add patties. Cook for about 10 minutes on each side and dish out to serve hot.
- You can store the raw patties in the freezer for about 3 weeks for meal prepping.
- Place patties in a container and place parchment paper in between the patties to avoid stickiness.

Nutritional information: Calories: 153; Fat: 10 g; Carbs: 6.8 g

8. Cayenne Rib Eye Steak

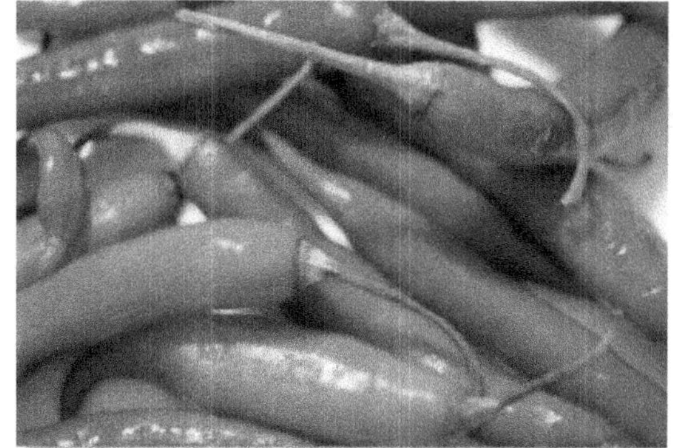

Serving: 2

Difficulty: 1

Preparation Time: 10 minutes

Cooking Time: 13 minutes

Optavia Counts: 1 lean/ 0 green/ 3 healthy fat/ 5 condiments

Ingredients:

- 1-pound rib eye steak.
- 1 tsp. Salt.
- 1 tsp. Cayenne pepper.
- ½ Tsp. Chili flakes.
- 1 tbsp. Cream.
- 1 tsp. Olive oil.
- 1 tsp. Lemongrass.
- 1 tbsp. Butter.
- 1 tsp. Garlic powder.

Preparation:

- Preheat the Air Fryer to 360°F.
- Take a shallow bowl and combine the cayenne pepper, salt, chili flakes, lemongrass, and garlic powder.
- Mix the spices gently.
- Sprinkle the rib eye steak with the spice mixture.
- Melt the butter and combine it with cream and olive oil.
- Churn the mixture.
- Pour the churned mixture into the Air Fryer basket tray.
- Add the rib eye steak.
- Cook the steak for 13 minutes. Do not stir the steak during the cooking.
- When the steak is cooked, transfer it to a paper towel to soak all the excess fat.
- Serve the steak. You can slice the steak if desired.

Nutritional information: Calories: 708; Fat: 59 g; Carbs: 2.3 g; Protein: 40.4 g.

9. Pasta With Avocado And Cream

Serving: 2

Difficulty: 1

Preparation Time: 10 minutes

Cooking Time: 6 minutes

Optavia Counts: 0 lean/ 0 green/ 2 healthy fat/ 3 condiments

Ingredients:

- ½ Tsp. Dried basil
- ⅛ Cup heavy cream
- ½ Avocado
- ½ Pack of shirataki noodles, cooked
- Salt
- Black pepper

Preparation:

- Fill a medium saucepan halfway with water and bring to a boil over medium heat; then add pasta and cook for 2 minutes.

- Then drain the pasta and set aside until ready to use.

- Put the avocado in a bowl and mash it with a fork. Transfer to a blender, add remaining **Ingredients** and blend until smooth.

- Take a pan, put it on medium heat and when it is hot, add the noodles. Pour in the avocado mixture, stir well and cook for 2 minutes until hot.

- Serve immediately.

Nutritional information: Calories: 131 kcal; Protein: 1.2 g; Fat: 12.6 g; Carbs: 4.9 g.

10. Spaghetti Squash With Cheese And Pesto

Serving: 2

Difficulty: 2

Preparation Time: 10 minutes

Cooking Time: 35 minutes

Optavia Counts: 1 lean/ 0 green/ 3 healthy fat/ 3 condiments

Ingredients:

- 1 Cup cooked spaghetti squash
- Salt to taste
- Black pepper
- ½ Tbsp. Olive oil
- ¼ Cup ricotta cheese
- 4 oz. Fresh mozzarella cheese
- ⅛ Cup basil pesto

Preparation:

- Preheat oven to 375°F.

- Take a bowl, put the drained spaghetti squash in it and season it with salt and black pepper.

- Using a baking dish, grease it with oil, put the squash mixture in it, cover it with ricotta cheese and cubed mozzarella and bake it for 10 minutes until cooked.

- Drizzle pesto over and serve.

Nutritional information: Calories: 169 kcal; Protein: 11.9 g; Fat: 11.3 g; Carbs: 6.2 g.

11. Eggs In Pepper Rings

Serving: 2

Difficulty: 1

Preparation Time: 10 minutes

Cooking Time: 6 minutes

Optavia Counts: 1 lean/ 1 green/ 0 healthy fat/ 4 condiments

Ingredients:

- 1 bell pepper
- 4 eggs
- 1 tbsp. Parsley
- 1 tbsp. Chives
- Salt
- Pepper

Preparation:

- Heat a lightly greased nonstick skillet over medium fire.
- Cut the bell pepper into 4 rings.
- Place 4 bell pepper rings in the skillet and cook for about 2 minutes.
- Carefully flip the rings.
- Crack an egg into the center of each pepper ring and sprinkle with salt and black pepper.
- Fry for about 2-4 minutes or until the eggs have reached the desired doneness.
- Carefully transfer the pepper rings to serving plates and serve garnished with chopped parsley and chopped chives.

Nutritional information: Calories: 278 kcal; Protein: 18.94 g; Fat: 19.39 g; Carbs: 6.47 g.

12. Fish Lettuce Tacos

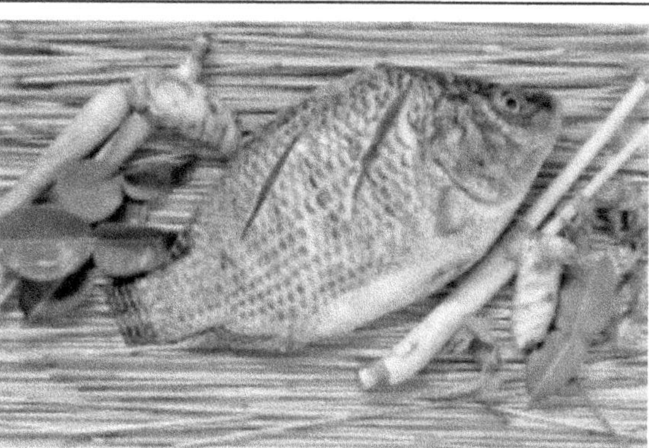

Serving: 2

Difficulty: 2

Preparation Time: 10-15 minutes

Cooking Time: 25-30 minutes

Optavia Counts: 1 lean/ 0 green/ 1 healthy fat/ 6 condiments

Ingredients:

- ½ Tsp. Chili powder
- 20 oz. Raw tilapia
- ½ Tsp. Ground cumin

Toppings:

- 2 tsp. Lime juice
- 4 tbsp. Dressing of choice
- 3 oz. Avocado
- Salt
- Black pepper

Preparation:

- Preheat the oven to 375°F.
- Line a baking sheet with parchment paper. Sprinkle both sides of the tilapia with salt, pepper, cumin and chili powder.
- Bake for 20 to 25 minutes, or until cooked through.
- Spoon some fish in a lettuce boat to hold it. Drizzle each serving with 1 teaspoon of lime juice and 2 tablespoons of dressing. Serve with avocado.

Nutritional information: Calories: 68 kcal; Protein: 1 g; Fat: 6 g; Carbs: 3 g.

13. Meatball Lasagna

Serving: 2

Difficulty: 1

Preparation Time: 15 - 10 minutes

Cooking Time: 15-20 minutes

Optavia Counts: 1 lean/ 2 green/ 3 healthy fat/ 2 condiments

Ingredients:

- 4 tsp. Grated parmesan cheese
- 2 cups zucchini
- ½ Cup skim ricotta cheese
- ½ Cup 2% mozzarella cheese
- 12 turkey meatballs
- ½ Tsp. Basil
- 1 cup tomatoes
- Garlic salt

Preparation:

- Preheat the oven to 350°F.
- Layer zucchini slices in a medium-sized casserole dish. Spread ricotta cheese over the squash. Sprinkle garlic salt and basil over.
- Mix diced tomatoes with meatballs in a bowl. Pour over ricotta cheese. Sprinkle mozzarella over meatballs and then top with grated parmesan cheese. Bake for 25 minutes or until cheese is melted.
- Drain the water from the dish by tilting carefully.
- Serve.

Nutritional information: Calories: 584 kcal; Protein: 46 g; Fat: 41 g; Carbs: 4 g.

14. Lettuce Salad With Beef Strips

Serving: 3

Difficulty: 1

Preparation Time: 10 minutes.

Cooking Time: 12 minutes.

Optavia Counts: 1 lean/ 2 green/ 3 healthy fat/ 5 condiments

Ingredients:

- 2 cups lettuce
- 10 oz. Beef brisket
- 2 tbsp. Sesame oil
- 1 tbsp. Sunflower seeds
- 1 cucumber
- 1 tsp. Ground black pepper
- 1 tsp. Paprika
- 1 tsp. Italian spices
- 1 tsp. Butter
- 1 tsp. Dried dill
- 1 tbsp. Coconut milk

Preparation:

- Cut the beef brisket into strips.
- Sprinkle the beef strips with the ground black pepper, paprika, and dried dill.
- Preheat the Air Fryer to 365°F.
- Put the butter in the Air Fryer basket tray and melt it.
- Then add the beef strips and cook them for 6 minutes on each side.
- Meanwhile, tear the lettuce and toss it in a big salad bowl.
- Crush the sunflower seeds and sprinkle them over the lettuce.
- Chop the cucumber into the small cubes and add to the salad bowl.
- Then combine the sesame oil and Italian spices together. Stir the oil.
1. Combine the lettuce mixture with the coconut milk and stir it using 2 wooden spatulas.
2. When the meat is cooked, let it chill to room temperature.
3. Add the beef strips to the salad bowl.
4. Stir it gently and sprinkle the salad with the sesame oil dressing.
5. Serve the dish immediately.

Nutritional information: Calories: 199 kcal; Fat: 12.4 g; Carbs: 3.9 g; Protein: 18.1 g.

15. Mozzarella, Tomatoes And Pesto Chicken

Serving: 3

Difficulty: 2

Preparation Time: 5-15 minutes

Cooking Time: 20-25 minutes

Optavia Counts: 1 lean/ 1 green/ 1 healthy fat/ 3 condiments

Ingredients:

- ½ Cup part-skim mozzarella
- 1 cup tomato
- 4 tsp. Pesto
- 16 oz. Chicken breast
- Salt
- Pepper

Preparation:

- Cut chicken breast horizontally into 4 thinner cutlets. Season with salt and pepper.
- Preheat the oven to 400°F.
- Line a baking sheet with parchment paper. Place the chicken and spread 1 teaspoon of pesto over.
- Bake 15 minutes or until chicken is no longer pink in the center.
- Remove from oven, top with diced tomatoes, shredded mozzarella and parmesan cheese.
- Bake for an extra 3 to 5 minutes or until cheese is melted.
- Serve

Nutritional information: Calories: 601 kcal; Protein: 59 g; Fat: 38 g; Carbs: 2 g.

16. Cheesy Jalapeños

Serving: 3

Difficulty: 2

Preparation Time: 10-15 minutes

Cooking Time: 20-25 minutes

Optavia Counts: 0 lean/ 1 green/ 3 healthy fat/ 1 condiments

Ingredients:

- 2 light cream cheese triangles
- ¼ cup 2% reduced-fat Cheese Blend
- ⅛ Tsp. Worcestershire sauce
- 3 to 4 jalapeños
- 1 tbsp. Parmesan cheese

Preparation:

- Cut jalapenos in half lengthwise; remove seeds and membranes.
- In a large saucepan, boil peppers in water for 5-10 minutes (the longer you boil the peppers, the milder they become).
- Drain and rinse in cold water; set aside.
- Preheat oven to 400°F.
- In a small mixing bowl, beat the light cream cheese, cheddar cheese and Worcestershire sauce (optional).
- Scoop 2 teaspoons into each jalapeño half; sprinkle with grated Parmesan cheese.
- Place on a greased baking sheet.
- Bake at 400°F for 5-10 minutes or until the cheese is melted.
- Serve warm.

Nutritional information: Calories: 158 kcal; Protein: 10.3 g; Fat: 10.8 g; Carbs: 4.5 g.

17. Avocados Stuffed With Salmon

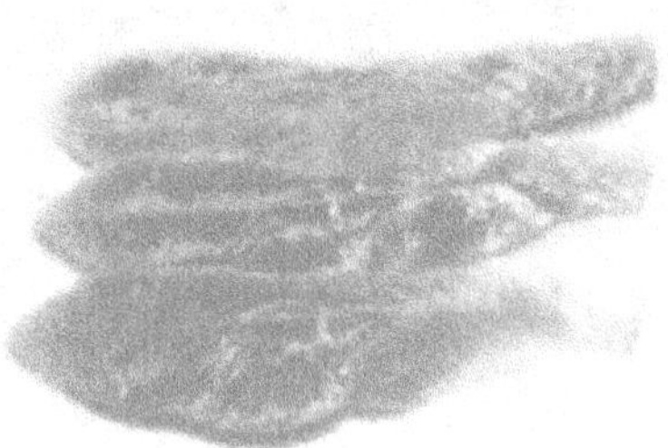

Serving: 3

Difficulty: 1

Preparation Time: 5 minutes

Cooking Time: 5 minutes

Optavia Counts: 1 lean/ 1 green/ 3 healthy fat/ 2 condiments

Ingredients:

- 2 oz. Smoked salmon
- 2 tbsp. Olive oil
- Lemon juice
- 1 avocado
- 1 oz. Goat cheese
- Sea salt
- Pepper

Preparation:

- Combine the salmon, lemon juice, oil, cheese, salt and pepper in your food processor and pulse well.
- Spread this mixture over the avocado halves and serve.

Nutritional information: Calories: 300 kcal; Protein: 16.7 g; Fat: 15.1 g; Carbs: 8.8 g.

18. Chicken Gordon Bleu

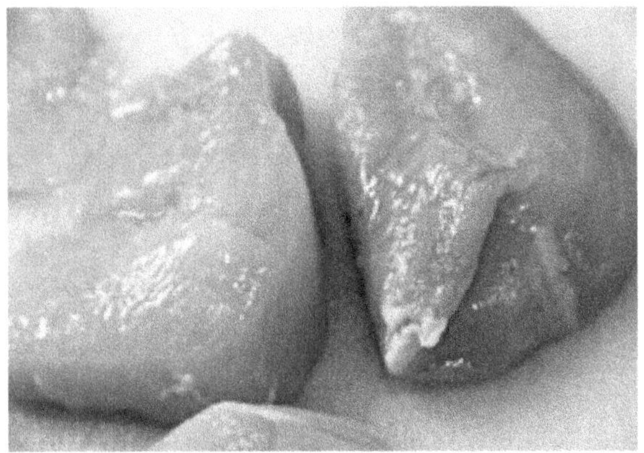

Serving: 3

Difficulty: 3

Preparation Time: 5-10 minutes

Cooking Time: 25-30 minutes

Optavia Counts: 1 lean/ 1 green/ 3 healthy fat/ 2 condiments

Ingredients:

- ½ Cup tomato
- 18 oz. Boneless, skinless chicken breasts
- 4 oz. Part-skim mozzarella cheese
- 2 cups spinach

Italian dressing:

- 1 tbsp. Dijon mustard
- 1 tbsp. White wine vinegar
- 1 packet Splenda
- 1 tsp. Olive oil
- ½ Tsp. Italian mixed herbs
- 3 cups red pepper flakes
- Sea salt
- Black pepper

Preparation:

- Preheat the oven to 350°F.
- Whisk Italian dressing Ingredients together in a bowl.
- Cut a pocket in each chicken breast, being careful not to cut all the way through. Coat the chicken with the Italian Dressing, inside and outside.
- Fill the chicken as much as you can with sun-dried tomato, top with cheese then finish with spinach leaves.
- Seal using toothpicks.
- Heat oil in a skillet over high fire. Add chicken and fry for 1 ½ minutes on each side, until golden brown.
- Transfer to oven and cook for 15 minutes, until the cheese is melted and bubbly and chicken is cooked through.
- Let rest for 3 minutes before serving, and drizzle with the juices from the pan.

Nutritional information: Calories: 684 kcal; Protein: 135 g; Fat: 65 g; Carbs: 5 g.

19. Chicken & Zucchini Pancakes

Serving: 4

Difficulty: 3

Preparation Time: 15 minutes

Cooking Time: 32 minutes

Optavia Counts: 2 lean/ 2 green/ 2 healthy fat/ 2 condiments

Ingredients:

- 4 cups zucchinis
- ¼ Cup chicken
- ¼ Cup scallion
- 1 egg
- ¼ Cup coconut flour
- 1 tbsp. Olive oil
- Salt
- Black pepper

Preparation:

- In a colander, place the shredded zucchini and sprinkle it with salt.
- Set aside for about 8-10 minutes.
- Squeeze the zucchinis well and transfer into a bowl.
- Shred the chicken and finely chop the scallion.
- In the bowl of zucchini, add the rest of the Ingredients and mix until well combined.
- In a large nonstick skillet, heat the oil over medium fire.
- Add ¼ cup of zucchini mixture into the preheated skillet and spread in an even layer.
- Cook for about 3-4 minutes per side.
- Repeat with the remaining mixture.
- Serve warm.

Nutritional information: Calories: 89 kcal; Protein: 4.43 g; Fat: 6.87 g; Carbs: 2.68 g.

20. Lemon Parmesan Salmon

Serving: 4

Difficulty: 2

Preparation Time: 10 minutes

Cooking Time: 25 minutes

Optavia Counts: 1 lean/ 2 green/ 2 healthy fat/ 2 condiments

Ingredients:

- ¼ Pound salmon fillet
- ¼ Tsp. Thyme leaves dried
- 1 tbsp. Scallions
- 1 tsp. Grated lemon peel
- ¾ Cup white breadcrumbs
- 2 tbsp. Butter,
- ¼ Tsp. Salt
- ¼ Cup grated parmesan cheese

Preparation:

- Preheat the oven to 350°F.
- Mist cooking spray onto a baking pan. Fill with pat-dried salmon. Brush salmon with melted butter before sprinkling with salt.
- Combine the breadcrumbs with chopped scallions, thyme, lemon peel, cheese, and remaining butter.
- Cover salmon with the breadcrumb mixture. Air-fry for 15 to 25 minutes.

Nutritional information: Calories: 290 kcal; Protein: 30 g; Fat: 10 g; Carbs: 0 g.

21. Tasty Pancakes

Serving: 4

Difficulty: 1

Preparation Time: 12 minutes

Cooking Time: 3 minutes

Optavia Counts: 1 lean/ 1 green/ 1 healthy fat/ 2 condiments

Ingredients:

- 2 eggs
- 1 tsp. Stevia
- 4 oz. Cream cheese
- ½ Tsp. Cinnamon powder
- Cooking spray

Preparation:

- Place eggs in a blender with the cream cheese, stevia, cinnamon and blend well.
- Heat skillet with spray over medium-high fire. Pour in ¼ of the batter, spread well, bake for 2 minutes, flip and bake for 1 minute more.
- Transfer to a plate and repeat with the rest of the batter.
- Serve immediately.

Nutritional information: Calories: 344 kcal; Protein: 16.7 g; Fat: 23 g; Carbs: 3.7 g.

22. Bacon Frittata With Asparagus

Serving: 4

Difficulty: 2

Preparation Time: 20 minutes

Cooking Time: 20 minutes

Optavia Counts: 2 lean/ 1 green/ 0 healthy fat/ 2 condiments

Ingredients:

- 4 bacon slices
- Sea salt
- Black pepper
- 8 eggs
- Bunch asparagus

Preparation:

- Heat a frying pan, add crumbled bacon, stir and fry for 5 minutes.
- Add cleaned and cut asparagus, salt and pepper, stir and cook for another 5 minutes.
- Add the eggs, spread in the pan, place in oven and bake at 350°F for 20 minutes.
- Divide and serve on plates.

Nutritional information: Calories: 251 kcal; Protein: 7 g; Fat: 6 g; Carbs: 16 g.

23. Spaghetti Squash Casserole

Serving: 4

Difficulty: 4

Preparation Time: 20-25 minutes

Cooking Time: 100-120 minutes

Optavia Counts: 2 lean/ 1 green/ 4 healthy fat/ 3 condiments

Ingredients:

- 4 pounds spaghetti squash
- 8 oz. Part-skim ricotta
- 8 oz. Reduced-fat mozzarella cheese
- 2 tbsp. Eggbeaters
- 2 tbsp. Parmesan cheese
- 2 cups tomatoes
- ¼ Tsp. Garlic powder
- ⅛ Tsp. Salt
- ⅛ Tsp. Pepper
- 2 tsp. Olive oil
- 6 oz. Seasoned ground turkey

Preparation:

- Preheat oven to 400°F.
- Prick squash with fork or metal skewer and roast in the oven for an hour or until it seems soft when you press on it. Then take it out and leave on the counter until cool.
- When squash is cool, cut in half and scoop out the seeds and discard.
- Use a fork or spoon to scoop out the rest of the squash and set it aside in a bowl.
- Measure out 4 cups of spaghetti squash and store the rest in the fridge.
- Add oil to a skillet over medium heat.
- Sauté the 4 cups of squash for a few minutes until it begins to brown. Then add garlic powder, salt and pepper if desired.
- Mix ricotta cheese, grated parmesan, eggbeaters and 4 oz. Or 1 cup of mozzarella cheese together.
- Preheat oven to 375°F.
- Pour 1 cup of the diced tomatoes on the bottom of a casserole dish and spread evenly.
- Add squash.
- Top the squash with the ricotta cheese mixture.
- Then top the ricotta cheese mixture with the cooked ground turkey.

- Spread 1 cup of diced tomatoes over the meat.
- Bake for 35 minutes.
- Spread the rest of the mozzarella cheese over the top and bake an additional 25 minutes until cheese is melted and lightly brown.
- Let rest for 10 minutes or so to serve.

Nutritional information: Calories: 593 kcal; Protein: 39.6 g; Fat: 25.7 g; Carbs: 54.6 g.

24. Tuna Cobbler

Serving: 4

Difficulty: 2

Preparation Time: 15 minutes

Cooking Time: 25 minutes

Optavia Counts: 1 lean/ 2 green/ 1 healthy fat/ 3 condiments

Ingredients:

- 2 oz. Hot peppers
- 10 oz. Canned tuna
- 1 tsp. Lemon juice
- ⅓ Cup cold water
- 1 ½ cups mixed vegetables, frozen
- 10 ¾ oz. Cream of chicken
- 1 tbsp. Sweet pickle relish
- Paprika

Directions:

- Preheat the Air Fryer at 375°F.
- Mist cooking spray into a round casserole.
- Mix the frozen vegetables with milk, cream, lemon juice, relish, sliced hot peppers, and tuna in a saucepan. Cook for 8 minutes over medium heat.
- Fill the casserole with the mixture.
- Mix the biscuit mixture with cold water to make a soft dough. Beat for half a minute and then pour by spoonsful into the casserole.
- Season with paprika.
- Fry in the Air Fryer for 25 minutes.

Nutritional information: Calories: 320 kcal; Protein: 20 g; Fat: 10 g; Carbs: 30 g.

25. Chicken Zucchini Noodles

Preparation Time: 10 minutes
Cooking Time: 25 minutes
Servings: 2

Ingredients:

- 1 large zucchini, spiralized
- 1 chicken breast, skinless & boneless
- 1/2 tablespoon jalapeno, minced
- 2 garlic cloves, minced
- 1/2 teaspoon ginger, minced
- 1/2 tablespoon fish sauce
- 2 tablespoon coconut cream
- 1/2 tablespoon honey
- 1/2 lime juice
- 1 tablespoon peanut butter
- 1 carrot, chopped
- 2 tablespoons cashews, chopped
- 1/4 cup fresh cilantro, chopped
- 1 tablespoon olive oil
- Pepper, salt

Preparation:

- Heat olive oil in a pan over medium-high heat. Season chicken breast with pepper and salt.
- Once the oil is hot, add chicken breast into the pan and cook for 3-4 minutes per side or until cooked.
- Remove chicken breast from pan. Shred chicken breast with a fork and set aside.
- In a small bowl, mix peanut butter, jalapeno, garlic, ginger, fish sauce, coconut cream, honey, and lime juice. Set aside.

- In a large mixing bowl, combine spiralized zucchini, carrots, cashews, cilantro, and shredded chicken. Pour peanut butter mixture over zucchini noodles and toss to combine. Serve immediately and enjoy.

Nutritional information:

Calories: 353

Fat: 21.1 g

Carbohydrates: 20.5 g

Sugar: 10.8 g

Protein: 24.5 g

Cholesterol: 54 mg

26. Garlic Chicken With Zoodles

Preparation Time: 15 minutes
Cooking Time: 15 minutes
Servings: 4

Ingredients:

- 3-6 tomatoes, sun-dried
- 1 tablespoon of garlic, chopped
- 1 ½ cup of zucchini, cut into thin noodle-like strands
- 1 ½ lb. Of boneless, skinless chicken breasts
- 1 tablespoon of olive oil
- 1 cup of plain Greek yogurt, low fat
- ½ cup of chicken broth
- ½ teaspoon of garlic powder
- ½ teaspoon of Italian seasoning
- ¼ cup of parmesan cheese

Preparation:

- Heat the olive oil in a large skillet on medium heat. Pat the chicken breast dry using paper towels, add salt and pepper to taste, then place it into the hot oil. Cook it on medium high for approximately 3 to 5 minutes on each side, or until each side is golden brown.

- After it is done cooking, set aside the chicken breasts on a plate.

- Now, add the yogurt, chicken broth, garlic powder, Italian seasoning, and parmesan cheese into the large skillet. Keep whisking over medium heat until it starts to thicken.

- Add the spinach and sun-dried tomatoes and simmer until the spinach wilts. Add the chicken back to the skillet and serve over the zucchini noodles.

Nutritional information:

Calories: 414

Protein: 60 g

Carbohydrate: 8 g

Fat: 15 g

27. Herbed Lemon Chicken

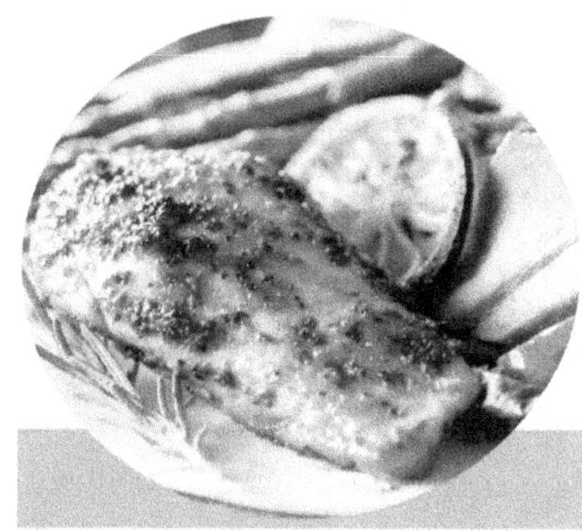

Preparation Time: 10 minutes

Cooking Time: 30 minutes

Servings: 4

Ingredients:

- 1 ½ lb. Of boneless, skinless chicken thighs

- 4 teaspoons of lemon oil (oil, fresh lemon juice, and fresh lemon zest)

- 2 tablespoons of herbs (thyme, parsley, rosemary, chives etc.), freshly chopped

Preparation:

- Preheat grill to medium high (around 3500F).

- Add all Ingredients to a large bowl. Toss well to coat the chicken properly.

- Grill for about 7 to 12 minutes on each side, or until meat is fully cooked.

- Alternatively, you can use your oven to cook this dish. Place in a single layer on a cookie sheet or roasting dish and bake at 3500F for 20 to 35 minutes.

Nutritional information:

Calories: 234

Protein: 36.1 g

Carbohydrate: 0 g

Fat: 8.8 g

28. Honey Mustard Chicken Skillet

Preparation Time: 10 minutes

Cooking Time: 20 minutes

Servings: 4

Ingredients:

- ¼ cup of almonds, slivered

- 1 ½ tablespoon of olive oil, divided

- 1 tablespoon of fresh garlic, minced

- 1 pound of chicken breasts, cut into strips

- 4 cups of zucchini, sliced

- 2 cups of asparagus, chopped

- 1 cup of chicken broth, low sodium

- 4 tablespoons of honey

- ¼ cup of Dijon mustard

- 1 tablespoon of Balsamic vinegar

- 1 tablespoon of Tapioca starch

- 2 teaspoon of soy sauce, low sodium

- Pinch of sea salt

- Sliced fresh basil, for garnish

Preparation:

- Preheat your oven to 4000F. Using parchment paper, line a small baking sheet and toast the almonds in the oven until they are a light golden brown. Then, set them aside.

- Using a large pan, heat the olive oil over medium high heat. Add the garlic and cook for about 1 minute, or until it is golden brown.

- Now, add the chicken breast strips and cook over medium heat until they are no longer pink. Transfer to a bowl, cover, and set aside.

- Turn the heat back up to medium high and add in the remaining oil. After letting it heat, add in the zucchini and asparagus. Cook until they are light brown. Now, add in the chicken strips and cook for about 1 to 2 minutes.

- In a medium-sized bowl, add the chicken broth, honey, mustard, vinegar, tapioca starch, soy sauce, and sea salt. Whisk together and make sure the tapioca is properly dissolved.

- Now, add the sauce into the pan. Stir and bring to a boil for 1 minute. Reduce the heat to medium and bring to a simmer for about 3 to 5 minutes, until the sauce is nice and thick.

- Pour the sauce on the chicken strips, zucchini, and asparagus. Garnish with toasted almonds and basil.

Nutritional information:

Calories: 335

Protein: 31.2 g

Carbohydrate: 28.1 g

Fat: 5.5 g

Ingredients:

- 1 tablespoon of Dijon mustard

- 1 tablespoon of whole grain mustard

- 1 cup of chicken broth, low sodium

- 4 teaspoons of roasted garlic oil

- 4 cups of broccoli florets, fresh

- 1 tablespoon of garlic, parsley, lemon, and onion, freshly crushed

- 1 ½ lb. Of boneless, skinless chicken breasts

Preparation:

- Put mustard and chicken broth in a bowl and whisk. Set aside. In a large frying pan with a lid, put oil and heat over medium heat. Add broccoli and season with freshly crushed garlic, parsley, lemon, and onion. Stir well and cook for about 2 minutes.

- Pour broccoli into a bowl and set aside.

- Now, place the pan back over medium high heat and add the chicken. Cook it for about 4 to 5 minutes, or until golden brown on both sides.

- Reduce the heat to medium and pour chicken broth and mustard mixture over the chicken. Add the broccoli. Cover the pan with a lid and let it simmer for about 5 to 7 minutes, or until the chicken is cooked and broccoli is bright green and tender crisp.

Nutritional information:

Calories: 277

Protein: 39.6 g

Carbohydrate: 7.4 g

Fat: 9.4 g

29. Chicken Broccoli Dijon

Preparation Time: 10 minutes

Cooking Time: 15 minutes

Servings: 4

30. Glazed Ginger Chicken And Green Beans

Preparation Time: 5 minutes

Cooking Time: 30 minutes

Servings: 4

Ingredients:

- ⅓ Cup of white sesame seeds + ⅓ cup of black sesame seeds

- 2 tablespoons of ginger, dried crushed or minced

- 1 tablespoon of dried minced garlic

- 1 teaspoon of red pepper flakes

- 1 tablespoon of salt

- 1 teaspoon of toasted sesame oil

- 1 ½ lb. Of boneless, skinless chicken breasts or thighs

- ¼ Cup of soy sauce, low sodium

- ½ Cup of water

- 4 cups of fresh green beans, ends snipped

Preparation:

- Make a toasted sesame-ginger spice mix by combining white sesame seeds, black sesame seeds, dried crushed or minced ginger, dried minced garlic, red pepper flakes, and salt in a small bowl.

- Heat the sesame oil over medium low heat in a nonstick skillet and toast the spice mix for about 10 to 12 minutes, or until the sesame seeds are light golden brown. Stir occasionally.

- Now, sprinkle the toasted sesame-ginger spice mix over the chicken. Pat it to stick and let it sit for around 15 minutes.

- Spray a large frying pan with non-stick cooking spray and heat over medium high heat. Then, place the chicken in the frying pan with the sesame side down and let it cook for 5 to 7 minutes, or until the sides are opaque. Turn the

chicken over and cook for 5 to 7 more minutes, or until the chicken is thoroughly cooked.

- Remove the chicken from the pan and set aside. Pour the water and soy sauce into the pan and scrape off the stuck residue off the bottom. This will serve as part of the sauce for the chicken.

- Turn the heat back up to medium high and bring to a boil. Then, add the beans and cook for 5 to 7 minutes, making sure to stir occasionally.

- When the beans are fork tender, add to plate with the chicken, and pour the sauce over the chicken and beans.

Nutritional information:

Calories: 284

Protein: 43.4 g

Carbohydrate: 3.8 g

Fat: 9.7 g

31. Creamy Chicken And Asparagus

Preparation Time: 10 minutes

Cooking Time: 15 minutes

Servings: 4

Ingredients:

- 4 teaspoons of roasted garlic oil

- 1 ¾ lb. Boneless, skinless chicken breasts, cut into chunks

- ½ cup chicken broth, low sodium

- 1 clove of garlic, chopped

- 8 tablespoons of cream cheese, light

- 4 cups of fresh asparagus, cut into 2" pieces

- Salt and pepper to taste

Preparation:

- Place a large skillet over medium high heat and add oil. When hot, add chicken breasts and cook for about 7 to 10 minutes, or until the chicken is slightly brown.

- When the chicken is cooked, place onto a plate and set aside.

- Pour the broth into the pan and add garlic, cream cheese, and asparagus. Turn the heat up to high. Stir continually and allow the cream cheese to melt evenly into the sauce. Bring to a boil and simmer until a thick sauce has formed.

- Divide the chicken into four equal portions and pour sauce on top, sprinkle salt and pepper to taste.

Nutritional information:

Calories: 302

Fat: 12.8 g

Carbohydrate: 7.1 g

Protein: 39 g

32. High Protein Chicken Meatballs

Preparation Time: 5 minutes

Cooking Time: 25 minutes

Servings: 2

Ingredients:

- 1 lb. Lean chicken

- 3/4 cup oats, rolled

- 2 onions, grated

- 2 teaspoons all spice, ground

- Salt and black pepper, to taste

Preparation:

- Heat a large skillet over medium heat, then grease using cooking spray.

- Add in the onions, chicken, oats, allspice and a dash of salt and black pepper in a large-sized bowl, stir well to mix.

- Shape mixture into small meatballs.

- Place into the greased skillet. Cook for roughly 5 minutes until golden brown on all sides.

- Remove meatballs from heat, then serve immediately.

Nutritional information:

Calories: 519 Cal

Protein: 57g

Carbohydrates: 32 g

Fat: 15 g

33. Pan Seared Balsamic Chicken And Vegetables

Preparation Time: 5 minutes

Cooking Time: 25 minutes

Servings: 4

Ingredients:

- ½ teaspoon of basil, dried

- 1 ½ teaspoon of oregano, dried

- ½ teaspoon of rosemary

- 1 teaspoon of marjoram

- ½ teaspoon of sage

- 1 teaspoon of thyme, dried

- ½ teaspoon of fennel seeds

- 1 teaspoon of garlic powder

- 1 ½ lb. Boneless, skinless chicken thighs

- 4 tablespoons of balsamic reduction

- 1 tablespoon of Dijon mustard

- 2 cups of zucchini, sliced

- ⅓ cup of water

Preparation:

- Put basil, oregano, rosemary, marjoram, sage, thyme, fennel seeds, and garlic powder into a mortar and pestle and grind to break up the fennel seeds. Then, place into a small jar. This will serve as your Tuscan seasoning.

- In a bowl that is large enough to hold the chicken, whisk together the balsamic reduction, Dijon mustard, and 1 tablespoon of Tuscan seasoning. Add the chicken and toss to coat.

- Preheat the oven to 4250F. Place a well-seasoned cast iron skillet over medium high heat. After shaking off the excess marinade, place the chicken into the pan and cook for about 5 minutes, or until it is slightly browned. Flip the chicken and cook for 5 minutes more.

- Scatter the vegetables around the pan and season with salt and pepper to taste.

- Add water to the remaining marinade, whisk to combine, and pour the mixture over the vegetables and chicken. Toss to combine. Finally, place in the preheated oven for around 15 minutes.

Nutritional information:

Calories: 280

Carbohydrate: 7.5 g

Protein: 38.7 g

Fat: 9.9 g

---

34. Chicken With Artichokes And Garlic

Preparation Time: 5 minutes

Cooking Time: 15 minutes

Seervings: 4

Ingredients:

- 1 teaspoon of parsley, dried

- ½ Teaspoon of oregano, dried

- ½ Teaspoon of basil, dried

- ¼ Teaspoon of garlic powder

- ¼ Teaspoon of onion powder

- ¼ Teaspoon of salt

- 4 teaspoons of roasted garlic oil

- 1 ½ boneless chicken breasts, cut into small cubes

- 1 12-15 oz. Jar artichoke hearts in water, drained well and chopped

- ¼ Cup of green onions (scallions), tops only for garnish

Preparation:

- Heat roasted garlic oil in a large skillet over medium high heat.

- Add chicken and cook for 5 to 7 minutes on each side, or until brown and firm.

- Put parsley, oregano, basil, garlic powder, onion powder, and salt in a small bowl. Mix well. This will serve as your seasoning.

- Add artichokes and 1 tablespoon of seasoning to the skillet. Turn heat to medium and simmer for 5 more minutes, or until artichokes are thoroughly heated and the chicken is fully cooked.

Nutritional information:

Calories: 294

Fat: 9 g

Carbohydrate: 13 g

Protein: 40.3 g

35. Tomato Braised Cauliflower With Chicken

Preparation Time: 10 minutes

Cooking Time: 30 minutes

Servings: 4

Preparation:

- 4 garlic cloves, sliced
- 3 scallions, to be trimmed and cut into 1-inch pieces
- ¼ teaspoon dried oregano
- ¼ teaspoon crushed red pepper flakes
- 4 ½ cups cauliflower
- 1 ½ cups diced canned tomatoes
- 1 cup fresh basil, gently torn
- ½ teaspoon each pepper and salt, divided
- 1 ½ teaspoon olive oil
- 1 ½ lb. Boneless, skinless chicken breasts

Preparation:

- Get a saucepan and combine the garlic, scallions, oregano, crushed red pepper, cauliflower, and tomato, and add ¼ cup of water. Get everything boiled together and add ¼ teaspoon of pepper and salt for seasoning, then cover the pot with a lid.
- Let it simmer for 10 minutes and stir as often as possible until you observe that the cauliflower is tender. Now, wrap up the seasoning with the remaining ¼ teaspoon of pepper and salt.
- Toss the chicken breast with oil, olive preferably and let it roast in the oven with the heat of 4500F for 20 minutes and an internal temperature of 1650F.
- Allow the chicken to rest for like 10 minutes. Now slice the chicken, and serve on a bed of tomato braised cauliflower.

Nutritional information: Calories: 290 - Fat: 10 g - Carbohydrate: 13 g -Protein: 38 g

36. Chipotle Chicken & Cauliflower Rice Bowls

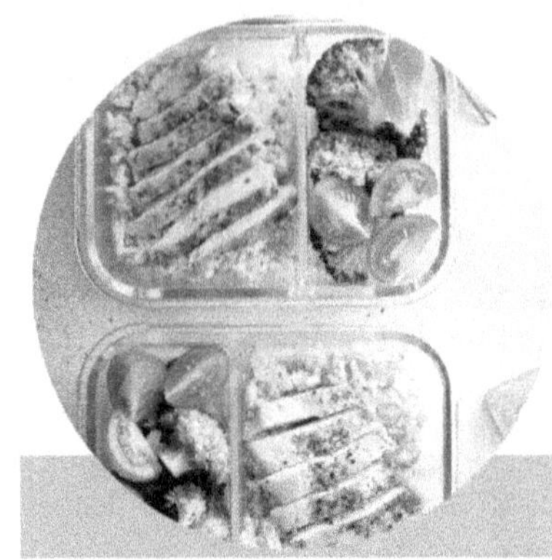

Preparation Time: 10 minutes

Cooking Time: 20 minutes

Servings: 4

Ingredients:

- 1/3 cup salsa
- 1 quantity 14.5 oz. Can fire-roasted diced tomatoes
- 1 canned chipotle pepper + 1 teaspoon of sauce
- ½ teaspoon of dried oregano
- 1 teaspoon of cumin
- 1 ½ lb. Boneless, skinless chicken breast
- ¼ teaspoon salt
- 1 cup reduced-fat shredded Mexican cheese blend
- 4 cups frozen riced cauliflower
- ½ medium-sized avocado, sliced

Preparation:

- Combine the first **Ingredients** in a blender and blend until they become smooth
- Place chicken inside your instant pot, and pour the sauce over it. Cover the lid and close the pressure valve. Set it to 20 minutes at high temperature. Let the pressure release on its own before opening. Remove the piece and the chicken and then add it back to the sauce.
- Microwave the riced cauliflower according to the **Directions** on the package
- Before you serve, divide the riced cauliflower, cheese, avocado, and chicken equally among the 4 bowls.

Nutritional information: Calories: 287 - Protein: 35g - Carbohydrate: 19g -Fat: 12 g

37. Sheet Pan Chicken Fajita Lettuce Wraps

Preparation Time: 15 minutes

Cooking Time: 30 minutes

Servings: 2

Ingredients:

- 1 lb. Chicken breast, thinly sliced into strips
- 2 teaspoons olive oil
- 2 bell peppers, thinly sliced into strips
- 2 teaspoons fajita seasoning
- 6 leaves from a romaine heart
- Half a lime juice
- ¼ cup plain of non-fat Greek yogurt

Preparation:

- Preheat your oven to about 4000F. Combine all the Ingredients except for lettuce in a large plastic bag that can be resealed. Mix very well to coat vegetables and chicken with oil and seasoning evenly.

- Spread the contents of the bag evenly on a foil-lined baking sheet. Bake it for about 25-30 minutes, until the chicken is thoroughly cooked.

- Serve on lettuce leaves and topped with Greek yogurt if you like.

Nutritional information:

Calories: 387

Fat: 6 g

Carbohydrate: 14 g

Protein: 18 g

38. Lemon Garlic Oregano Chicken With Asparagus

Preparation Time: 5 minutes

Cooking Time: 40 minutes

Servings: 4

Ingredients:

- 1 small lemon, juiced (this should be about 2 tablespoons of lemon juice)
- 1 ¾ lb. Bone-in, skinless chicken thighs
- 2 tablespoons fresh oregano, minced
- 2 cloves garlic, minced
- 2 lbs. Asparagus, trimmed
- ¼ teaspoon each or less for black pepper and salt

Preparation:

- Preheat the oven to about 3500F. Put the chicken in a medium-sized bowl. Now, add the garlic, oregano, lemon juice, pepper, and salt and toss together to combine.

- Roast the chicken in the air fryer oven until it reaches an internal temperature of 1650F in about 40 minutes. Once the chicken thighs have been cooked, remove and keep aside to rest.

- Now, steam the asparagus on a stovetop or in a microwave to the desired doneness.

- Serve asparagus with the roasted chicken thighs.

Nutritional information:

Calories: 350

Fat: 10 g

Carbohydrate: 10 g

Protein: 32 g

39. Lean And Green Chicken Pesto Pasta

Preparation Time: 5 minutes

Cooking Time: 15 minutes

Servings: 2

Ingredients:

- 3 cups raw kale leaves
- 2 tablespoon olive oil
- 2 cups fresh basil
- 1/4 teaspoon salt
- 3 tablespoon lemon juice
- 3 garlic cloves
- 2 cups cooked chicken breast
- 1 cup baby spinach
- 6 ounces uncooked chicken pasta
- 3 ounces diced fresh mozzarella
- Basil leaves or red pepper flakes to garnish

Directions:

- Start by making the pesto, add the kale, lemon juice, basil, garlic cloves, olive oil, and salt to a blender and blend until it's smooth. Add salt and pepper to taste.
- Cook the pasta and strain off the water. Reserve 1/4 cup of the liquid.
- Get a bowl and mix everything, the cooked pasta, pesto, diced chicken, spinach, mozzarella, and the reserved pasta liquid.
- Sprinkle the mixture with additional chopped basil or red pepper flakes (optional).
- Now your salad is ready. You may serve it warm or chilled. Also, it can be taken as a salad mix-ins or as a side dish. Leftovers should be stored in the refrigerator inside an air-tight container for 3-5 days.

Nutritional information:

Calories: 244 Cal

Protein: 20.5 g

Carbohydrates: 22.5 g

Fats: 10 g

40. Buffalo Chicken Sliders

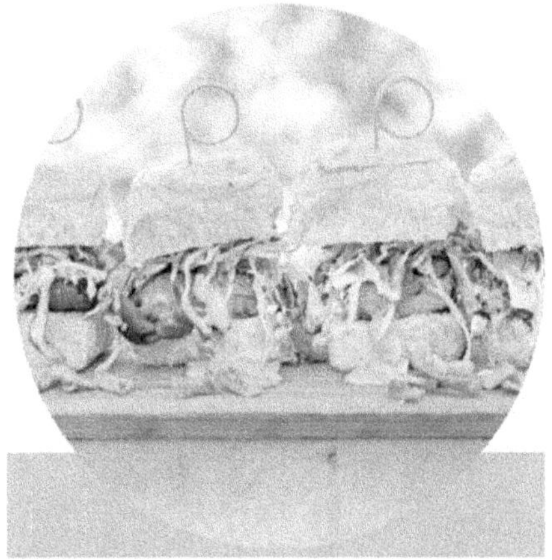

Preparation Time: 10 minutes

Cooking Time: 15 minutes

Servings: 12

Ingredients:

- 2 lb. Chicken breasts, cooked, shredded
- 1 cup wing sauce
- 1 pack ranch dressing mix
- 1/4 cup blue cheese dressing, low fat
- Lettuce, for topping
- 12 buns, slider

Directions:

- Add the chicken breasts (shredded, cooked) in a large bowl along with the ranch dressing and wing sauce.
- Stir well to combine, then place a piece of lettuce onto each slider roll. Top off using chicken mixture.
- Drizzle blue cheese dressing over chicken, then top off using top buns of slider rolls. Serve.

Nutritional information:

Calories: 300

Fat: 14 g

Cholesterol: 25 mg

Dinner

1. Chicken Tetrazzini

Preparation Time: 10 minutes

Cooking Time: 20 minutes

Servings: 2

Ingredients:

- 16 ounces of uncooked linguine pasta
- 4 ounces of butter
- 24 ounces of fresh mushrooms, sliced
- 8 ounces of onion, minced
- 8 ounces of green bell pepper, minced
- 21 ½ ounces condensed cream of mushroom soup
- 16 ounces of chicken broth
- 16 ounces of Cheddar cheese, shredded
- 10 ounces of frozen green peas
- 4 ounces of cooking sherry
- 1 teaspoon of Worcestershire sauce
- 1 teaspoon of salt
- 1/4 teaspoon of ground black pepper
- 32 ounces of boneless and skinless cooked chicken breast, chopped
- 8 ounces of Parmesan cheese, grated
- A pinch of paprika

Preparation:

- Boil a large pot of salted water and cook pasta for 10 minutes or until noodles are tender but firm to the taste
- Preheat oven to 375 degrees Fahrenheit

- Heat butter in a large pan on medium heat and cook mushrooms, onions and pepper in the butter until tender
- Add mushroom soup and broth until warmed through. Add the pasta, cheddar cheese, peas, Worcestershire, sherry, salt, pepper and chicken to the mushroom soup and mix thoroughly
- Transfer mixture to a large baking dish and sprinkle Parmesan and paprika over the top. 6. Bake for 35 minutes.

Nutritional information:

Carbohydrates: 32 g

Fat: 12 g

Protein: 33 g

2. Baked Ricotta With Pears

Preparation time: 5 minutes

Cooking time: 25 minutes

Servings: 4

Level of difficulty: Normal

Category: green

Ingredients:

- Nonstick cooking spray
- 1 (16-ounce) container whole-milk ricotta cheese
- 2 large eggs
- 1/4 cup white whole-wheat flour
- 1 tablespoon sugar
- 1 teaspoon vanilla extract
- 1/4 teaspoon ground nutmeg
- 1 pear, cored and diced
- 2 tablespoons water
- 1 tablespoon honey

Preparation:

- Preheat the oven to 400°F. Oiled four 6-ounce ramekins with nonstick cooking spray. Beat the ricotta, eggs, flour, sugar, vanilla, and nutmeg in a large bowl. Spoon into the ramekins.

- Bake for 22 to 25 minutes, or until the ricotta is just about set. Remove from the oven and cool slightly on racks.

- While the ricotta is baking, in a small saucepan over medium heat, simmer the pear in the water for 10 minutes, until slightly softened.

- Remove, then stir in the honey. Serve the ricotta ramekins topped with the warmed pear.

Nutritional information:

Calories: 312

Fat: 17g

Carbohydrates: 23g

Protein: 17g

---

3. Herbed Wild Rice

Preparation time: 10 minutes

Cooking time: 4-6 hours

Servings: 8

Level of difficulty: Normal

Category: green

Ingredients:

- 3 cups wild rice, rinsed and drained

- 6 cups Vegetable Broth

- 1 onion, chopped

- 1/2 teaspoon salt

- 1/2 teaspoon dried thyme leaves

- 1/2 teaspoon dried basil leaves

- 1 bay leaf

- 1/3 cup chopped fresh flat-leaf parsley

Preparation:

- In a 6-quart slow cooker, mix the wild rice, vegetable broth, onion, salt, thyme, basil, and bay leaf. Cover and cook on low for 4 to 6 hours, or until the wild rice is tender but still firm.

- You can cook this dish longer until the wild rice pops, taking about 7 to 8 hours. Remove and discard the bay leaf. Stir in the parsley and serve.

Nutritional information:

Calories: 258 Carbohydrates: 54 g

Fat: 2 g Protein: 6 g

---

4. Buffalo Chicken Sliders

Preparation time: 10 minutes

Cooking time: 15 minutes

Servings: 12

Level of difficulty: Normal

Category: leaner

Ingredients:

- 2 lb. Chicken breasts, cooked, shredded

- 1 cup Wing sauce

- 1 pack Ranch dressing mix

- ¼ cup Blue cheese dressing, low fat

- Lettuce, for topping

- 12 Buns, slider

Preparation:

- Add the chicken breasts (shredded, cooked) in a large bowl along with the ranch dressing and wing sauce. Stir well to incorporate, then place a piece of lettuce onto each slider roll.

- Top off using the chicken mixture. Drizzle blue cheese dressing over chicken, then top off using top buns of slider rolls. Serve.

Nutrition:

Calories: 330 Carbs: 32g

Fat: 6g Protein: 35g

5. High Protein Chicken Meatballs

Preparation time: 5 minutes
Cooking time: 25 minutes
Servings: 2
Level of difficulty: Normal
Category: lean

Ingredients:

- 1 lb. Chicken, lean, ground
- ¾ cup Oats rolled
- 2 Onions, grated
- 2 tsp Allspice, ground
- Salt and black pepper

Preparation:

- Heat a skillet (large) over medium heat, then grease using cooking spray. Add in the onions (grated), chicken (lean, ground), oats (rolled), allspice (earth), and a dash of salt and black pepper in a large-sized bowl, stir well to incorporate.

- Shape mixture into meatballs (small). Place into the skillet (greased). Cook for roughly within 5 minutes until golden brown on all sides. Remove meatballs from heat, then serve immediately.

Nutritional information:

Calories: 519
Protein: 57g
Carbohydrates: 32 g
Fat :15 g

6. Barley Risotto

Preparation time: 15 minutes
Cooking time: 7-8 hours
Servings: 8
Level of difficulty: Normal
Category: green

Ingredients:

- 21/4 cups hulled barley, rinsed
- 1 onion, finely chopped
- 4 garlic cloves, minced
- 1 (8-ounce) package button mushrooms, chopped
- 6 cups low-sodium vegetable broth
- 1/2 teaspoon dried marjoram leaves
- 1/8 teaspoon freshly ground black pepper
- 2/3 cup grated Parmesan cheese

Preparation:

- In a 6-quart slow cooker, mix the barley, onion, garlic, mushrooms, broth, marjoram, and pepper.

- Cover and cook on low within 7 to 8 hours, or until the barley has absorbed most of the liquid and is tender, and the vegetables are tender. Stir in the Parmesan cheese and serve.

Nutritional information: Calories: 288
Carbohydrates: 45 g
Fat: 6 g Protein: 13 g

7.   Risotto With Green Beans, Sweet Potatoes, And Peas

Preparation time: 20 minutes
Cooking time: 4-5 hours
Servings: 8
Level of difficulty: Normal
Category: green

Ingredients:

- 1 large, sweet potato, peeled and chopped
- 1 onion, chopped
- 5 garlic cloves, minced
- 2 cups short-grain brown rice
- 1 teaspoon dried thyme leaves
- 7 cups low-sodium vegetable broth
- 2 cups green beans, cut in half crosswise
- 2 cups frozen baby peas
- 3 tablespoons unsalted butter
- 1/2 cup grated Parmesan cheese

Preparation:

- In a 6-quart slow cooker, mix the sweet potato, onion, garlic, rice, thyme, and broth. 2Cover and cook on low for 3 to 4 hours, or until the rice is tender.
- Stir in the green beans plus frozen peas. Cover and cook on low for 30 to 40 minutes or until the vegetables are tender. Stir in the butter and cheese. Cover and cook on low for 20 minutes, then stir and serve.

Nutritional information:

Calories: 385
Carbohydrates: 52 g
Fat: 10 g
Protein: 10 g

8.   Maple Lemon Tempeh Cubes

Preparation time: 10 minutes
Cooking time: 30-40 minutes
Servings: 4
Level of difficulty: Normal
Category: green

Ingredients:

- 1 packet tempeh
- 2-3 tsp coconut oil
- 3 tbsp lemon juice
- 2 tsp maple syrup
- 1-2 tsp Bragg's liquid aminos or low-sodium tamari (optional)
- 2 tsp water
- ¼ Tsp dried basil
- ¼ Tsp powdered garlic
- Black pepper (freshly grounded); to taste

Preparation:

- Heat your oven to 400 ° C. Cut your tempeh block into squares in bite form. Heat coconut oil over medium to high heat in a nonstick skillet.
- When melted and heated, add the tempeh and cook on one side for 2-4 minutes, or until the tempeh turns down into a golden-brown color.
- Flip the tempeh bits, and cook for 2-4 minutes. Mix the lemon juice, tamari, maple syrup, basil, water, garlic, and black pepper while tempeh is browning.
- Drop the mixture over tempeh, then swirl to cover the tempeh. Sauté for 2-3 minutes, then turn the tempeh and sauté 1-2 minutes more. The tempeh, on both sides, should be soft and orange. Serve.

Nutritional information: Calories: 22 - Fats: 17 g - Carbs: 5 g -

Protein: 21 g

9. Bok Choy With Tofu Stir Fry

Preparation time: 15 minutes

Cooking time: 15 minutes

Servings: 4

Level of difficulty: Normal

Category: green

Ingredients:

- 1 lb. Super-firm tofu drained and pressed
- 1 tbsp coconut oil
- 1 clove of garlic, minced
- 3 heads baby bok choy, chopped
- Low-sodium vegetable broth
- 2 tsp maple syrup
- Braggs liquid aminos
- 1-2 tsp chili sauce
- 1 scallion or green onion, chopped
- 1 tsp grated ginger
- Quinoa/rice, for serving

Preparation:

- With paper towels, Pat pressed the tofu dry and cut into tiny pieces of bite-size around 1/2 inch wide.
- Heat coconut oil in a wide skillet onto a warm. Remove tofu and stir-fry until painted softly. Stir-fry for 1-2 minutes before the choy of the Bok starts to wilt.
- When this occurs, you'll want to apply the vegetable broth and all the remaining Ingredients to the skillet.
- Hold the mixture stir-frying until all components are well coated and the bulk of the liquid evaporates, around 5-6 minutes. Serve over brown rice or quinoa.

Nutritional information: Calories: 263.7 Fat 4.2 g

Protein: 0 g Carbohydrate: 35.7 g

10. Three-Bean Medley

Preparation time: 15 minutes

Cooking time: 6-8 hours

Servings: 8

Level of difficulty: Easy

Category: green

Ingredients:

- 11/4 cups dried kidney beans, rinsed and drained
- 11/4 cups dried black beans, rinsed and drained
- 11/4 cups dried black-eyed peas, rinsed and drained
- 1 onion, chopped
- 1 leek, chopped
- 2 garlic cloves, minced
- 2 carrots, peeled and chopped
- 6 cups low-sodium vegetable broth
- 11/2 cups water
- 1/2 teaspoon dried thyme leaves

Preparation:

- In a 6-quart slow cooker, mix all of the ingredients. Cover and cook on low for 6 to 8 hours, or until the beans are tender and the liquid is absorbed. Serve.

Nutritional information: Calories: 284 Carbohydrates: 56 g

Fat: 0 g Protein: 1 9g

11. Herbed Garlic Black Beans

Preparation time: 10 minutes

Cooking time: 7-9 hours

Servings: 8

Level of difficulty: Easy

Category: green

Ingredients:

- 3 cups dried black beans, rinsed and drained

- 2 onions, chopped

- 8 garlic cloves, minced

- 6 cups low-sodium vegetable broth

- 1/2 teaspoon salt

- 1 teaspoon dried basil leaves

- 1/2 teaspoon dried thyme leaves

- 1/2 teaspoon dried oregano leaves

Directions:

- In a 6-quart slow cooker, mix all the ingredients. Cover and cook on low within 7 to 9 hours, or until the beans have absorbed the liquid and are tender. Remove and discard the bay leaf. Serve.

Nutritional information:

Calories: 250 Carbohydrates: 47 g

Fat: 0 g Protein: 15 g

12. Quinoa With Vegetables

Preparation time: 10 minutes

Cooking time: 5-6 hours

Servings: 8

Level of difficulty: Easy

Category: green

Ingredients:

- 2 cups quinoa, rinsed and drained

- 2 onions, chopped

- 2 carrots, peeled and sliced

- 1 cup sliced cremini mushrooms

- 3 garlic cloves, minced

- 4 cups low-sodium vegetable broth

- 1/2 teaspoon salt

- 1 teaspoon dried marjoram leaves

- 1/8 teaspoon freshly ground black pepper

Directions:

- In a 6-quart slow cooker, mix all of the ingredients. Cover and cook on low for 5 to 6 hours, or until the quinoa and vegetables are tender. Stir the mixture and serve.

Nutritional information:

Calories: 204

Carbohydrates: 35 g

Fat: 3 g

Protein: 7 g

13. Pan-Fried Salmon

Preparation time: 5 minutes

Cooking time: 20 minutes

Servings: 4

Level of difficulty: Normal

Category: lean

Ingredients:

- 4 salmon fillets

- 1 teaspoon dried oregano

- Salt and pepper

- 3 tbsp olive oil

- 1 tsp dried basil

Preparation:

- Marinate the fish with pepper, oregano, salt, and basil. Warm the oil in a pan and put the salmon in the cooking oil.

- Fry on per side for around 2 minutes until it turns golden brown and odorous. Serve the salmon fresh and warm.

Nutritional information: Calories: 327 Fat: 25g

Protein: 36g Carbohydrates: 0.3g

14. Mediterranean Chickpea Salad

Preparation time: 5 minutes

Cooking time: 20 minutes

Servings: 6

Level of difficulty: Easy

Category: green

Ingredients:

- 1 red onion, sliced

- 1 can chickpeas, drained

- 1 teaspoon dried oregano

- Chopped parsley (2 tablespoons)

- 1 teaspoon dried basil

- 1 fennel bulb, sliced

- 2 tablespoons lemon juice

- 2 tbsp olive oil

- Salt

- 4 garlic cloves, minced

- Pepper

Directions:

- Add the chickpeas, oil, red onion, fennel, herbs, S

15. Zucchini Salmon Salad

Preparation time: 5 minutes

Cooking time: 10 minutes

Servings: 3

Level of difficulty: Normal

Category: lean

Ingredients:

- 2 salmon fillets

- Pepper and salt

- 2 tbsp soy sauce (2 tablespoons)

- 2 tablespoons olive oil

- 2 zucchinis, sliced

- 2 tablespoons sesame seeds

Preparation:

- Mix the salmon with soy sauce. Heat a grill vessel to medium flame. Cook salmon on the grill and heat per side for around 2-3 minutes

- Marinate the zucchini with pepper and salt and put it on the grill as well as salmon. Cook on per side until golden brown. Place the salmon, zucchini, and the rest of the components in a bowl. Serve.

Nutritional information: Calories: 224 Fat: 19g

Protein: 18g Carbohydrates: 0g

16. Greek Roasted Fish

Preparation time: 5 minutes

Cooking time: 30 minutes

Servings: 4

Category: lean

Level of difficulty: Easy

Ingredients:

- 4 salmon fillets

- 2 tbsp olive oil

- 1 teaspoon dried basil

- 1 red onion, sliced

- 1 tablespoon chopped oregano

- 1 carrot, sliced

- 1 zucchini, sliced

- 1 lemon, sliced

- Salt and pepper

Preparation:

- Preheat the oven to 350F. Mix all the components to the baking pan. Add pepper and salt and then cook for around 20 minutes. Serve the vegetables and fish warm.

Nutritional information: Calories: 328 Fat: 13g

Protein: 38g Carbohydrates: 8g

17. Oregano Pork Mix

Preparation time: 5 minutes

Cooking time: 7 hours & 6 minutes

Servings: 5

Level of difficulty: Normal

Category: lean

Ingredients:

- 1 yellow onion, chopped
- 2 pounds' pork roast
- 1 cup beef stock
- Olive oil (2 tablespoons)
- 2 tablespoons fresh oregano chopped
- 1 tablespoon garlic, minced
- 2 tablespoons ground cumin
- ½ Cup fresh thyme, chopped
- 7 ounces' tomato paste

Preparation:

- Heat a saucepan with the oil over average temperature. Add the roast and brown it for around 3 minutes per side. Then shift to your slow cooker.

- Add the rest of the components and stir—Cook at a low temperature for around 7 hours. Slice the roast, distribute it between plates.

Nutritional information:

Calories 623 Carbs 19.3 g

Fat 30.1 g Protein 69.2 g

18. Simple Beef Roast

Preparation time: 10 minutes

Cooking time: 8 hours

Servings: 8

Level of difficulty: Normal

Category: lean

Ingredients:

- 5 pounds' beef roast
- 1 cup beef stock
- 3 tbsp olive oil
- 1 tbsp sweet paprika
- 2 tablespoons Italian seasoning

Preparation:

- Mix all the components in your slow cooker. Lid it, and cook on low temperature for 8 hours. Slice the roast, divide it between plates. Serve them and enjoy

Nutritional information: Calories 587 Fat 24.1g

Carbs 0.9g Protein 86.5g

19. Pork And Peppers Chili

Preparation time: 5 minutes

Cooking time: 8 hours & 5 minutes

Servings: 4

Level of difficulty: Normal

Category: lean

Ingredients:

- 2 pounds' pork
- 2 red bell peppers, chopped
- 4 garlic cloves, minced
- 1 red onion, chopped
- 25 ounces' fresh tomatoes crushed
- ¼ Cup green chilies, chopped
- 1 celery stalk, chopped
- A pinch of black pepper and salt
- Fresh oregano chopped (olive oil 2 tablespoons)
- 2 tablespoons chili powder

Preparation:

- Heat a saucepan with the oil above medium temperature. Add the garlic, onion, and meat, mix them well and put aside.
- Cook for 5 minutes, and then transfer to your slow cooker. Add the rest of the Components. Lid it and cook on low for 8 hours. Distribute everything into bowls.

Nutritional information: Calories 448 Carbs 20.2 g

Fat 13g protein 63 g

20. Chicken Breast Soup

Preparation time: 5 minutes

Cooking time: 4 hours

Servings: 4

Level of difficulty: Normal

Category: leaner

Ingredients:

- 2 celery stalks, chopped
- 2 tbsp olive oil
- 3 chicken breasts, boneless and cubed
- 1 red onion, chopped
- 4 cups chicken stock
- 3 garlic cloves, minced
- 2 carrots, chopped
- 1 tbsp parsley, chopped

Preparation:

- Mix all the components except the parsley in your slow cooker. Lid it and cook on high temperature for 4 hours. Add the parsley, stir well. Ladle the soup into bowls

Nutritional information: Calories 445 Carbs 7.4g

Fat 21.1g Protein 54.3g

21. Tomato Fish Bake

Preparation time: 5 minutes

Cooking time: 30 minutes

Servings: 4

Level of difficulty: Easy

Category: leanest

Ingredients:

- 4 cod fillets

- 4 garlic cloves

- 1 tsp fennel seeds

- 1 celery stalk, sliced

- 4 tomatoes, sliced

- 1 cup vegetable stock

- 1 shallot, sliced

- Salt and pepper

Directions:

- Preheat the oven to 350F. Cover the tomatoes and cod fillets in a baking pan. Add all the **Ingredients** and add pepper and salt. Cook in the oven for around 20 minutes. Serve the dish chilled or warm.

Nutritional information:

Calories: 299 Fat: 3g

Carbohydrates: 2g Protein: 64g

22. Warm Chorizo Chickpea Salad

Preparation time: 5 minutes

Cooking time: 20 minutes

Servings: 6

Level of difficulty: Easy

Category: green

Ingredients:

- 4 chorizo links, sliced

- Pepper and salt

- 1 tablespoon olive oil

- 1 can chickpeas, drained

- 2 cups cherry tomatoes

- 1 red onion, sliced

- 4 roasted red bell peppers, chopped

- 2 tablespoons balsamic vinegar

Directions:

- Cook the oil in a saucepan and add the chorizo. Cook briefly just until fragrant, and then add the bell peppers, chickpeas, and onion.

- Cook for 2 extra minutes. Put the mixture in a salad bowl, and then add the vinegar, salt, tomatoes, and pepper. Mix them properly and serve.

Nutritional information:

Calories: 359

Fat: 18g

Protein: 15g

Carbohydrates: 21g

23. Chicken Broccoli Salad With Avocado Dressing

Preparation time: 5 minutes

Cooking time: 0 minutes

Servings: 1

Level of difficulty: Easy

Category: leaner

Ingredients:

- 1-pound broccoli, cut into florets
- ¼ Teaspoon cumin powder
- 2 chicken breasts
- 2 garlic cloves
- 1 avocado, peeled and pitted
- ¼ Teaspoon chili powder
- ½ Lemon, juiced
- Pepper and salt

Preparation:

- Heat the chicken in a big pan of salty water. Remove water and chop the chicken into a small piece. Then place them in a bowl.
- Put the broccoli and mix well. Add the lemon juice, salt, garlic, avocado, cumin powder, chili powder, and pepper in a blender and beat until smooth. Add them to the salad and mix properly. Serve.

Nutritional information: Calories: 195 Fat: 11g

Protein: 14g Carbohydrates: 3g

24. Balsamic Beef And Mushrooms Mix

Preparation time: 5 minutes

Cooking time: 0 minutes

Servings: 1

Level of difficulty: Easy

Category: lean

Ingredients:

- 1 cup brown mushrooms, sliced
- ¼ Cup balsamic vinegar
- 1 tbsp ginger
- 1 tsp ground cinnamon
- 2 cups beef stock
- 2 pounds' beef, cut into strips
- ½ Cup of lemon juice(1/2cup)
- A pinch of black pepper and salt

Preparation:

- In your slow cooker, mix all the components. Lid it and heat on low for around 8 hours. Distribute everything between plates. Serve.

Nutritional information:

Calories 446

Protein 70.8g

Fat 14g

Carbs 2.9g

25. Garlicky Tomato Chicken Casserole

Preparation time: 5 minutes

Cooking time: 50 minutes

Servings: 4

Level of difficulty: Normal

Category: leaner

Ingredients:

- 1 can diced tomatoes

- 4 chicken breasts

- 1 shallot, chopped

- 2 tomatoes, sliced

- 1 bay leaf

- 2 garlic cloves, chopped

- ½ Cup dry white wine

- ½ Cup chicken stock

- 1 thyme sprig

- Pepper and salt

Directions:

- Preheat the oven to 330F. Add the chicken and all the components to a deep bowl baking pan. Add pepper and salt.

- Close the pot with a cover or aluminum foil, then cook them in the oven for around 40 minutes. Serve them while warm.

Nutritional information:

Calories: 313 Protein: 47g

Carbohydrates: 6g Fat: 8g

26. Fennel Wild Rice Risotto

Preparation time: 5 minutes

Cooking time: 35 minutes

Servings: 6

Level of difficulty: Normal

Category: green

Ingredients:

- 2 cups chicken stock

- 1 shallot, chopped

- 2 garlic cloves

- 2 tablespoons olive oil

- 1 fennel bulb, chopped

- 1 cup wild rice

- 1 teaspoon grated orange zest

- ¼ Cup dry white wine

- Pepper and salt

Directions:

- Warm the oil in a pan. Add the shallot, fennel, and garlic. Cook them for a few minutes. Mix in the rice, heat for two extra minutes.

- Then add the orange zest and wine, with pepper and salt to taste. Cook on low heat for around 20 minutes. Serve them while warm.

Nutritional information:

Calories: 162

Protein: 8g

Fat: 2g

Carbohydrates: 20g

27. Garlic Chicken Balls

Preparation time: 5 minutes

Cooking time: 0 minutes

Servings: 1

Level of difficulty: Normal

Category: lean

Ingredients:

- 1 teaspoon minced garlic
- 1/3 carrot, grated
- 1 egg, beaten
- 1 teaspoon dried dill
- 2 cups ground chicken
- ¼ Cup coconut flakes
- ½ Teaspoon salt
- 1 tbsp olive oil

Directions:

- Mix up together minced garlic, egg, dried dill, ground chicken, carrot, and salt in a bowl. Mash the chicken with the help of the fingertips until homogenous.

- Then make average balls from the mixture. Cover every chicken ball in coconut flakes—heat olive oil in the skillet. Put chicken balls into the oil; cook them for 3 minutes from each side or brownish color.

Nutritional information: Calories 200

Carbs 1.7g

Fat 11.5g

Protein 21.9g

28. Sliced Steak With Canadian Crust

Preparation Time: 10 minutes

Cooking Time: 20 minutes

Servings: 5

Level of difficulty: Normal

Category: lean

Ingredients:

- 2- 10-ounce steaks, about 1 and one-half thick
- 1 tablespoon dry steak seasonings

Directions

- Preheat broiler. Rub on both sides of the steak the dry steak seasonings. Place steak under a preheated broiler.

- Broil each side to taste within 5 minutes per side for medium-rare—slice steak in thin, 3/4" slices against the grain.

- Arrange slices on a serving platter and top with a generous amount of butter. Serve and enjoy with a side salad.

Nutritional information:

Calories: 51

Protein: 6.58 g

Fat: 2.02 g

Carbohydrates: 1.03 g

29. Fork Tender Beef Goulash With Peppercorn & Sage

Preparation Time: 15 minutes

Cooking Time: 35 minutes

Servings: 4

Level of difficulty: Normal

Category: lean

Ingredients:

- 2 tbsp olive oil
- 2 onions, chopped roughly
- 4 garlic cloves, crushed
- 2 celery stalks, sliced
- 800 g beef rump steaks, or use stewing steak, cut into 3cm cubes
- 1 tbsp paprika
- ½ Bottle red wine
- 1 tin chopped tomato, approx. 420g
- 1 tbsp balsamic vinegar
- 1/2 peppercorn
- 2 tsp brown sugar
- 1 stalk sage, leaves only
- 1 pinch chili flakes
- 1 pottle sour cream, for serving

Preparation:

- In a heavy saucepan, sauté the onion, celery, and garlic till soft. Add the meat and brown well.
- Set aside a small amount of the meat, sliced thinly, and return the rest to the pan along with the paprika, wine, chopped tomatoes, balsamic vinegar, and sugar.
- Preheat the oven to 160°C. Gently simmer for 20–30 minutes, adding the whole peppercorn and sage bundle. With a sharp knife, remove the peppercorn and sage.

- Increase the heat and simmer vigorously for another 10 minutes. Serve garnished with the reserved meat slices, sour cream, and chili flakes.

Nutritional information:

Calories: 417

Protein: 44.36 g

Fat: 18.21 g

Carbohydrates: 17.78 g

30. Mexican Chicken In Orange Juice

Preparation Time: 2 hours

Cooking Time: 20 minutes

Level of difficulty: Normal

Servings: 4

Category: leaner

Ingredients

- 1 cup fresh orange juice
- 2 tbsp. Fresh lime juice
- 1 dried chipotle chili pepper, stemmed and seeded
- 1 cup mild salsa
- 1/4 c. Olive oil
- 1 tsp. Salt
- 4 boneless, skinless chicken breast halves
- 1 orange, sliced into rings
- 1/4 cup chopped fresh cilantro leaves

Preparation:

- Place all Ingredients except chicken and orange slices in the blender. Blend until smooth. Store in refrigerator overnight to allow flavors to blend.
- Add chicken to orange juice mixture and marinate for 2 hours. Prepare grill for medium heat. Remove chicken from marinade; reserve marinade.

- Place chicken on grill rack coated with nonstick cooking spray and grill 10 minutes. Turn and cook until juices run clear. Move the chicken to your cutting board, then cut into thin bite-size slices.

- Pour reserved marinade into a small saucepan. Boil it on high heat, then adjust the heat to medium and boil for 5 minutes. Add orange slices to the saucepan and mix well. Heat through.

- Divide cilantro evenly among 4 dinner plates. Top each of the plates evenly with orange slices and sauced chicken. Garnish with lime slices and serve.

Nutritional information:

Calories: 489

Protein: 55.23 g

Fat: 19.98 g

Carbohydrates: 20.47 g

31. Chicken Sancho

Preparation Time: 5 minutes

Cooking Time: 1 hour

Servings: 6

Level of difficulty: Normal

Category: leaner

Ingredients:

- 1 teaspoon olive oil

- 5 scallions, chopped

- 1 tomato, chopped

- 4 cloves garlic, chopped

- 1/2 onion, chopped

- 6 skinless chicken thighs on the bone

- 1 cup chopped cilantro

- 3 medium potatoes, peeled and chopped into 2-inch pieces

- 1 small green plantain, peeled & chopped into 1" pieces

- 1 tsp cumin

- 2 chicken bouillon cubes

- Salt to taste

Preparation:

- Heat the oil in a large skillet, brown the chicken, skin side first over medium heat for 2-3 minutes, then take them out.

- Preheat the oven to 350F. Chop the scallions, tomatoes, onions, and garlic in a food processor

- Heat the skillet and add the scallion, onion, and garlic; cook for a minute or until the onion is translucent. Add the cilantro and chicken, stir.

- Prepare the chicken broth by adding the chicken bouillon cubes to a large saucepan and adding 2 cups of water. Bring to a boil, reduce the heat and simmer for 5 min until it is fully dissolved.

- Add the potatoes, yucca, corn, and plantain to the skillet, stir. Pour in the chicken broth, then cook until the vegetables are tender. Add a pinch or two of salt to taste.

- Prepare the Arroz con coco (rice with coconut milk). Add 1/2 cup of the coconut milk to rice and cook according to the Directions.

- Add the chicken mixture into the rice and mix well. Garnish with cilantro.

Nutritional information:

Calories: 552 Protein: 37.75 g

Fat: 38.68 g Carbohydrates: 134.47 g

Sides

1. Caramelized Onion Quesadilla

Preparation Time: 10 minutes
Cooking Time: 25 minutes
Servings: 4
Level of difficulty: Normal
Category: green

Ingredients:

- A whole grain of tortilla
- 1 big caramelize onion, slice
- 1 cup of fresh spinach
- Black beans - Cheese (Nonfat)

Directions:

- On medium heat, heat the onion, use dry sautéing to caramelize. Add a pinch of salt so that it can bring the moisture out of the onion.
- Cook it until the color changes to brown and translucent, then set it aside. Heat your tortilla in a skillet. Then add your beans, spinach, and onion mixture on one side of the tortilla. Add your cheese and fold over the tortilla. Serve.

Nutritional information: Calories: 350Protein: 13.9 g
Carbohydrates: 40.9 g Fat: 26 g

2. Roasted Garlic Potatoes

Preparation Time: 5 minutes
Cooking Time: 1 hour
Servings: 6
Level of difficulty: Normal
Category: green

Ingredients:

- 1 teaspoon of dried or fresh chopped rosemary
- 6 cups of potatoes, unpeeled
- 1 teaspoon of onion powder
- 1 teaspoon of pepper, freshly ground

Directions:

- Preheat the oven to 425°F. Toss the potatoes and mix with rosemary, garlic, onion powder, salt, and pepper to coat.
- On an even layer over the already prepared baking sheet, spread the potatoes and bake for 20 minutes.
- Stir potatoes to promote even browning of the potatoes. Continue for about 3 to 10 minutes until the potato becomes browner and more tender. Remove from the oven and serve it warm.

Nutritional information: Calories: 100 Protein: 2.8 g
Carbohydrates: 23.5 g Fat: 7.9 g

3. Asian Noodle Salad

Preparation Time: 20 minutes

Cooking Time: 5 minutes

Servings: 12

Level of difficulty: Normal

Category: green

Ingredients:

- Whole wheat of noodles, e.g., spaghetti/soba
- 24 ounces of Mann's broccoli
- 5 grated carrots
- 1/4 cup of EVOO or any preferred oil
- 1/5 cup of rice vinegar
- 4 tablespoons of honey
- 4 tablespoons of creamy butter
- 1 tablespoon mashed garlic
- 3/4 cup roasted peanuts roughly chopped

Preparation:

- Cook and drain the noodles. If you are using soba noodles, you should add a tablespoon of salt to your water, and salt won't be necessary when using Chinese noodles.

- After draining the noodles, rinse with cold water and then spread out the noodles on a pan to dry. Steam the broccoli by viding it in boiled water and steam for about 4 minutes, rinse with cold water, and set aside.

- In your mixing bowl, whisk together the olive or cooking oil, honey, rice vinegar, creamy butter, ginger, and garlic.

- Pour it inside the noodle and toss. Then add the roasted peanuts at this point and toss it again. Serve chilled or at room temperature.

Nutritional information:

Calories: 175

Fats: 10.6 g

Carbohydrates: 18.3 g

Protein: 3.9 g

4. Protein Pumpkin Spiced Donuts

Preparation Time: 10 minutes

Cooking Time: 25 minutes

Servings: 8

Level of difficulty: Normal

Category: green

Ingredients:

- 1 cup oat flour
- 3/4 cup xylitol
- 1 scoop, powdered vanilla protein
- 1 tbsp ground flaxseed
- 1 tbsp ground cinnamon
- 2 tsp. Baking powder
- 1 tsp sea salt
- 3 beaten eggs
- 1/2 cup canned pumpkin
- 1 tbsp coconut oil, melted
- 2 tsp vanilla
- 1 tsp apple cider vinegar

Ingredients for the frosting:

- ½ cup Cream cheese, whipped
- ½ tsp Liquid stevia

Preparation:

- Place the xylitol, oat flour, ground flaxseed, powdered protein, baking powder, ground cinnamon, and a dash of sea salt in a large bowl. Preheat your oven to 350 degrees Fahrenheit.

- Add the egg (beaten) into another bowl (large) along with the pumpkin (canned), pure vanilla and vinegar, and coconut oil (melted).

- Whisk until mixed (evenly), then pour the mixture into the flour. Stir until thoroughly mixed. Use a cooking spray, grease a large donut pan.

- Pour batter into the donut pan (greased). Place batter into the oven and bake for approximately 10 minutes until thoroughly baked.

- Remove from heat and set donuts onto a wire rack to cool. Add in the cream cheese (whipped) and liquid stevia in a small bowl, whisk until smooth.

- Frost donuts using the frosting and serve with a sprinkle of cinnamon (ground) over the top.

Nutritional information: Calories 95 Fats 0.3 g

Carbohydrates 9.3 g Protein 12.5 g

Vegan

1. Zucchini Muffins

Preparation Time: 10 minutes
Cooking Time: 25 minutes
Servings: 16

Ingredients:

- 1 tablespoon ground flaxseed
- 3 tablespoons alkaline water
- 1/4 cup walnut butter
- 3 medium over-ripe bananas
- 2 small grated zucchinis
- 1/2 cup coconut milk
- 1 teaspoon vanilla extract
- 2 cups coconut flour
- 1 tablespoon baking powder
- 1 teaspoon cinnamon
- 1/4 teaspoon sea salt

Preparation:

- Tune the temperature of your oven to 375°f. Grease the muffin tray with the cooking spray.
- In a bowl, mix the flaxseed with water. In a glass bowl, mash the bananas then stir in the remaining Ingredients.
- Properly mix and then divide the mixture into the muffin tray. Bake it for 25 minutes. Serve.

Nutritional information:

Calories: 127 kcal

Fat: 6.6g

Carbs: 13g

Protein: 0.7g

2. Crunchy Quinoa Meal

Preparation Time: 5 minutes
Cooking Time: 25 minutes
Servings: 2

Ingredients:

- 3 cups coconut milk
- 1 cup rinsed quinoa
- 1/8 teaspoon ground cinnamon
- 1 cup raspberry
- 1/2 cup chopped coconuts

Preparation:

- In a saucepan, pour milk and bring it to a boil over moderate heat.
- Add the quinoa to the milk and then bring it to a boil once more.
- Let it simmer for at least 15 minutes on medium heat until the milk is reduced.
- Stir in the cinnamon then mix properly.
- Cover and cook for 8 minutes until the milk is completely absorbed.
- Add the raspberry and cook the meal for 30 seconds. Serve and enjoy.

Nutritional information:

Calories: 271

Fat: 3.7 g

Carbs: 54 g

Proteins: 6.5 g

3. Jackfruit Vegetable Fry

Preparation Time: 5 minutes
Cooking Time: 5 minutes
Servings: 6

Ingredients:

- 2 finely chopped small onions
- 2 cups finely chopped cherry tomatoes
- 1/8 teaspoon ground turmeric
- 1 tablespoon olive oil
- 2 seeded and chopped red bell peppers
- 3 cups seeded and chopped firm jackfruit
- 1/8 teaspoon cayenne pepper
- 2 tablespoons chopped fresh basil leaves
- Salt

Directions:

- In a greased skillet, sauté the onions and bell peppers for about 5 minutes.
- Add the tomatoes and stir. Cook for 2 minutes.
- Then add the jackfruit, cayenne pepper, salt, and turmericup. Cook for about 8 minutes.
- Garnish the meal with basil leaves. Serve warm.

Nutritional information:

Calories: 236
Fat: 1.8 g
Carbs: 48.3 g
Protein: 7 g

4. Banana Barley Porridge

Preparation Time: 15 minutes
Cooking Time: 5 minutes
Servings: 2

Ingredients:

- 1 cup divided unsweetened coconut milk
- 1 small peeled and sliced banana
- 1/2 cup barley
- 3 drops liquid stevia
- 1/4 cup chopped coconuts

Directions:

- In a bowl, properly mix barley with half of the coconut milk and stevia.
- Cover the mixing bowl then refrigerate for about 6 hours.
- In a saucepan, mix the barley mixture with coconut milk. Cook for about 5 minutes on moderate heat.
- Then top it with the chopped coconuts and the banana slices. Serve.

Nutritional information:

Calories: 159
Fat: 8.4 g
Carbs: 19.8 g
Proteins: 4.6 g

5. Pumpkin Spice Quinoa

Preparation Time: 10 minutes
Cooking Time: 0 minutes
Servings: 2

Ingredients:

- 1 cup cooked quinoa
- 1 cup unsweetened coconut milk
- 1 large mashed banana
- 1/4 cup pumpkin puree
- 1 teaspoon pumpkin spice
- 2 teaspoons chia seeds

Preparation:

- In a container, mix all the Ingredients.
- Seal the lid then shake the container properly to mix.
- Refrigerate overnight. Serve.

Nutritional information:

Calories: 212
Fat: 11.9 g
Carbs: 31.7 g
Protein: 7.3 g

6. Quinoa Porridge

Preparation Time: 5 minutes
Cooking Time: 25 minutes
Servings: 2

Ingredients:

- 2 cups coconut milk
- 1 cup rinsed quinoa
- 1/8 teaspoon ground cinnamon
- 1 cup fresh blueberries

Preparation:

- In a saucepan, boil the coconut milk over high heat. Add the quinoa to the milk then bring the mixture to a boil.
- You then let it simmer for 15 minutes on medium heat until the milk is reduced. Add the cinnamon and mix it properly in the saucepan.
- Cover the saucepan and cook for at least 8 minutes until the milk is completely absorbed.
- Add in the blueberries then cook for 30 more seconds. Serve.

Nutritional information:

Calories: 271
Fat: 3.7 g
Carbs: 54 g
Protein: 6.5 g

7. Hemp Seed Porridge

Preparation Time: 5 minutes
Cooking Time: 5 minutes
Servings: 6

Ingredients:

- 3 cups cooked hemp seed

- 1 packet Stevia

- 1 cup coconut milk

Preparation:

- In a saucepan, mix the rice and the coconut milk over moderate heat for about 5 minutes as you stir it constantly.

- Remove the pan from the burner then add the Stevia. Stir.

- Serve in 6 bowls. Enjoy.

Nutritional information:

Calories: 236

Fat: 1.8 g

Carbs: 48.3 g

Protein: 7 g

8. Millet Porridge

Preparation Time: 10 minutes
Cooking Time: 20 minutes
Servings: 2

Ingredients:

- Sea salt

- 1 tablespoon finely chopped coconuts

- 1/2 cup unsweetened coconut milk

- 1/2 cup rinsed and drained millet

- 1-1/2 cups alkaline water

- 3 drops liquid stevia

Preparation:

- Sauté the millet in a non-stick skillet for about 3 minutes. Add salt and water then stir.

- Let the meal boil then reduce the amount of heat.

- Cook for 15 minutes then add the remaining Ingredients. Stir. Cook the meal for 4 extra minutes.

- Serve the meal with a topping of the chopped nuts.

Nutritional information:

Calories: 219

Fat: 4.5 g

Carbs: 38.2 g

Protein: 6.4 g

9. Veggie Fritters

Preparation Time: 10 minutes
Cooking Time: 10 minutes
Servings: 4

Ingredients:

- 2 garlic cloves, minced
- 2 yellow onions, chopped
- 4 scallions, chopped
- 2 carrots, grated
- 2 teaspoons cumin, ground
- ½ Teaspoon turmeric powder
- Salt and black pepper to the taste
- ¼ Teaspoon coriander, ground
- 2 tablespoons parsley, chopped
- ¼ Teaspoon lemon juice
- ½ Cup almond flour
- 2 beets, peeled and grated
- 2 eggs, whisked
- ¼ Cup tapioca flour
- 3 tablespoons olive oil

Directions:

- In a bowl, combine the garlic with the onions, scallions, and the rest of the Ingredients except the oil, stir well and shape medium fritters out of this mix.
- Heat oil in a pan over medium-high heat, add the fritters, cook for 5 minutes on each side, arrange on a platter and serve.

Nutritional information:

Calories 209, Fat 11.2 g, Fiber 3 g, Carbs 4.4 g, Protein 4.8 g

10. Potato Hash With Cilantro-Lime Cream

Preparation Time: 20 minutes
Cooking Time: 30 minutes
Servings: 2

Ingredients:

For the cilantro-lime cream

- 1 avocado, halved and pitted
- ¼ Cup packed fresh cilantro leaves and stems
- 2 tablespoons freshly squeezed lime juice
- 1 garlic clove, peeled
- 1 teaspoon kosher salt
- ½ Teaspoon ground cumin
- 2 tablespoons extra-virgin olive oil

For the hash

- ½ Teaspoon kosher salt
- 1 large sweet potato, cut into ¾-inch pieces
- 2 tablespoons extra-virgin olive oil
- 1 onion, thinly sliced
- 2 garlic cloves, crushed
- 1 red bell pepper, thinly sliced
- 1 teaspoon ground cumin
- ¼ Teaspoon ground turmeric
- A pinch of freshly ground black pepper
- 2 tablespoons fresh cilantro leaves, chopped
- ½ Jalapeño pepper, seeded and chopped (optional)
- Hot sauce, for serving (optional)

Preparation:

To make the cilantro-lime cream

- Add the avocado flesh in a food compressor. Add the cilantro, lime juice, garlic, salt, and cumin. Whirl until smooth. Taste and adjust seasonings, as needed. If you do not have a food processor or blender, simply mash the avocado well with a fork; the results will have more texture, but will still work. Cover and refrigerate until ready to serve.

To make the hash

- Boil salt water in a medium pot over high heat. Add the sweet potato and cook for about 20 minutes until tender. Drain thoroughly.

- Heat olive oil in a big skillet over low heat until it shimmers. Add the onion and sauté for about 4 minutes until translucent. Put the garlic and cook, turning, for about 30 seconds. Add the cooked sweet potato and red bell pepper. Season the hash with cumin, salt, turmeric, and pepper. Sauté for 5 to 7 minutes, until the sweet potatoes are golden and the red bell pepper is soft.

- Divide the sweet potatoes between 2 bowls and spoon the sauce over them. Scatter the cilantro and jalapeño (optional) over each and serve with hot sauce (optional).

Nutritional information:

Calories: 520, Total fat: 43 g, Cholesterol: 0 mg, Fiber: 2 g, Protein: 12 g, Sodium: 1719 mg

11. Black Beans And Sweet Potato Tacos

Preparation Time: 10 minutes

Cooking Time: 30 minutes

Servings: 6

Ingredients:

- 1-pound sweet potato (about 2 medium teaspoons), remove skin and cut into 1/2-inch pieces

- 2 tablespoons of olive oil, divided

- 1 tablespoon kosar salt, divided

- ¼ Teaspoon fresh black pepper on large white or yellow onion, finely chopped

- 2 teaspoons of red pepper

- 1 teaspoon of cumin

- 1 (15 oz.) Can black beans, drained

- 1 cup of water

- ¼ Cup freshly chopped garlic

- 12 pieces Corn

To serve:

- Guacamole

- Sliced cheese or feta cheese (optional)

- Wood wedge

Preparation:

- In the oven, set out a tray in the middle rack and preheat to 425 degrees Fahrenheit. Set a big sheet of aluminum foil on the work surface. Collect the tortillas from the top and wrap them completely in foil. Put it aside.

- Put sweet potatoes on a small baking sheet. Mix with one tablespoon oil and sprinkle with 1/2 teaspoon salt and 1/4 teaspoon black pepper. Mix it properly and arrange it in a single layer on the sheet. Fry for 20 minutes. Cover the potatoes with a flat lid and set aside.

- Put the foil wrapping in the oven and continue to cook for about 10 minutes until the sweet potatoes are browned and stained and the seasonings are heated. Also, cook the beans.

- Thereafter, heat one tablespoon oil in a large skillet over low heat. Add the onions and cook, occasionally stirring, until translucent, about 3 minutes. Mix the pepper powder, cumin, and 1/2 teaspoon salt. Add the beans and water.

- Shield the pan and reduce the heat to low heat. Cook for 5 minutes, then slice and use the back of the fork to chop the beans a little, about half of the total. Continue cooking till the water content of the mixture is evaporated, and a semi-solid state is reached.

- Peel the sweet potatoes and add the cantaloupe to the black beans and mix. Fill the taco cavity with a mixture of black beans and top with guacamole and cheese. Serve with lime wedges.

Nutritional information:

Calories: 251

Total fat: 4 g, Cholesterol: 94 mg, Fiber: 2 g, Protein: 15 g, Sodium: 329 mg

12. Spicy Waffle With Jalapeno

Preparation Time: 5 minutes

Cooking Time: 10 minutes

Servings: 2

Ingredients:

- 2 teaspoon coconut flour
- ½ Tablespoon chopped jalapeno pepper
- 2 teaspoon cream cheese
- 1 egg
- 2 oz shredded mozzarella cheese
- ¼ Teaspoon salt
- 1/8 teaspoon ground black pepper

Preparation:

- Switch on a mini waffle maker and let it preheat for 5 minutes.
- Meanwhile, take a medium bowl, place all the Ingredients in it and then mix by using an immersion blender until smooth.
- Ladle the batter evenly into the waffle maker, shut with lid, and let it cook for 3 to 4 minutes until firm and golden brown. Serve.

Nutritional information:

Calories 153

Fats 10.7 g

Protein 11.1 g

Net Carb 1 g

Fiber 1 g

13. Wheat Pita Bread Wedges

Preparation Time: 10 minutes

Cooking Time: 7 minutes

Servings: 24

Ingredients:

- 230 ml. (or a cup) lukewarm water
- 2 teaspoons honey
- 2 teaspoons yeast (dry)
- 1 teaspoon salt
- 1½ cup whole wheat flour (180grams)
- 1 teaspoon extra virgin oil or any cooking oil.

Preparation:

- Mix the water, yeast and honey in your mixing bowl allowing it to sit for 4 or 5 minutes.
- Then add the flours, olive oil and salt, nixing it for a couple of minutes until it sticks together. Take a little flour and sprinkle it on the surface, making a dough.
- Add more flour if necessary, to the dough until it becomes smooth and more elastic. This might take up to 5 minutes.
- Make a ball with it and cover it an oiled bowl for about an hour until it is doubled
- Remove the dough and divide it equally into 9 parts with each part circle shaped like a ball. Cover with a clean damp cloth.
- Preheat the oven to 230C and bake for 4 to 5 minutes. Allow the homemade whole wheat pita bread to cool before serving.

Nutritional information:

Protein: 3.2 g

Carbohydrates: 17.7 g

Dietary Fiber: 2.4 g

Sugars 0.3 g

Fat: 5.3 g

14. Chili Mango And Watermelon Salsa

Preparation Time: 5 minutes
Cooking Time: 0 minutes
Servings: 8
Ingredients:

- 1 red tomato, chopped

- Salt and black pepper to the taste

- 1 cup watermelon, seedless, peeled and cubed

- 1 red onion, chopped

- 2 mangos, peeled and chopped

- 2 chili peppers, chopped

- ¼ Cup cilantro, chopped

- 3 tablespoons lime juice

- Pita chips for serving

Preparation:

- In a bowl, mix tomato with watermelon, onion, and rest of the ingredients except the pita chips and toss well.

- Divide the mix into small cups and serve with pita chips on the side.

Nutritional information:

Calories 62
Fat g
Fiber 1.3 g
Carbs 3.9 g
Protein 2.3 g

15. Cucumber Sandwich Bites

Preparation Time: 5 minutes
Cooking Time: 0 minutes
Servings: 12
Ingredients:

- 1 cucumber, sliced

- 8 slices whole-wheat bread

- 2 tablespoons cream cheese, soft

- 1 tablespoon chives, chopped

- ¼ Cup avocado, peeled, pitted, and mashed

- 1 teaspoon mustard

- Salt and black pepper to the taste

Preparation:

- Spread the mashed avocado on each bread slice, also spread the rest of the ingredients except the cucumber slices.

- Divide the cucumber slices on the bread slices, cut each slice in thirds, arrange on a platter and serve as an appetizer.

Nutritional information:

Calories 187
Fat 12.4 g
Fiber 2.1 g
Carbs 4.5 g
Protein 8.2 g

16. Zucchini Noodles With Creamy Avocado Pesto

Preparation Time: 5 minutes

Cooking Time: 20 minutes

Servings: 4

Ingredients:

- 6 cups spiralized zucchini

- 1 tablespoon olive oil

- 6 oz. Avocado

- 1 basil leaf

- 3 garlic cloves

- 1/3 oz. Pine nuts

- 2 tablespoon lemon juice

- 1/2 teaspoon salt

- 1/4 teaspoon black pepper

Preparation:

- Spiralize the courgettes and set them aside on paper towels to absorb the excess water.

- In a food processor, put avocados, lemon juice, basil leaves, garlic, pine nuts, and sea salt and pulse until chopped.

- Then put olive oil in a slow stream till emulsified and creamy. Drizzle olive oil in a skillet over medium-high heat and put zucchini noodles, cooking for about 2 minutes till tender.

- Put zucchini noodles in a big bowl and toss with avocado pesto.

- Season with cracked pepper and a little Parmesan and serve.

Nutritional information:

Calories: 362 Cal, Carbohydrates: 16 g, Protein: 4.6 g, Fat: 34.1 g, Sodium: 28 mg, Potassium: 1043 mg, Fiber: 9.1 g, Sugar: 4.1 g, Calcium: 40 mg

17. Herbed Wild Rice

Preparation Time: 10 minutes

Cooking Time: 5/ 6 hours

Servings: 8

Ingredients:

- 3 cups wild rice, rinsed and drained

- 6 cups Roasted Vegetable Broth

- 1 onion, chopped

- 1/2 teaspoon salt

- 1/2 teaspoon dried thyme leaves

- 1/2 teaspoon dried basil leaves

- 1 bay leaf

- 1/3 cup chopped fresh flat-leaf parsley

Preparation:

- In a 6-quart slow cooker, mix the wild rice, vegetable broth, onion, salt, thyme, basil, and bay leaf.

- Cover and cook on low for 4 to 6 hours, or until the wild rice is tender but still firm.

- You can cook this dish longer until the wild rice pops, taking about 5 to 6 hours.

- Remove and discard the bay leaf. Stir in the parsley and serve.

Nutritional information: Calories: 258 Cal - Carbohydrates: 54 g

Sugar: 3 g

Fiber: 5 g

Fat: 2 g

Saturated Fat: 0 g

Protein: 6 g,

Sodium: 257 mg

18. Celeriac Stuffed Avocado

Preparation Time: 10 minutes
Cooking Time: 0 minutes
Servings: 2

Ingredients:

- 1 avocado
- 1 celery root, finely chopped
- 2 tablespoon mayonnaise
- ½ Of a lemon, juiced, zested
- 2 tablespoon mayonnaise
- ¼ Teaspoon salt

Preparation:

- Prepare avocado and for this, cut avocado in half and then remove its pit.
- Place remaining Ingredients in a bowl, stir well until combined, and evenly stuff this mixture into avocado halves. Serve.

Nutritional information:

Calories 285
Fats 27 g
Protein 2.8 g
Net Carb 4.4 g
Fiber 2.6 g

19. Squash Hash

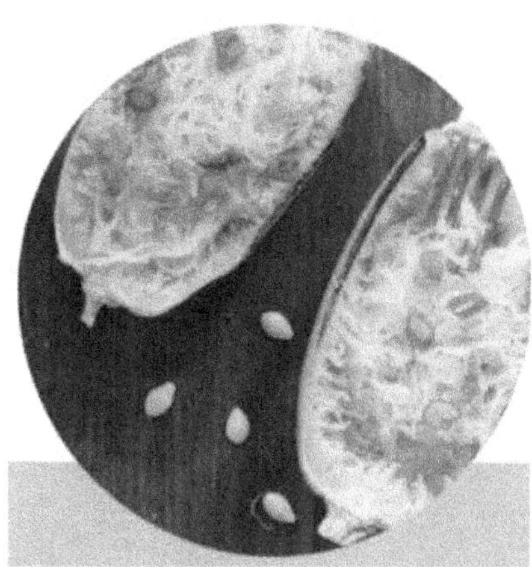

Preparation Time: 2 minutes
Cooking Time: 10 minutes
Servings: 2

Ingredients:

- 1 teaspoon onion powder
- ½ Cup finely chopped onion
- 2 cups spaghetti squash
- ½ Teaspoon sea salt

Preparation:

- Using paper towels, squeeze extra moisture from spaghetti squash.
- Place the squash into a bowl then add the salt, onion, and the onion powder. Stir properly to mix them.
- Spray a non-stick cooking skillet with cooking spray then place it over moderate heat. Add the spaghetti squash to the pan. Cook the squash for about 5 minutes.
- Flip the hash browns using a spatula. Cook for 5 minutes until the desired crispness is reached. Serve.

Nutritional information:

Calories: 44
Fat: 0.6 g
Carbs: 9.7 g
Protein: 0.9 g

20. Peanut Sauce, Green Vegetables And Tempeh

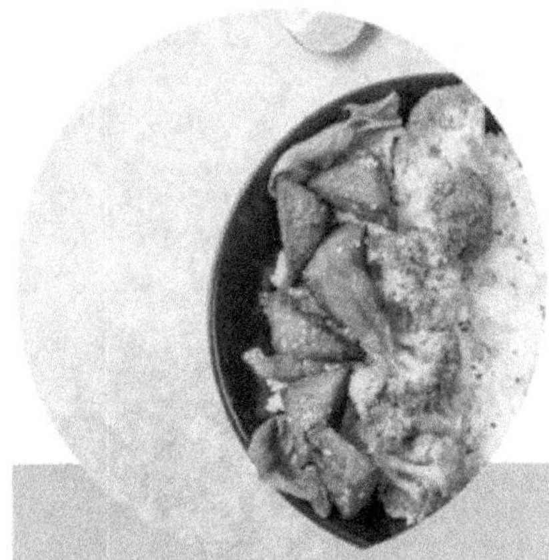

Preparation Time: 25 minutes

Cooking Time: 5 minutes

Servings: 4

Ingredients:

Veggies:

- 3 ounces tempeh, cubed
- 1/2 cup frozen spinach
- 1/2 cup green bell pepper, chopped
- 1/2 cup broccoli
- 1/4 cup ycllow onion, chopped
- 1/2 cup unshelled edamame
- 1/4 cup vegetable broth, low-sodium
- 1/4 clove minced garlic

Sauce:

- 1 tablespoon of unsalted peanut butter
- 1 tablespoon of soy sauce, low-sodium
- 1 tablespoon of apple cider vinegar
- 1/4 teaspoon of garlic powder

Preparation:

- Pour vegetable broth into a saucepan at low pressure.
- In the sauce, add tempeh, bell pepper, spinach, cabbage, broccoli, edamame, along with garlic and simmer until the vegetables are tender and the vegetable broth is soaked in.
- Whisk all sauce Ingredients together in a separate bowl while the vegetables and tempeh are cooking; if needed, add a little water for a thinner consistency.
- Place aside sauce. If vegetables are ready to cook, apply the peanut sauce and cover uniformly.

Nutritional information:

Calories: 441 Cal ,Carbohydrates 43.3 g ,Protein 21.2 g ,Fats 23.7 g

21. Green Pea Guacamole

Preparation Time: 15 minutes

Cooking Time: 35 minutes

Servings: 4

Ingredients:

- 1 teaspoon crushed garlic
- 1 chopped tomato
- 3 cups frozen green peas (chopped)
- 5 green onions, chopped
- 1/6 teaspoon hot sauce
- 1/2 teaspoon grounded cumin
- 1/2 cup lime juice

Preparation:

- Blend the peas, garlic, lime juice and cumin until it is smoothened
- Stir in the tomatoes, green onion and hot sauce into the mixture. Then add salt to taste
- Cover it and put into the refrigerator for a minimum of 30 minutes.
- This will allow the flavor to blend very well.

Nutritional information:

Calories: 40.7 Cal

Fat: 0.2 g

Cholesterol: 0.0 mg

Sodium: 157.4 mg

Carbohydrates: 7.6g

Dietary Fiber: 1.7 g

Protein: 2.7 g

22. Stewed Herbed Fruit

Preparation Time: 15 minutes
Cooking Time: 6 to 8 hours
Servings: 12

Ingredients:

- 2 cups dried apricots
- 2 cups prunes
- 2 cups dried unsulfured pears
- 2 cups dried apples
- 1 cup dried cranberries
- 1/4 cup honey
- 6 cups water
- 1 teaspoon dried thyme leaves
- 1 teaspoon dried basil leaves

Preparation:

- In a 6-quart slow cooker, mix all the Ingredients.
- Cover and cook on low for 6 to 8 hours, or until the fruits have absorbed the liquid and are tender.
- Store in the refrigerator up to 1 week.
- You can freeze the fruit in 1-cup portions for more extended storage.

Nutritional information:

Calories: 242

Carbohydrates: 61 g

Sugar: 43 g

Fiber: 9 g

Fat: 0 g

Saturated Fat: 0 g

Protein: 2 g

Sodium: 11 mg

23. Maple Lemon Tempeh Cubes

Preparation Time: 10 minutes
Cooking Time: 35minutes
Servings: 4

Ingredients:

- 1 packet of tempeh
- 2 to 3 teaspoons of coconut oil
- 3 tablespoons of lemon juice
- 2 teaspoons of maple syrup
- 1 to 2 teaspoons of Bragg's Liquid aminos or low-sodium tamari (optional);
- 2 teaspoons of water;
- 1/4 teaspoon of dried basil
- 1/4 teaspoon of powdered garlic;
- Black pepper (freshly grounded); to taste

Preparation:

- Heat your oven to 400 ° C. Cut your tempeh block into squares in bite form.
- Heat coconut oil over medium to high heat in a non-stick skillet. When melted and heated, add the tempeh and cook on one side for 2-4 minutes, or until the tempeh turns down into a golden-brown color.
- Flip the tempeh bits, and cook for 2-4 minutes. Mix the lemon juice, tamari, maple syrup, basil, water, garlic, and black pepper while tempeh is browning.
- Drop the mixture over tempeh, then swirl to cover the tempeh.
- Sauté for 2-3 minutes, then turn the tempeh and sauté 1-2 minutes more. The tempeh, on both sides, should be soft and orange.

Nutritional information: Carbohydrates: 22 Cal, Fats: 17 g, Sugar: 5 g, Protein: 21 g, Fiber: 9 g

24. Bok Choy With Tofu Stir Fry

Preparation Time: 15 minutes
Cooking Time: 15 minutes
Servings: 4

Ingredients:

- 1 lb. Super-firm tofu, drained and pressed
- 1 tablespoon coconut oil
- 1 clove garlic, minced
- 3 heads Baby bok choy; chopped
- Low-sodium vegetable broth
- 2 teaspoons Maple syrup
- Braggs liquid aminos
- 1 to 2 teaspoons Sambal oelek, similar chili sauce
- Scallion or green onion, chopped
- 1 teaspoon freshly grated ginger
- Quinoa/rice, for serving

Directions:

- With paper towels, pat the tofu dry and cut into tiny pieces of bite-size around 1/2 inch wide.
- Heat coconut oil in a wide skillet till it becomes warm. Remove tofu and stir-fry until painted softly.
- Stir-fry for 1-2 minutes, until the choy of the Bok starts to wilt.
- When this occurs, apply the vegetable broth and all the remaining Ingredients to the skillet.
- Keep stir-frying until all components are well coated, and the bulk of the liquid evaporates, around 5-6 minutes. Serve over brown rice or quinoa.

Nutritional information:

Calories: 263.7 Cal

Fat 4.2 g

Cholesterol: 0.3 mg

Sodium: 683.6 mg

Potassium: 313.7 mg

Carbohydrate: 35.7 g

25. Mini Zucchini Bites

Preparation Time: 10 minutes
Cooking Time: 10 minutes
Servings: 6

Ingredients:

- 1 zucchini, cut into thick circles
- 3 cherry tomatoes, halved
- 1/2 cup of parmesan cheese, grated
- Salt and pepper, to taste
- 1 teaspoon of chives, chopped

Directions:

- Preheat the oven to 390 degrees F. Add wax paper on a baking sheet.
- Arrange the zucchini pieces. Add the cherry halves on each zucchini slice. Add parmesan cheese, chives, and sprinkle with salt and pepper.
- Bake for 10 minutes. Serve.

Nutritional information:

Fat: 1.0 g

Cholesterol: 5.0 mg

Sodium: 400.3 mg

Potassium: 50.5 mg

Carbohydrates: 7.3 g

26. Three-Bean Medley

Preparation Time: 15 minutes

Cooking Time: 6 hours

Servings: 8

Ingredients:

- 1 ¼ cups of dried kidney beans, rinsed and drained

- 1 ¼ cups of dried black beans, rinsed and drained

- 1 ¼ cups of dried black-eyed peas, rinsed and drained

- 1 onion, chopped

- 1 leek, chopped

- 2 garlic cloves, minced

- 2 carrots, peeled and chopped

- 6 cups of low-sodium vegetable broth

- 1 ½ cups of water

- 1/2 teaspoon of dried thyme leaves

Directions:

- Add all the Ingredients into a 6-quart pot.

- Cover and cook on low heat for 6 hours, or until the beans are tender and the liquid is absorbed.

Nutritional information:

Calories: 284

Carbohydrates: 56 g

Sugar: 6 g

Fiber: 19 g

Fat: 0 g

Saturated Fat: 0 g,

Protein: 1 9g

Sodium: 131 mg

27. Herbed Garlic Black Beans

Preparation Time: 10 minutes

Cooking Time: 6 hours

Servings: 8

Ingredients:

- 3 cups dried black beans, rinsed and drained

- 2 onions, chopped

- 8 garlic cloves, minced

- 6 cups low-sodium vegetable broth

- 1/2 teaspoon salt

- 1 teaspoon dried basil leaves

- 1/2 teaspoon dried thyme leaves

- 1/2 teaspoon dried oregano leaves

Directions:

- Add all the Ingredients into a 6-quart pot.

- Cover and cook on low for 7 to 9 hours, or until the beans have absorbed the liquid and are tender.

- Remove and discard the bay leaf.

Nutritional information:

Calories: 250 Cal

Carbohydrates: 47 g

Sugar: 3 g

Fiber: 17 g

Fat: 0 g

Saturated Fat: 0 g

Protein: 15 g

Sodium: 253 mg

28. Quinoa With Vegetables

Preparation Time: 10 minutes

Cooking Time: 1 hours

Servings: 8

Ingredients:

- 2 cups quinoa, rinsed and drained

- 2 onions, chopped

- 2 carrots, peeled and sliced

- 1 cup sliced cremini mushrooms

- 3 garlic cloves, minced

- 4 cups low-sodium vegetable broth

- 1/2 teaspoon salt

- 1 teaspoon dried marjoram leaves

- 1/8 teaspoon freshly ground black pepper

Preparation:

- Add all the Ingredients into a 6-quart pot.

- Cover and cook on low for 1 hour, or until the quinoa and vegetables are tender.

- Stir the mixture and serve.

Nutritional information:

Calories: 204

Carbohydrates: 35 g

Sugar: 4 g

Fiber: 4 g

Fat: 3 g

Saturated Fat: 0 g

Protein: 7 g

Sodium: 229 mg

29. Barley Risotto

Preparation Time: 15 minutes

Cooking Time: 45' minutes

Servings: 8

Ingredients:

- 2 ¼ cups hulled barley, rinsed

- 1 onion, finely chopped

- 4 garlic cloves, minced

- 1 (8-ounce) package button mushrooms, chopped

- 6 cups low-sodium vegetable broth

- 1/2 teaspoon dried marjoram leaves

- 1/8 teaspoon freshly ground black pepper

- 2/3 cup grated Parmesan cheese (optional)

Preparation:

- In a 6-quart slow cooker, mix the barley, onion, garlic, mushrooms, broth, marjoram, and pepper.

- Cover and cook on low for 45 minutes, or until the barley has absorbed most of the liquid and is tender, and the vegetables are tender.

- Stir in the Parmesan cheese and serve. (optional)

Nutritional information:

Calories: 288 cal

Carbohydrates: 45 g

Sugar: 2 g

Fiber: 9 g

Fat: 6 g

Saturated Fat: 3 g

Protein: 13 g

Sodium: 495 mg

30. Spring Pasta

Preparation Time: 10 minutes

Cooking Time: 60' minutes

Servings: 8

Ingredients:

- 8 ounces uncooked penne pasta

- 1 ounce olive oil

- 2 ounces onion, chopped

- 1 minced clove garlic

- 25 ounces tomatoes, chopped

- 8 ounces packed spinach leaves

- A pinch salt and pepper

- 1 pinch red pepper flakes

Preparation:

- Boil a large pot of salted water and cook pasta for 5-10 minutes or until the noodles are soft but firm to the taste. Drain the water from the pot.

- Heat oil in a large frying pan on Medium-High heat. Sauté onion and garlic until translucent.

- Add tomatoes, mushrooms, spinach, salt, pepper and red flakes in the pan and mix thoroughly, cooking for 2-3 minutes or until mixture is heated through. . Stir thoroughly until heated completely and serve

Nutritional information:

Carbohydrates: 51,8 g

Fiber: 4,6 g

Protein: 18,8 g

Healthy Recipes

Throughout this book, there have been many recipes. We have put all of these recipes here to help guide you along the path to a healthy lifestyle and achieving your weight-loss goal. The last fifteen recipes listed below are some of our favorites. They're delicious, nutritious and ridiculously easy to make. If you follow all of these recipes, you should have no problem managing to easily maintain your weight loss without feeling like you are losing out. We have separated the recipes into the three different types of proteins to help you navigate through them a little easier.

1. Mason Jar Chicken Parmesan Soup

Yield: 1 serving

Per serving: 1 leaner. 3 green. 1 healthy fat. 1 condiments.

Total time: 10 minutes

Ingredients:

- ¼ Cup no-sugar added tomato sauce

- 2 tbsp Italian salad dressing

- 1 zucchini, cut or spiralized into noodles

- 6 oz. Chicken breasts cut into pieces, cooked

- 2 tbsp grated parmesan

- 1 tbsp chopped fresh basil

- 8 oz. Hot water

Preparation:

- Add tomato sauce and the Italian dressing to the bottom of the jar.

- Layer the zucchini noodles, chicken breast, parmesan and basil on top.

- Pour in hot water, add the lid and let sit for five minutes. Serve.

2. Cheesy Pepper Taco Bake

Yield: 4 serving

Per serving: 1 leaner. 2 ½ green. 1 healthy fat. 3 condiments.

Total time: 40 minutes

Ingredients:

- 1 lb 95–97% lean ground meat (beef, chicken or turkey)

- 1 tbsp_garlic, cumin, paprika, cayenne, salt, black pepper, onion, and parsley

- 1 cup no-sugar, fresh vegetable salsa

- 1 ½ lbs fresh peppers (any color), cut in two and seeded.

- ½ Cup of low fat cheddar cheese

- 4 tbsp of sour cream

Preparation:

- Preheat the oven to 350°F.

- Add ground meat, spices, and salsa to a large bowl.

- Combine all Ingredients using your hands.

- Divide the meat mixture equally among the pepper halves, stuffing each.

- Place on the bottom of a large baking dish.

- Sprinkle the cheese over the peppers.

- Bake in the oven for 30 minutes, or until the meat is properly cooked through.

- Remove from the oven and divide into 4 equal servings.

- Top off each pepper with 1 tablespoon of sour cream and salsa.

- Serve warm or when ready.

3. Cashew Chicken & Cauliflower Rice

Yield: 4 serving

Per serving: 1 leaner. 3 green. 1 healthy fat. 3 condiments.

Total time: 35 minutes

Ingredients:

- 4 tsp unrefined coconut oil

- 3 scallions sliced into medallions

- 1 ½ lbs boneless skinless chicken breast sliced into strips

- 1 cup green bell pepper chopped into strips

- 1 cup red bell pepper chopped into strips

- 2 cups vegetables of your choice

- 1 tbsp fresh garlic, chives, salt, pepper, onion and parsley

- ½ Cup low-sodium chicken broth

- 2 cups of cauliflower rice

- 24 cashews, cut into pieces

Preparation:

- Add the oil to a large frying pan on a medium heat.

- Once hot, add the scallion and cook for 1 minute or until fragrant.

- Add the chicken and cook for 5–7 minutes until it changes in color.

- Add the rest of the vegetables and sprinkle with spice

- Begin to prepare the cauliflower rice while the chicken is cooking.

- Once cooked, remove chicken mixture from heat.

- Equally serve cauliflower rice into 4 equal portions. Do the same with the chicken mixture.

- Place the chicken over the rice and sprinkle with 1/4 of the crushed cashews. Serve hot and enjoy

4. Cheesy Chicken Caprese

Yield: 4 servings

Per serving: 1 leaner. ½ green. 1 healthy fat. 3 condiments.

Total time: 35 minutes

Ingredients:

- 4 teaspoons oil and fresh garlic

- 1 ½ lbs chicken breasts, flattened

- 2 tsp garlic, red pepper, black pepper, parsley, onion, garlic powder

- 1 cup chopped up tomatoes

- 8 tbsp (½ cup) low fat mozzarella cheese

Preparation:

- Set the oven to 350 degrees.

- Flatten the chicken by placing between 2 pieces of plastic wrap and beating with a rolling pin.

- Add oil to a large, oven-safe frying pan and put on a medium-high heat.

- Season each chicken breast. When the oil is hot, put the chicken in the pan.

- Cook chicken for 5–7 minutes on one side then flip.

- Turn off the stove. Scoop ¼ of a cup of tomatoes on to the top of each chicken breast.

- Sprinkle 2 tablespoons of mozzarella, and a pinch of spices, on each chicken breast.

- Place in the oven for 7–10 minutes until chicken is fully cooked and cheese is melted

5. Creamy Skillet Chicken And Asparagus

Yield: 4 servings

Per serving: 1 leaner. 2 green. 1 healthy fat. 3 condiments.

Total time: 25 minutes

Ingredients:

- 4 tsp of oil mixed with fresh garlic
- 1 ¾ lbs boneless and skinless chicken breast, cut into chunks
- ½ Cup low-sodium chicken broth
- 1 tbsp fresh chopped garlic, parsley and chives
- 8 tbsp light cream cheese
- 4 cups of fresh asparagus, cut into small pieces.
- Pinch of salt and pepper

Preparation:

- Place oil in a large skillet and heat to a medium high heat.
- Once hot, add chicken breasts and cook for 7–10 minutes, stirring occasionally. The chicken should look slightly browned in color.
- Add the broth into the pan and scrape all the browned bits of chicken left behind, off the bottom of the pan.
- Throw in the seasoning, cream cheese and asparagus. Change the heat to high.
- Continuously stir the Ingredients, waiting for the cream cheese to melt evenly into the sauce.
- Bring Ingredients to a boil and then simmer until a thick sauce has formed. Divide this into 4 equal portions.

Seafood

1. Smoky Shrimp Chipotle

Yield: 4 servings

Per servings: 1 leanest. 1 green. 1 healthy fat. 3 condiments.

Total time: 20 minutes

Ingredients:

- 4 tsp of oil
- 1 cup chopped scallions
- 2 lbs raw shrimp
- 1 can diced tomatoes
- 1 tbsp chipotle pepper, cinnamon, salt and pepper to taste
- 4 lime wedges (optional)
- 4 tbsp fresh cilantro (optional)

Preparation:

- Put oil in a frying pan over medium temperature.
- Cook the scallions for 1 minute, until changed in look.
- Add the shrimp and cook for 1 minute on each side.
- Pour in the tomatoes and Chipotle. Cook for an additional 3–5 minutes, stirring often, until everything is fully cooked.
- If you prefer, sprinkle with cilantro and squeeze on the lemon wedge.

2. Tender And Tasty Fish

Yield: 4 servings

Per serving: 1 leanest. 1 healthy fat. 1 condiments.

Total time: 30 minutes

Ingredients:

- 1 ¾ lbs any white meat fish
- 1 tbsp cilantro, garlic, onion, red pepper flakes, paprika, parsley, salt, & pepper
- 4 tsp oil

Preparation:

- Make sure the fish has been pat dry and slice into small pieces
- Coat the fish in a sprinkle of the spices.
- Heat the oil in a large, nonstick frying pan over medium temperature.
- Add fish and cook for 10–12 minutes, until fish has changed in color and becomes flaky.

3. Seared Mahi Mahi With Lemon Basil Butter

Yield: 4 servings

Per serving: 1 leanest. 2 healthy fats. 3 condiments.

Total time: 20 minutes

Ingredients:

- 4 tbsp butter
- 1 tbsp chopped garlic, parsley and chives
- 2 tbsp fresh basil
- 1 tbsp lemon juice
- 2 lb Mahi Mahi filets (or any white fish)
- Pinch salt and pepper

Preparation:

- Melt the butter on a low heat, in a small saucepan. Throw in the garlic, basil and lemon. Stir to ensure they are all combined. Set aside and be ready to reheat later.
- Spray a large frying pan with non-stick spray.
- Sprinkle seasonings on the fish.
- Once the pan is hot, cook the fish for 2–3 minutes making sure to cook evenly on both sides.
- Gently remove the fish from the pan and pour on melted butter.

4. Garlic Shrimp & Broccoli

Yield: 4 servings

Per serving: 1 leanest. 3 green. 2 healthy fat. 3 condiments.

Total time: 25 minutes

Ingredients:

- 4 tsp of fresh garlic and oil
- 1 ¾ lbs shrimp
- 2 cups broccoli
- 2 tsp tarragon, black pepper, salt, lemon, parsley, chives, garlic, and onion
- 1 tsp of fresh garlic, lemon and onion
- ⅓ Cup low-sodium chicken broth
- 4 cups alternative "noodles"
- 2 tbsp butter

Preparation:

- Put the garlic and the oil in a medium heat pan and let combine.
- Once the oil is hot, add shrimp and cook for 1 minute until changed in color.
- Introduce the seasonings and broth to the shrimp. Stir until combined.
- Add in the broccoli and place the lid on the pan. Bring to a boil and reduce temperature. Let simmer until broccoli is cooked through.
- Take off the lid and add the butter. Stir thoroughly and add the noodles. Serve as soon as possible.

5. Oven Roasted Cod With Poblano Pepper Garlic Cream Sauce

Yield: 4 servings

Per serving: 1 leanest. 3 green. 1 ½ condiments.

Total time: 35 minutes

Ingredients:

- 5.5 oz. Poblano peppers
- 1 cup sour cream
- 1 tbsp sea salt, scallions, fresh garlic & parsley
- 5 cups riced cauliflower, raw
- ¼ Cup water
- 2 lb white fish (cod, flounder)

Preparation:

- Set the oven to 375 degrees.
- Use a food processor to pulse the peppers, sour cream and seasonings until combined.
- Place cauliflower on the bottom of a baking dish. Put the fish on top of the cauliflower. Season with salt and pepper.
- Place a spoonful of the pepper mixture over the fish.
- Pour water into the corner of the dish to saturate the cauliflower.
- Bake in the oven for 25–35 minutes.

Vegetarian

1. Turmeric Ginger Spiced Cauliflower

Yield: 4 servings
Per serving: 1 lean. 2 condiments.
Total time: 35 minutes

Ingredients

- 4 cups cauliflower
- 2 cups carrots or any bell pepper cut into strips
- 4 tsp oil
- ½ Tsp salt and pepper
- ¼ Cup low sodium chicken broth
- 1 teaspoon fresh garlic, parsley and lemon spritz
- ½ Tsp curry powder

Preparation

- Set the oven on broil and place the shelf in the middle of the oven.
- Coat the vegetables in oil, salt, and pepper.
- Spread the vegetables on a cooking sheet and let look for 10 minutes before turning and broil for a further 10 minutes.
- In a large pan add the garlic, parsley and lemon. Once vegetables are finished broiling add them to this mixture and cook for 5 minutes until there is no liquid.

2. Lemon Dill Roasted Radishes

Yield: 4 servings
Per serving:
Total time: 35 minutes

Ingredients:

- 4 cups radish halves
- 2 tsp cooking oil
- ½ tbsp dill
- ½ tbsp lemon juice

Preparation:

- Set the oven to 350 degrees.
- Wash and cut the radishes in halves. Smaller radishes can be kept whole.
- Place all the Ingredients into a bowl and stir until well coated.
- In an oven safe dish, place the radishes and let cook for 30 minutes.

3. Roasted Garlic Zoodles

Yield: 4 servings
Per Serving: 3 Green. 0.75 Healthy fats. 1 Condiments.
Total time: 10 minutes

Ingredients:

- 1 tbsp butter or any other choice of fats
- 6 cups zucchini noodles
- 1/2 tsp chopped garlic, salt and pepper
- Pinch of salt and pepper

Preparation:

- Add the butter to a frying pan and heat until melted.
- Place the zucchini noodles in the pan and season with garlic salt and pepper.
- Let sit for 2–3 minutes, tossing occasionally.
- Season with a pinch of salt and pepper

4. Thanksgiving Low Carb Stuffing

Yield: 4 servings

Per serving: ½ leanest. 1 green. 2 condiments.

Total time: 20 minutes

Ingredients:

- 16 oz cauliflower, finely chopped
- 4 tbsp milk OR 4 tbsp chicken broth
- 1 tbsp rosemary
- 1 tsp of salt and pepper
- 2 packages Medifast/Lean and green Parmesan Cheese Puffs

Preparation:

- Put the oven on 350 degrees to preheat.
- Crush the puffs into pieces and split into 2 equal portions.
- Pce 1 package of parm puffs in a bowl with the other Ingredients and mix through.
- Put the cauliflower into a square baking dish. Sprinkle with remaining "breadcrumbs."
- For a crunchy stuffing bake for 30 minutes. If a less crunchy texture is desired, cook for 45 minutes

5. Greek Stuffed Mushrooms With Feta

Nutritional information:

Yield: 4 servings

Per serving: 1 lean. 1 green. 2 condiments.

Total time: 35–40 minutes

Ingredients:

- 1 ½ pounds lean ground soya mince
- 1 tbsp basil, oregano, onion, pepper, rosemary, sage and parsley.
- ¼ Tsp salt and pepper
- ½ Cup feta cheese crumbled
- 4 portobello mushroom caps

Preparation:

- Combine the soya, seasoning spices, and feta in a large bowl. Combine the mixture, using your hands. Measure out into 4 equal size balls and leave to the side.
- Place the mushrooms gills up in a baking dish. Season with a pinch of salt and pepper.
- Place a ball of filling into a mushroom cap, gently pushing it down.
- Put the dish in the oven and let sit for 25–30 minutes.

Sauces, Soup, and Stew Recipes

1. Cranberry Sauce

Preparation Time: 5 minutes
Cooking Time: 8 minutes
Servings: 2

Ingredients:

- ¾ Cup fresh cranberries
- 2 tbsp. Raw honey
- ½ Cup pure squeezed orange juice
- ½ Tsp. Cinnamon
- 1 tbsp. Stevia

Preparation:

- Put all the Ingredients: in the Instant Pot.
- Secure the lid and turn the pressure release handle to the "sealed" position.
- Select the MANUAL functions, set to HIGH PRESSURE, and adjust the timer to 8 minutes.
- After the beep, "QUICK-RELEASE" the steam and remove the lid.
- Serve when cool, or save in a bottle for later use.

Nutritional information:

Calories: 62

Fat: 0 g

Carbohydrate: 17 g

Protein: 0.1 g

2. Béarnaise Sauce

Preparation Time: 5 minutes
Cooking Time: 3 minutes
Servings: 2

Ingredients:

- ½ Cup butter
- 2 egg yolks, beaten
- 2 tsp. Lemon juice, freshly squeezed
- ¼ Tsp. Onion powder
- 2 tbsp. Fresh tarragon

Preparation:

- Press the SAUTÉ button on the Instant Pot.
- Melt the butter for 3 minutes and transfer it into a mixing bowl.
- While whisking the melted butter, slowly add the egg yolks.
- Continue stirring so that no lumps form.
- Add the lemon juice, onion powder, and fresh tarragon.
- Serve.

Nutritional information:

Calories: 603

Fat: 62 g

Carbs: 4 g

Protein: 5 g

3. Chili Sauce

Preparation Time: 8 minutes
Cooking Time: 15 minutes
Servings: 2
Ingredients:

- 2 oz. Hot peppers
- 2 cups of apple cider vinegar
- 1 tsp. Salt

Preparation:

- Trim away the stems from the peppers and chop.
- Add all Ingredients: to the Instant Pot.
- Secure the lid and MANUALLY set the timer to 15 minutes under HIGH pressure.
- Quick-release the pressure and serve the sauce into bowls.

Nutritional information:
Calories: 2
Fat: 0 g
Carbs: 0.7 g
Protein: 1 g

4. Vanilla Caramel Sauce

Preparation Time: 5 minutes
Cooking Time: 13 minutes
Servings: 2
Ingredients:

- 2 tbsp. Coconut oil
- 1 cup sugar
- 1 tsp vanilla extract
- 1/3 cup condensed coconut milk
- 1/3 cup water

Preparation:

- Warm up the Instant Pot using the SAUTÉ function.
- Add the water and sugar, then stir and sauté for 13 minutes.
- Stir in the milk, coconut oil, and vanilla.
- Whisk until creamy and add to a glass container.
- Cool completely and serve when ready.

Nutritional information:
Calories: 80
Carbs: 14 g
Fat: 5 g

Protein: 0 g

5. Delicious Chicken Soup

Preparation Time: 10 minutes
Cooking Time: 4 hours 30 minutes
Servings: 4
Ingredients:

- 1 lb. Chicken breasts, boneless and skinless
- 2 Tbsp. Fresh basil, chopped
- 1 1/2 cups mozzarella cheese, shredded
- 2 garlic cloves, minced
- 1 Tbsp. Parmesan cheese, grated
- 2 Tbsp. Dried basil
- 2 cups chicken stock
- 28 oz. Tomatoes, diced
- 1/4 tsp pepper
- 1/2 tsp salt

Preparation:

- Add chicken, Parmesan cheese, dried basil, tomatoes, garlic, pepper, and salt to a crock pot and stir well to combine.
- Cover and cook on low for 4 hours.
- Add fresh basil and mozzarella cheese and stir well.
- Cover again and cook for 30 more minutes or until cheese is melted.
- Remove chicken from the crock pot and shred using forks.
- Return shredded chicken to the crock pot and stir to mix.
- Serve and enjoy.

Nutritional information:
Calories 299
Fat 16 g
Carbohydrates 3 g
Sugar 6 g
Protein 38 g
Cholesterol 108 mg

6. Flavorful Broccoli Soup

Preparation Time: 10 minutes
Cooking Time: 4 hours 15 minutes
Servings: 6
Ingredients:

- 20 oz. Broccoli florets

- 4 oz. Cream cheese

- 8 oz. Cheddar cheese, shredded

- 1/2 tsp paprika

- 1/2 tsp ground mustard

- 3 cups chicken stock

- 2 garlic cloves, chopped

- 1 onion, diced

- 1 cup carrots, shredded

- 1/4 tsp baking soda

- 1/4 tsp salt

Preparation:

- Add all Ingredients except cream cheese and cheddar cheese to a crock pot and stir well.

- Cover and cook on low for 4 hours.

- Purée the soup using an immersion blender until smooth.

- Stir in the cream cheese and cheddar cheese.

- Cover and cook on low for 15 minutes longer.

- Season with pepper and salt.

- Serve and enjoy.

Nutritional information:

Calories 275,Fat 19 g,Carbohydrates 19 g,Sugar 4 g,Protein 14 g, Cholesterol 60 mg

7. Healthy Spinach Soup

Preparation Time: 10 minutes
Cooking Time: 3 hours
Servings: 8
Ingredients:

- 3 cups frozen spinach, chopped, thawed, and drained

- 8 oz. Cheddar cheese, shredded

- 1 egg, lightly beaten

- 10 oz. Can cream of chicken soup

- 8 oz. Cream cheese, softened

Preparation:

- Add spinach to a large bowl. Purée the spinach.

- Add egg, chicken soup, cream cheese, and pepper to the spinach purée and mix well.

- Transfer spinach mixture to a crock pot.

- Cover and cook on low for 3 hours.

- Stir in cheddar cheese and serve.

Nutritional information:

Calories 256, Fat 29 g,Carbohydrates 1 g,Sugar 0.5 g,Protein 11 g,Cholesterol 84 mg,

8. Healthy Chicken Kale Soup

Preparation Time: 10 minutes
Cooking Time: 6 hours 15 minutes
Servings: 6
Ingredients:

- 2 lb. Chicken breasts, skinless and boneless

- 1/4 cup fresh lemon juice

- 5 oz. Baby kale

- 32 oz. Chicken stock

- 1/2 cup olive oil

- 1 large onion, sliced

- 14 oz. Chicken broth

- 1 Tbsp. Extra-virgin olive oil

- Salt

Preparation:

- Heat the extra-virgin olive oil in a pan over medium heat.

- Season chicken with salt and place in the hot pan.

- Cover pan and cook chicken for 15 minutes.

- Remove chicken from the pan and shred it using forks.

- Add shredded chicken to a crock pot.

- Add sliced onion, olive oil, and broth to a blender and blend until combined.

- Pour the blended mixture into the crock pot.

- Add remaining Ingredients to the crock pot and stir well.

- Cover and cook on low for 6 hours.

Stir well and serve.

Nutritional information:

Calories 493, Fat 33 g,Carbohydrates 8 g,Sugar 9 g,Protein 47 g,Cholesterol 135 mg,

9. Spicy Chicken Pepper Stew

Preparation Time: 10 minutes
Cooking Time: 6 hours
Servings: 6

Ingredients:

- 3 chicken breasts, skinless and boneless, cut into small pieces
- 1 tsp garlic, minced
- 1 tsp ground ginger
- 2 tsp olive oil
- 2 tsp soy sauce
- 1 Tbsp. Fresh lemon juice
- 1/2 cup green onions, sliced
- 1 Tbsp. Crushed red pepper
- 8 oz. Chicken stock
- 1 bell pepper, chopped
- 1 green chili pepper, sliced
- 2 jalapeño peppers, sliced
- 1/2 tsp black pepper
- 1/4 tsp sea salt

Preparation:

- Add all Ingredients to a large mixing bowl and mix well. Place in the refrigerator overnight.
- Pour marinated chicken mixture into a crock pot.
- Cover and cook on low for 6 hours.
- Stir well and serve.

Nutritional information:

,Calories 171, Fat 4 g, Carbohydrates 7 g, Sugar 7 g, Protein 22 g, Cholesterol 65 mg

10. Creamy Broccoli Cauliflower Soup

Preparation Time: 10 minutes
Cooking Time: 6 hours
Servings: 6

Ingredients:

- 2 cups cauliflower florets, chopped
- 3 cups broccoli florets, chopped
- 3 1/2 cups chicken stock
- 1 large carrot, diced
- 1/2 cup shallots, diced
- 2 garlic cloves, minced

- 1 cup plain yogurt
- 6 oz. Cheddar cheese, shredded
- 1 cup coconut milk
- Pepper
- Salt

Preparation:

- Add all Ingredients except milk, cheese, and yogurt to a crock pot and stir well.
- Cover and cook on low for 6 hours.
- Purée the soup using an immersion blender until smooth.
- Add cheese, milk, and yogurt and blend until smooth and creamy.
- Season with pepper and salt.
- Serve and enjoy.

Nutrition:

Calories 281, Fat 20 g, Carbohydrates 14 g, Sugar 9 g,Protein 11g, Cholesterol 32 mg

11. Mexican Chicken Soup

Preparation Time: 10 minutes
Cooking Time: 4 hours
Servings: 6

Ingredients:

- 1 1/2 lb. Chicken thighs, skinless and boneless
- 14 oz. Chicken stock
- 14 oz. Salsa
- 8 oz. Monterey Jack cheese, shredded

Preparation:

- Place chicken into a crock pot.
- Pour remaining Ingredients over the chicken.
- Cover and cook on high for 4 hours.
- Remove chicken from crock pot and shred using forks.
- Return shredded chicken to the crock pot and stir well.
- Serve and enjoy.

Nutritional information:

Calories 371,Fat 15 g,Carbohydrates 7 g,Sugar 2 g,Protein 41 g,Cholesterol 135 mg

12. Beef Stew

Preparation Time: 10 minutes
Cooking Time: 5 hours 5 minutes
Servings: 8

Ingredients:

- 3 lb. Beef stew meat, trimmed
- 1/2 cup red curry paste
- 1/3 cup tomato paste
- 13 oz. Can coconut milk
- 2 tsp ginger, minced
- 2 garlic cloves, minced
- 1 medium onion, sliced
- 2 Tbsp. Olive oil
- 2 cups carrots, julienned
- 2 cups broccoli florets
- 2 tsp fresh lime juice
- 2 Tbsp. Fish sauce
- 2 tsp sea salt

Preparation:

- Heat 1 tablespoon of oil in a pan over medium heat.
- Brown the meat on all sides in the pan.
- Add brown meat to a crock pot.
- Add remaining oil to the same pan and sauté the ginger, garlic, and onion over medium-high heat for 5 minutes.
- Add coconut milk and stir well.
- Transfer pan mixture to the crock pot.
- Add remaining Ingredients except for carrots and broccoli.
- Cover and cook on high for 5 hours.
- Add carrots and broccoli during the last 30 minutes of cooking.
- Serve and enjoy.

Nutritional information:

Calories 537
Fat 26 g
Carbohydrates 13 g
Sugar 16 g
Protein 54 g
Cholesterol 152 mg

13. Tasty Basil Tomato Soup

Preparation Time: 10 minutes
Cooking Time: 6 hours
Servings: 6

Ingredients:

- 28 oz. Can whole peeled tomatoes
- 1/2 cup fresh basil leaves
- 4 cups chicken stock
- 1 tsp red pepper flakes
- 3 garlic cloves, peeled
- 2 onions, diced
- 3 carrots, peeled and diced
- 3 Tbsp. Olive oil
- 1 tsp salt

Preparation:

- Add all Ingredients to a crock pot and stir well.
- Cover and cook on low for 6 hours.
- Purée the soup until smooth using an immersion blender.
- Season soup with pepper and salt.
- Serve and enjoy.

Nutritional information:

Calories 126
Fat 5 g
Carbohydrates 13 g
Sugar 7 g
Protein 5 g
Cholesterol 0 mg

14. Beef Chili

Preparation Time: 10 minutes
Cooking Time: 8 hours
Servings: 6

Ingredients:

- 1 lb. Ground beef
- 1 tsp garlic powder
- 1 tsp paprika
- 3 tsp chili powder
- 1 Tbsp. Worcestershire sauce
- 1 Tbsp. Fresh parsley, chopped
- 1 tsp onion powder
- 25 oz. Tomatoes, chopped
- 4 carrots, chopped
- 1 onion, diced
- 1 bell pepper, diced
- 1/2 tsp sea salt

Preparation:

- Brown the ground meat in a pan over high heat until meat is no longer pink.
- Transfer meat to a crock pot.
- Add bell pepper, tomatoes, carrots, and onion to the crock pot and stir well.
- Add remaining Ingredients and stir well.
- Cover and cook on low for 8 hours.
- Serve and enjoy.

Nutritional information:

Calories 152
Fat 4 g
Carbohydrates 4 g
Sugar 8 g
Protein 18 g
Cholesterol 51 mg

Chapter 11: Seafood

1. Mozzarella Fish

Preparation Time: 5 minutes

Cooking Time: 10-15 minutes

Servings: 6-8

Ingredients:

- 2 lbs. Of bone gold sole
- Salt and pepper to taste
- ½ Teaspoon dried oregano
- 1 cup grated mozzarella cheese
- 1 large fresh tomato, sliced thinly

Directions:

- Excellent source of cooking the butter. Organize a single layer of trout. Add salt, pepper, and oregano.
- Top with sliced cheese slices and tomatoes.
- Cook, covered, for 10 to 15 minutes at 425°F.

Nutritional information:

Calories: 156

Fat: 6g

Net Carbs: 5g

Protein: 8g

2. Cucumber Ginger Shrimp

Preparation Time: 5 minutes

Cooking Time: 10 minutes

Servings: 1

Ingredients:

- 1 large cucumber, sliced into 1/2-inch round
- 10-15 large shrimp/prawns
- 1 teaspoon (1 g) fresh ginger, grated
- Salt to taste
- Coconut oil to cook with

Directions:

- Pour 1 Tablespoon (15 ml) of coconut oil into a frying pan on medium heat.
- Put the ginger and the cucumber and sauté for 2-3 minutes.
- Add in the shrimp then cook until they turn pink and are no longer translucent.
- Add salt to taste and serve.

Nutritional information:

Calories: 250

Fat: 16 g

Net Carbohydrates: 4 g

Protein: 20 g

3. Salmon With Pesto

Preparation Time: 10 minutes

Cooking Time: 15 minutes

Servings: 4

Ingredients:

- 4 salmon fillets
- 2 teaspoons olive oil
- Pinch of salt
- ½-Cup pesto

Directions:

- Arrange the greased Cook & Crisp Basket in the pot of Ninja Foodi.
- Close the Ninja Foodi with crisping lid and select Air Crisp.
- Set the temperature to 270 degrees F for 5 minutes.
- Press Start/Stop to begin preheating.
- Drizzle the salmon fillets with oil evenly and sprinkle with a pinch of salt.
- After preheating, open the lid.
- Place the salmon fillets into the Cook & Crisp Basket.
- Close the Ninja Foodi with crisping lid and select Air Crisp.
- Set the temperature to 270 degrees F for 20 minutes.
- Press Start/Stop to begin cooking.
- Transfer the salmon fillets onto a platter and top with the pesto.
- Serve immediately.

Nutritional information:

Calories: 380

Fats: 25.8g

Carbohydrates: 2g

Proteins: 36g

4. Salmon In Dill Sauce

Preparation Time: 10 minutes
Cooking Time: 2 hours
Servings: 6
Ingredients:

- 2 cups water

- 1-cup homemade chicken broth

- 2 tablespoons fresh lemon juice

- ¼ Cup fresh dill, chopped

- 6 salmon fillets

- 1 teaspoon cayenne pepper

- Salt and ground black pepper

Directions:

- In the pot of Ninja Foodi, mix together the water, broth, lemon juice, lemon juice, and dill.

- Organize the salmon fillets on top, skin side down, and sprinkle with cayenne pepper, salt black pepper.

- Close the Ninja Foodi with a crisping lid and select Slow Cooker.

- Set on Low for 1-2 hours.

- Press Start/Stop to begin cooking.

- Serve hot.

Nutritional information:

Calories: 164, Fats: 7.4g, Carbohydrates 1.6 g, Proteins: 23.3g

5. Seasoned Catfish

Preparation Time: 15 minutes
Cooking Time: 23 minutes
Servings: 4
Ingredients:

- 4 catfish fillets

- 2 tablespoons Italian seasoning

- Salt and ground black pepper

- 1 tablespoon olive oil

- 1 tablespoon fresh parsley, chopped

Directions:

- Arrange the greased Cook & Crisp Basket in the pot of Ninja Foodi.

- Close the Ninja Foodi with a crisping lid and select Air Crisp.

- Set the temperature to 400 °F for 5 minutes.

- Press Start/Stop to begin preheating.

- Rub the fish fillets with seasoning, salt, and black pepper generously, and then coat with oil.

- After preheating, open the lid.

- Place the catfish fillets into the Cook & Crisp Basket.

- Close the Ninja Foodi with crisping lid and select Air Crisp.

- Set the temperature to 400°F for 20 minutes.

- Press Start/Stop to begin cooking.

- Flip the fish fillets once halfway through.

- Serve hot with the garnishing of parsley.

Nutritional information:

Calories: 205, Fats: 14.2g, Carbohydrates 0.8 g, Proteins: 17.7g

6. Parsley Tilapia

Preparation Time: 15 minutes
Cooking Time: 1 hour and 30 minutes
Servings: 6
Ingredients:

- 6 tilapia fillets

- Salt and ground black pepper

- ½ Cup yellow onion, chopped

- 3 teaspoons fresh lemon rind, grated finely

- ¼ Cup fresh parsley, chopped

- 2 tablespoon unsalted butter, melted

Directions:

- Grease the pot of Ninja Foodi.

- Spice the tilapia fillets with salt and black pepper generously.

- In the prepared pot of Ninja Foodi, place the tilapia fillets.

- Arrange the onion, lemon rind, and parsley over fillets evenly and drizzle with melted butter.

- Close the Ninja Foodi with crisping lid and select Slow Cooker.

- Set on Low for 1½ hours.

- Press Start/Stop to begin cooking.

- Serve hot.

Nutritional information:

Calories: 133, Fats: 4.9g, Carbohydrates: 1.3g, Proteins: 21.3g

7. Crispy Tilapia

Preparation Time: 15 minutes
Cooking Time: 14 minutes
Servings: 4

Ingredients:

- ¾ Cup pork rinds, crushed
- 1 packet dry ranch-style dressing mix
- 2½ tablespoons olive oil
- 2 organic eggs
- 4 tilapia fillets

Preparation:

- Arrange the greased Cook & Crisp Basket in the pot of Ninja Foodi.
- Close the Ninja Foodi with crisping lid and select Air Crisp.
- Set the temperature to 355 degrees F for 5 minutes.
- Press "Start/Stop" to begin preheating.
- In a shallow bowl, beat the eggs.
- In another bowl, add the pork rinds, ranch dressing, and oil and mix until a crumbly mixture form.
- Put the fish fillets into the egg then coat with the pork rind mixture.
- After preheating, open the lid.
- Arrange the tilapia fillets in the prepared Cook & Crisp Basket in a single layer.
- Close the Ninja Foodi with a crisping lid and select Air Crisp.
- Set the temperature to 350°F for 14 minutes.
- Press Start/Stop to begin cooking.
- Serve hot.

Nutritional information:

Calories: 304
Fats: 16.8g
Carbohydrates 0.4 g
Proteins: 38g

8. Cod With Tomatoes

Preparation Time: 15 minutes
Cooking Time: 16 minutes
Servings: 4

Ingredients:

- 1-pound cherry tomatoes halved
- 2 tablespoons fresh rosemary, chopped
- 4 cod fillets
- 2 garlic cloves, minced
- 1 tablespoon olive oil
- Salt and ground black pepper

Preparation:

- At the bottom of a greased a large heatproof bowl, place half of the cherry tomatoes followed by the rosemary.
- Arrange cod fillets on top in a single layer, followed by the remaining tomatoes.
- Sprinkle with garlic and drizzle with oil.
- At the bottom of Ninja Foodie, arrange the bowl.
- Close the Ninja Foodi with the pressure lid and place the pressure valve in the Seal position.
- Select Pressure and set to High for 6 minutes.
- Press Start/Stop to begin cooking.
- Switch the valve to Vent and do a quick release.
- Transfer the fish fillets and tomatoes onto serving plates.
- Sprinkle with salt and black pepper and serve.

Nutritional information:

Calories: 149
Fats: 5g
Carbohydrates 6 g
Proteins: 21.4g

9. Crab Casserole

Preparation Time: 10 minutes
Cooking Time: 30 minutes
Servings: 5

Ingredients:

- 2 tbsp. Of oil, for frying
- 1 onion, finely chopped
- 150 g finely chopped celery stalks
- Salt and pepper
- 300 ml homemade mayonnaise
- 4 eggs
- 450 g canned crab meat
- 325 g grated white cheddar cheese
- 2 tsp. Paprika
- ¼ Tsp. Cayenne pepper
- For filing
- 75 g leafy greens
- 2 tbsp. Of olive oil

Preparation:

- Set the oven to 350°F. Grease a 9x12 baking dish.
- Fry onion and celery in oil until translucent.
- In another bowl, add mayonnaise, eggs, crab meat, seasonings, and ⅔ chopped cheese. Add the fried onions and celery and stir.
- Add the mass to the baking dish. Sprinkle the remaining cheese on top and bake for about 30 minutes or until golden brown.
- Serve with salad and olive oil.

Nutritional information:

Carbohydrates: 6 g, Fats: 95 g, Proteins: 47 g, Calories: 400

10. Cod With Bell Pepper

Preparation Time: 15 minutes
Cooking Time: 1 hour and 30 minutes
Servings: 4

Ingredients:

- 1 bell pepper, seeded and sliced
- ½ Small onion, sliced
- 3 garlic cloves, minced
- 1 can sugar-free diced tomatoes
- 1 tablespoon fresh rosemary, chopped
- ¼ Cup homemade fish broth
- ¼ Teaspoon red pepper flakes
- Salt and ground black pepper
- 1-pound cod fillets

Preparation:

- In the pot of Ninja Foodi, add all the **Ingredients** except cod and stir to combine.
- Season cod fillets with salt and black pepper evenly.
- Arrange the cod fillets over broth mixture.
- Close the Ninja Foodi with a crisping lid and select Slow Cooker.
- Set on High for 1½ hours.
- Press Start/Stop to begin cooking.
- Serve hot.

Nutritional information:

Calories: 129, Fats: 1.6g, Carbohydrates 7.7 g, Proteins: 22.1g

11. Shrimp With Garlic

Preparation Time: 10 minutes
Cooking Time: 25 minutes
Servings: 2

Ingredients:

- 1 lb. Shrimp
- ¼ Teaspoon baking soda
- 2 tablespoons oil
- 2 teaspoon minced garlic
- ¼ Cup vermouth
- 2 tablespoons unsalted butter
- 1 teaspoon parsley

Preparation:

- In a bowl toss shrimp with baking soda and salt, let it stand for a couple of minutes
- In a skillet heat olive oil and add shrimp
- Add garlic, red pepper flakes and cook for 1-2 minutes
- Add vermouth and cook for another 4-5 minutes

When ready remove from heat and serve

Nutritional information:

Calories: 289,

Total Carbohydrate: 2 g, Cholesterol: 3 mg, Total Fat: 17 ,g Fiber: 2 g, Protein: 7 g, Sodium: 163 mg

12. Sabich Sandwich

Preparation Time: 5 minutes
Cooking Time: 15 minutes
Servings: 2
Ingredients:

- 2 tomatoes
- Olive oil
- ½ Lb. Eggplant
- ¼ Cucumber
- 1 tablespoon lemon
- 1 tablespoon parsley
- ¼ Head cabbage
- 2 tablespoons wine vinegar
- 2 pita bread
- ½ Cup hummus
- ¼ Tahini sauce
- 2 hard-boiled eggs

Preparation:

- In a skillet fry eggplant slice until tender
- In a bowl add tomatoes, cucumber, parsley, lemon juice, and season salad
- In another bowl toss cabbage with vinegar
- In each pita pocket add hummus, eggplant and drizzle tahini sauce
- Top with eggs, tahini sauce

Nutritional information:

Calories: 269
Total Carbohydrate: 2 g
Cholesterol: 3 mg
Total Fat: 14 g
Fiber: 2 g
Protein: 7 g
Sodium: 183 mg

13. Salmon With Vegetables

Preparation Time: 10 minutes
Cooking Time: 15 minutes
Servings: 4
Ingredients:

- 2 tablespoons olive oil
- 2 carrots
- 1 head fennel
- 2 squash
- ¼ Onion
- 1-inch ginger
- 1 cup white wine
- 2 cups water
- 2 parsley sprigs
- 2 tarragon sprigs
- 6 oz. Salmon fillets
- 1 cup cherry tomatoes
- 1 scallion

Preparation:

- In a skillet heat olive oil, add fennel, squash, onion, ginger, carrot, and cook until vegetables are soft
- Add wine, water, parsley and cook for another 4-5 minutes
- Season salmon fillets and place in the pan
- Cook for 5 minutes per side or until is ready
- Transfer salmon to a bowl, spoon tomatoes and scallion around salmon and serve

Nutritional information:

Calories: 301
Total Carbohydrate: 2 g
Cholesterol: 13 mg
Total Fat: 17 g
Fiber: 4 g
Protein: 8 g
Sodium: 201 mg

14. Moules Marinieres

Preparation Time: 10 minutes

Cooking Time: 30 minutes

Servings: 4

Ingredients:

- 2 tablespoons unsalted butter

- 1 leek

- 1 shallot

- 2 cloves garlic

- 2 bay leaves

- 1 cup white win

- 2 lb. Mussels

- 2 tablespoons mayonnaise

- 1 tablespoon lemon zest

- 2 tablespoons parsley

- 1 sourdough bread

Preparation:

- In a saucepan melt butter, add leeks, garlic, bay leaves, shallot, and cook until vegetables are soft

- Bring to a boil, add mussels, and cook for 1-2 minutes

- Transfer mussels to a bowl and cover

- Whisk in remaining butter with mayonnaise and return mussels to the pot

- Add lemon juice, parsley lemon zest, and stir to combine

Nutritional information:

Calories: 321

Total Carbohydrate: 2 g

Cholesterol: 13 mg

Total Fat: 17 g

Fiber: 2 g

Protein: 9 g

Sodium: 312 mg

15. Steamed Mussels With Coconut-Curry

Preparation Time: 15 minutes

Cooking Time: 20 minutes

Servings: 4

Ingredients:

- 6 sprigs cilantro

- 2 cloves garlic

- 2 shallots

- ¼ Teaspoon coriander seeds

- ¼ Teaspoon red chili flakes

- 1 teaspoon zest

- 1 can coconut milk

- 1 tablespoon vegetable oil

- 1 tablespoon curry paste

- 1 tablespoon brown sugar

- 1 tablespoon fish sauce

- 2 lb. Mussels

Preparation:

- In a bowl combine lime zest, cilantro stems, shallot, garlic, coriander seed, chili, and salt

- In a saucepan heat oil add, garlic, shallots, pounded paste, and curry paste

- Cook for 3-4 minutes, add coconut milk, sugar, and fish sauce

- Bring to a simmer and add mussels

- Stir in lime juice, cilantro leaves and cook for a couple of more minutes

- When ready remove from heat and serve

Nutritional information:

Calories: 209

Total Carbohydrate: 6 g

Cholesterol: 13 mg

Total Fat: 7 g

Fiber: 2 g

Protein: 17 g

Sodium: 193 mg

16. Salmon Burgers

Preparation Time: 10 minutes
Cooking Time: 15 minutes
Servings: 4

Ingredients:

* 1 lb. Salmon fillets
* 1 onion
* ¼ Dill fronds
* 1 tablespoon honey
* 1 tablespoon horseradish
* 1 tablespoon mustard
* 1 tablespoon olive oil
* 2 toasted split rolls
* 1 avocado

Preparation:

* Place salmon fillets in a blender and blend until smooth, transfer to a bowl, add onion, dill, honey, horseradish, and mix well
* Add salt and pepper and form 4 patties
* In a bowl combine mustard, honey, mayonnaise, and dill
* In a skillet heat oil add salmon patties and cook for 2-3 minutes per side
* When ready remove from heat
* Divided lettuce and onion between the buns
* Place salmon patty on top and spoon mustard mixture and avocado slices

Serve when ready

Nutritional information:

Calories: 189
Total Carbohydrate: 6 g
Cholesterol: 3 mg
Total Fat: 7 g
Fiber: 4 g
Protein: 12 g
Sodium: 293 mg

Desserts

1. Brown & White Mushroom Soup

Preparation time: 10 Minutes

Cooking time: 45 minutes

Servings: 1

Calories (100 gr): 266

Nutritional information: carbs: 15 gr; proteins: 26 gr; fats: 44 gr

Ingredients

- 1/2 cup Celery

- 1 cup Brown Mushrooms

- 1 cup White Mushrooms

- 1 cup Scallions

- 3/4 cup Onion

- 2 tablespoon Butter

- 1/4 tablespoon Salt

- 1/4 tablespoon Black Pepper

- 6 cup Low Sodium Chicken Broth

- 1 tablespoon Fresh Thyme

- 1 stalk Green Onions (optional)

Preparation

- Melt the butter in a stockpot over medium heat.

- To the stockpot, add the celery and onions. Cook and stir for 10 minutes, or until soft but not browned.

- Cook until the mushrooms are tender, about 5 minutes, after adding the thyme and mushrooms.

- Season with salt and pepper and pour in the chicken stock. Simmer for 30 minutes, covered, on low heat.

- Serve in a dish with a sprinkling of green onions on top.

2. Banana Chocolate And Peanut Butter Swirl Bread With Pecan Praline

Preparation time: 25 Minutes

Cooking time: 60 minutes

Servings: 12

Calories (100 gr): 467

Nutritional information: carbs: 32 gr; proteins: 47 gr; fats: 64 gr

Ingredients

- Banana Chocolate and Peanut Butter Swirl Bread

- 1 3/4 (210g) cups gluten-free flour blend (or use all-purpose flour)

- 1 tablespoon baking powder

- 1/2 tablespoon baking soda

- 1/2 tablespoon salt

- 1 tablespoon cinnamon

- 2 large ripe bananas (they should have a lot of dark spots on it)

- 2 large eggs

- 1/2 cup (270g) sugar

- 1/2 cup (130g) creamy peanut butter

- 1/3 cup coconut oil, melted (80ml)

- 1/3 cup (75g) unsweetened applesauce

- 2 tablespoon vanilla

- 1/2 cup (90g) semi-sweet chocolate chips

Pecan praline

- 3 tablespoon butter

- 4 tablespoon brown sugar

- 2 tablespoon low-fat milk

- 1 tablespoon vanilla

- 4 tablespoon chopped pecans

Preparation

- Preheat the oven to 375°F (180 degrees C). Line a loaf pan with parchment paper and coat it with cooking spray. This will make it simpler to get the bread out afterwards.

- In a medium mixing bowl, combine the flour, baking powder, baking soda, salt, and cinnamon.

- Mash the bananas in a large mixing basin until there are no pieces remaining. Incorporate the eggs, sugar, peanut butter, oil, applesauce, and vanilla extract. Mix in the flour mixture gradually. I often add the flour in three batches. Divide the batter evenly between two bowls.

- Microwave the chocolate chips until they are melted. Begin by heating it for 30 seconds, then continue heating it in 15-second increments until nearly all of the chips are glossy. Remove the chips from the microwave and whisk until a creamy chocolate mixture forms. Combine the chocolate with one-half of the batter.

- Fill the loaf pan with the batter, alternating between the light and dark mixtures. Swirl the batter on top using a knife, toothpick, or skewer. You don't need to overwork it, but you do want to make a pattern out of it.

- Bake for 55 to 60 minutes, or until a toothpick inserted into the center comes out clean. Allow the bread to cool for 10 minutes before removing it from the pan.

- Prepare The Pecan Praline: Melt the butter in a small pot. Then add the sugar and milk and combine everything until it looks like a sauce. Remove from the heat and whisk in the vanilla extract and pecans. Distribute the sauce over the bread. The praline hardens quite rapidly. If the sauce hardens before you pour it over the bread, simply reheat it.

- Refrigerate any leftovers in foil. It should last at least a week.

3. Blackberry Cheesecake Bars

Preparation time: 20 Minutes

Cooking time: 60 minutes

Servings: 6

Calories (100 gr): 484

Nutritional information: carbs: 53 gr; proteins: 6 gr; fats: 11 gr

Ingredients

Crust:

- One 11-ounce box vanilla wafers

- ½ cup pecans

- 1/2 cup butter, melted

- 1½ teaspoons vanilla

Filling:

- Three 8-ounce packages cream cheese, at room temperature

- 1½ cups sugar

- 4 eggs

- ½ cup sour cream

Topping:

- 4 cups fresh blackberries

- 1 cup sugar

- 4 teaspoons cornstarch

Preparation

Preheat the oven to 350 degrees Fahrenheit.

Nonstick foil should be used to line a 9-by-13-inch baking sheet. Set aside some time

In a food processor, combine the vanilla wafers and pecans. Using a food processor, pulsate until crumbs form. Add the melted butter and vanilla extract and pulse until mixed. Fill the prepared pan halfway with the mixture. Press the crumbs evenly into the bottom of the pan.

Using a paddle attachment, smooth up the cream cheese and sugar. Add the eggs one at a time, beating until each one is well mixed before adding the next. Mix with the sour cream again.

- Scrape the contents over the prepared crust, level the top, and bake for 50 minutes. Turn off the oven, open the door, and leave the pan in the oven for 15 minutes. Remove from the oven and put aside to cool.

- In a saucepan, combine the blackberries, sugar, and 14 cup water to form the topping. Bring to a boil over medium-high heat and simmer for 5 minutes, or until the fluids begin to thicken.

- Stir together the cornstarch and 2 tablespoons water in a small bowl until smooth. Add this mixture to the berries, bring to a boil, and continue to simmer for a few minutes. Turn off the heat and allow the mixture to cool.

- Pour the blackberries over the cheesecake and set it in the refrigerator for at least 2 hours to chill.

- When ready to serve, use the foil as a sling to transfer the bars to a cutting board. Cut into squares.

4. Bacon Cheeseburger Soup

Preparation time: 5 Minutes

Cooking time: 10 minutes

Servings: 3

Calories (100 gr): 456

Nutritional information: carbs: 32 gr; proteins: 59 gr; fats: 9 gr

Ingredients

- Oz 93% lean ground beef, cooked (1/2 Lean)

- 1 oz 2% reduced fat Mexican Cheese

- 2 slices turkey bacon, cooked and crumbled (1/2 Lean with the cheese)

- 1 cup low sodium beef broth (1 Condiment)

- 1 wedge Light Garlic and Herb Laughing Cow Cheese (1 Condiment)

- 1/2 cup Italian diced tomatoes in juice (1 Green)

Preparation

- In a sauce pan, combine all of the Ingredients and simmer over medium-high heat until the cheese has melted.

5. Balsamic Buttermilk Sherbet

Preparation time: 5 Minutes

Cooking time: 5 minutes

Servings: 1

Calories (100 gr): 111

Nutritional information: carbs: 26 gr; proteins: 2 gr; fats: 1 gr

Ingredients

- 2 cups strawberry slices frozen

- 1 cup mango cubes frozen - cube fresh mango into 1 inch cubes before freezing

- 2 bananas frozen - slice into 1/2 inch pieces before freezing

- 2 tablespoons honey

- 1 cup buttermilk low fat - makes your ice cream ultra rich & creamy

- 2 tablespoons white balsamic vinegar enhances the taste of the strawberries and mango

Preparation

- In the order stated above, combine all of the following Ingredients in a food processor or high duty blender such as a vitamix. Blend until smooth and creamy. Keep the food processor running until the fruit starts to mix. This procedure necessitates a few stops and stirrings, and it may take 3-5 minutes to thoroughly mix the components. Scoop out about three-thirds of a cup of servings each dish using an ice cream scoop or a big spoon.

- Consider garnishing with freshly chopped strawberries. YUM YUM YUM

- It is best to serve sherbet right away. Sherbet can be frozen if stored in an airtight, freezer-proof container...but the consistency is creamiest right away.

6. Baileys Crepe Cake

Preparation time: 60 Minutes

Cooking time: 60 minutes

Servings: 12

Calories (100 gr): 498

Nutritional information: carbs: 65 gr; proteins: 6.3 gr; fats: 8.3 gr

Ingredients

For the crepes:

- 2 Cups Whole wheat pastry flour 8oz

- 2 Cups BAILEYS Coffee Creamer Original Irish Cream Flavour

- 1 Cup Strong brewed coffee

- 4 tablespoon Olive oil

- 4 Eggs

For the ganache:

- 1 Cup + 2 Tablespoon Heavy whipping cream

- 3/4 Cup BAILEYS Coffee Creamer Original Irish Cream Flavour

- 3 Tablespoon Light corn syrup

- 18 Oz Semi-sweet chocolate roughly chopped

- Coffee beans for garnish (optional)

Preparation

- In a blender, mix all of the crepe Ingredients and blend until smooth and blended. Put the crepe batter in the fridge for at least an hour.

- Over medium heat, whisk together the whipped cream, 3/4 cup BAILEYS Coffee Creamer, and light corn syrup in a medium saucepan. Bring the mixture to a boil and then remove from the heat.

- Allow the chopped chocolate to stand for 30 seconds. Then, whisk until the chocolate is completely smooth and melted.

- Refrigerate the ganache in a large bowl for 3 hours, or until it is completely firm.

- After one hour, coat the acrepe pan (or small pan) with cooking spray and heat over medium heat.

- Using a scant 1/4 cup, spoon the batter into the pan and turn in a circular motion to evenly coat the pan.

- Cook the crepe until the edges start to become golden brown and lift away from the pan's sides. Lift the side of the crepe off the pan using a thin spatula, then swiftly flip the crepe with your fingers and cook for an additional 30 seconds. Place the cooked crepe on a platter and repeat with the remaining batter, stacking the crepes on the plate. Put the cooked crepes in the fridge to chill until the ganache is ready.

- Once the ganache is completely firm, whip it with an electric hand mixer until it lightens in color and becomes smooth and fluffy.

Cake assembly:

- Arrange one crepe on a dish. Drop a heaping tablespoon of whipped ganache on top and spread thinly to cover the whole crepe (an offset spatula will come in in here!) Place another crepe on top and continue until you reach the last crepe

- Smooth additional 2 tablespoons of ganache over the top of the cake. Then, using a spatula, spread part of the whipped ganache over the sides of the cake until you can no longer see the crepe's edges and it is smooth and even.

- Return the cake to the refrigerator for 30 minutes, or until the ganache has set.

- While the cake is setting, reheat the leftover ganache in the microwave for 10-20 seconds, or until it is just melted; you don't want it to be too hot. Pour it into a liquid measuring cup and put it aside to cool until the first layer of ganache hardens.

- Place the cake on a cooling rack set on top of a parchment-lined baking sheet once the first layer is set. Pour the ganache over the cake, allowing it to trickle down the edges (if making the entire recipe of ganache, start with half).

- Spread the ganache evenly over the entire cake. If preferred, garnish with coffee beans and store in the refrigerator until ready to serve

7. Butter And Rum Crêpes With Lemon Curd

Preparation time: 10 Minutes

Cooking time: 20 minutes

Servings: 3

Calories (100 gr): 661

Nutritional information: carbs: 103 gr; proteins: 5 gr; fats: 11 gr

Ingredients

For the crepes:

- 2 tablespoons sugar, plus more for sprinkling

- Finely grated zest of 1/2 lemon

- Finely grated zest of 1/4 orange

- Pinch of salt

- 2 large eggs

- 3/4 cup whole milk, plus a little more if needed

- 1 tablespoon dark rum or 1-1/2 teaspoons pure vanilla

- 2 teaspoons Grand Marnier (optional)

- 3 tablespoons unsalted butter, melted

- 1/2 cup all-purpose flour

- Canola oil or other flavorless oil, for the pan

For the sauce:

1/3 cup honey

1/3 cup fresh orange juice

1/4 cup fresh lemon juice

7 tablespoons unsalted butter, at cool room temperature

For the Lemon Curd:

- 1-1/4 cups sugar

- 4 large eggs

- 1 tablespoon light corn syrup

- 3/4 cup fresh lemon juice (from 4-5 lemons)

- 8 tablespoons (1 stick) unsalted butter, cut into chunks

Preparation

- Rub the sugar and zests together in a bowl with your hands until the sugar is wet and aromatic. In a food processor or blender, combine the sugar and zest.

- Blend in the salt, eggs, milk, rum or vanilla, and Grand Marnier, if using. Pour in the butter and process until everything is properly combined.

- Add the flour and pulse the machine to combine. Make sure the flour is well combined, but don't overmix. Cover and chill the batter for at least 2 hours in a pitcher or large measuring cup with a spout.

- When you're ready to create the crepes, put sugar on a dinner plate. Then, using an oiled paper towel, rub the surface of a 7-1/2-inch crepe pan or a similar-sized skillet. Preheat the oven to medium.

- When the pan is heated, remove it from the heat and immediately pour in 2 to 3 tablespoons of batter, swirling the pan to distribute the batter in a thin, uniform layer. Return the pan to the heat and cook the crepe until the top is set. Check the underside for brownness before flipping with your fingers or a spatula. Cook till the bottom is golden brown.

- Transfer the crepe to the sugared dish, sprinkle with sugar gently, and repeat with the remaining batter.

- Melt the honey in a microwave oven or a saucepan over low heat to produce the sauce. Allow the honey to cool for 5 minutes before adding the orange and lemon juices. Add the butter a spoonful at a time, blending or whisking it in. Refrigerate and reheat as required or use immediately.

- To fill the crepes, pour some lemon curd (see Directions below for how to prepare lemon curd) over the upper-right-hand quadrant of each crepe and fold in half, then in thirds to create triangles.

- Place the crepes on plates, sprinkle with the sauce, and serve immediately.

- Make lemon curd if you want the filling. In a heavy saucepan, mix together the sugar and eggs; stir in the other Ingredients.

- Stir continually over medium-low heat until the curd thickens and begins to boil. But don't let it get too hot. Place the curd in a heat-resistant container. Place a piece of plastic wrap on top of the surface. Cover, set aside to cool, and then refrigerate.

8. Chocolate Caramel Twix Cheesecake

Preparation time: 45 Minutes

Cooking time: 75 minutes

Servings: 2

Calories (100 gr): 780

Nutritional information: carbs: 72 gr; proteins: 8 gr; fats: 31 gr

Ingredients

Crust:

- 1 1/2 cups graham cracker crumbs
- 1 tablespoon sugar
- 6 tablespoons melted butter

Cheesecake:

- 32 ounces cream cheese, at room temperature
- 1 2/3 cups sugar
- 1/4 cup cornstarch
- 1 tablespoon pure vanilla
- 2 eggs
- 3/4 cup heavy whipping cream
- Caramel Sauce*:
- 40 Kraft caramels, unwrapped
- 1 can sweetened condensed milk
- 5 Tablespoons butter

Ganache:

- 2 cups heavy cream
- 12 ounces semisweet chocolate, chopped (I used three 4-ounce Ghirardelli semisweet chocolate bars)

Garnish:

- Fun-sized Twix bars, optional

Preparation

- To prepare the crust, mix all of the Ingredients together and press into a 9-inch springform pan. Bake for 8 minutes at 350°F. Allow to cool. To bake the cheesecake, keep the oven on.
- To prepare the cheesecake, in a stand mixer fitted with a paddle attachment, whip together 1 package of cream cheese, 13 cup of sugar, and the cornstarch on low until smooth, approximately 3 minutes, scraping down the sides of the bowl as required.
- Blend in the remaining cream cheese, one package at a time, beating thoroughly after each addition and scraping down the bowl.

- Increase the mixer speed to medium and add the remaining sugar, followed by the vanilla extract. Incorporate the eggs one at a time, beating vigorously after each addition. Just until combined, fold in the cream.
- The filling will be soft, creamy, and fluffy, resembling billowy clouds. Take care not to over-mix.
- Scrape the batter onto the crust gently. Wrap the pan's sides in aluminum foil.
- Place the cake pan in a big shallow pan with boiling water that comes halfway up the edge of the springform pan (approximately 1 inch). Bake for approximately 114 hours, or until the top is a very light golden brown and the middle hardly jiggles. Remove the cheesecake from the water bath and place it on a wire rack to cool for 2 hours. Chill until completely cold.
- To create the caramel, put all of the Ingredients in a heatproof dish and microwave in 1-minute increments until fully smooth and combined. Every minute, give it a good stir. Allow it cool for a few minutes. For this cheesecake, you'll only need approximately half of the caramel.
- To prepare the ganache, bring the cream to a boil and then pour it over the chopped chocolate in a heatproof bowl. Allow for a 2-minute rest. Stir until the chocolate is completely melted.
- Pour about half of the caramel into the center of the cheesecake, where it has deflated slightly. Chill for a few minutes to harden up the caramel. (Note: I did not create a caramel layer, but instead poured caramel over each slice as I served it.)
- Pour on the chocolate ganache and place in the refrigerator for several hours or overnight before removing from the pan. If desired, top with fun-sized Twix bars.
- To serve, gently remove the sides of the springform pan. Serve with caramel sauce and cut into pieces.

9. Chocolate Almond Meal Cake With Chocolate Whipped Coconut Cream

Preparation time: 60 Minutes

Cooking time: 180 minutes

Servings: 4

Calories (100 gr): 154

Nutritional information: carbs: 53 gr; proteins: 76 gr; fats: 38 gr

Ingredients:

For the cake:

- 2 cups almond meal
- 1/2 cup gluten-free oat flour

- 1/2 cup coconut sugar, or sucanat/pure cane sugar

- 6 tablespoons unsweetened cocoa powder

- 1 teaspoon baking soda

- 1/2 teaspoon baking powder

- 1/2 teaspoon salt

- 4 large eggs

- 1/2 cup pumpkin puree

- 1/4 cup honey or brown rice syrup/coconut nectar

- 3 tablespoons liquid from coconut milk can, or almond milk/soy/etc.

- 2 teaspoons pure vanilla extract

- 3 tablespoons unrefined coconut oil, melted and slightly cooled

- 1/3 cup chopped dark chocolate chips, dairy free if needed

For the frosting:

- Coconut cream from 1, 13.5oz can full fat coconut milk

- 2-3 tablespoons unsweetened cocoa powder

- 2-3 tablespoons powdered coconut sugar, or powdered sugar

- 1/2 teaspoon pure vanilla extract

Preparation

- Refrigerate the coconut cream, to separate it with milk place the can of coconut milk, right side up. Turn the can over and open it so that the liquid is now on top. Pour 3 tablespoons of the liquid into a container/bowl and put aside. [Store any leftover liquid in the fridge, covered, and use in smoothies, etc.] Place the firm coconut cream in a bowl and refrigerate.

Cake:

- Preheat your oven to 325°F and lightly coat an 8-inch circular pan with coconut oil.

- Mix the almond meal, oat flour, coconut sugar, cocoa powder, baking soda, baking powder, and salt in a large mixing basin. In a separate dish, whisk the eggs vigorously. Then, mix in the pumpkin, honey, coconut juice, and vanilla extract until well blended. Pour in the dry Ingredients after whisking in the melted coconut oil. Whisk or mix until just incorporated [when there is no longer any visible dry flour].

- Spread the batter in the pan with a spatula and bake for 32-37 minutes. Make the icing while the cake bakes. To check for doneness, use a toothpick [slightly wet but not sticky]. Set aside for 30 minutes on a cooling rack. To assist with

release, run a butter knife around the edge of the pan and gently push the edges with the knife if necessary. Turn the pan over with one hand on top of the cake and the other holding the pan. Place the cake, right side up, on a cooling rack and allow it cool completely before icing.

Whipped frosting:

- In a cold metal bowl, whip the solid coconut cream with a whisk attachment [hand mixer or stand mixer] on high speed until semi-stiff peaks form, 2-4 minutes. Incorporate the cocoa powder, powdered coconut sugar, and vanilla extract until blended. Place in the refrigerator until the cake has completely cooled.

- Spread the frosting on top of the cake and sprinkle with the chopped chocolate chips. Cut into slices and serve. Refrigerate leftovers for about 3 days, covered.

10. Chocolate Ice Cream Sandwiches

Preparation time: 10 Minutes

Cooking time: 35 minutes

Servings: 3

Calories (100 gr): 180

Nutritional information: carbs: 8 gr; proteins: 28 gr; fats: 21 gr

Ingredients

For cookies:

- 1 cup gluten-free rolled oats

- 1/3 cup cocoa

- 10 pitted dates

- 5 tablespoons cocoa butter

- 3 tablespoons water

For ice cream:

- 6 ounces chocolate chips

- 3 tablespoons hot coffee

- 3 frozen bananas cut into pieces

- 1 teaspoon vanilla paste or extract

Preparation

To make cookies:

- In a food processor, pulse oats until they form a fine powder. Process the cocoa and dates until they are mixed and powder-like. Pulse in the cocoa butter and water until a crumbly dough forms. Transfer the mixture to a piece of parchment and knead it with your hands to blend. Roll to a 1/4-inch thickness and cover with another piece of paper. Place in the refrigerator to cool. Empty the processor container.

To make ice cream:

- In a food processor container, combine chocolate chips and coffee; pulse until the mixture is melty and mixed. Add bananas and vanilla paste; process until well mixed and the consistency of soft-serve ice cream, stopping to scrape sides as required with a spatula. Fill an 8-inch parchment-lined container halfway with the mixture. 30 minutes in the freezer

To make sandwiches:

- Cut out cookies using a 2 ½ -inch circular cutter. Cut the ice cream using the same cutter and lay it on top of half of the cookies. Finish with the remaining cookies. Place in the freezer.

11. Chicken Zoodle Soup

Preparation time: 10 Minutes

Cooking time: 20 minutes

Servings: 3

Calories (100 gr): 133

Nutritional information: carbs: 32 gr; proteins: 54 gr; fats: 19 gr

Ingredients

- 1 1/4 cups or 162.5 g spiralized zucchini or yellow squash (2 1/2 Greens)

- 1 tablespoon olive oil

- 1/2 tablespoon minced garlic (1/2 Condiment)

- 1/4 cup celery or 25 g, chopped (1/2 Green)

- 6 oz rotisserie chicken breast, skin removed,cut into 1 inch pieces (1 Leaner)

- 2 cups chicken broth (2 Condiments)

- 1/2 tablespoon dried basil (1/4 Condiment)

- 1/4 tablespoon dried oregano (1/4 Condiment)

- 1/8 tablespoon black pepper (1/4 Condiment)

Preparation

- In a medium saucepan over medium-high heat, heat the olive oil. Sauté the garlic and celery until they are soft. Add the chicken broth, basil, oregano, black pepper, and chicken. Bring to a boil, then turn down the heat. Simmer for around 10 minutes. Simmer for 5 minutes, or until squash is soft or to desired tenderness.

12. Chicken And Vegetable Soup

Preparation time: 8 Minutes

Cooking time: 15 minutes

Servings: 2

Calories (100 gr): 195

Nutritional information: carbs: 21 gr; proteins: 45 gr; fats: 18 gr

Ingredients :

- 6 oz chicken breasts, cooked and chopped (1 Leaner Lean)

- 1/2 cup yellow squash, cubed (1 Green)

- 1/2 cup zucchini, cubed (1 Green)

- 1/2 cup green beans, chopped into 1 inch pieces (1 Green)

- 2 cups chicken broth (2 Condiments)

- 1/4 tablespoon oregano leaves (1/4 Condiment)

- 1/4 tablespoon basil leaves (1/8 Condiment)

- 1/8 tablespoon black pepper (1/4 Condiment)

Preparation

- In a medium saucepan, combine all of the Ingredients. Bring the water to a boil over medium-high heat. Cover and cook for 10 to 12 minutes, or until the vegetables are soft.

13. Crock Pot Beef Taco Soup

Preparation time: 80 Minutes

Cooking time: 360 minutes

Servings: 4

Calories (100 gr): 169

Nutritional information: carbs: 5 gr; proteins: 16 gr; fats: 9 gr

Ingredients

- 2 lbs 95 to 97% lean ground beef (4 Leaner)

- 4 1/2 ounces or 9 tablespoon reduced fat cream cheese (4 1/2 Healthy Fats)

- 2 (10 ounce) cans Rotel (5 Greens)

- 1 tablespoon low sodium taco seasoning (6 Condiments)

- 2 tablespoon Hidden Valley ranch seasoning mix (4 Condiments)

- 4 cups low sodium chicken broth (4 Condiments)

- 3/4 cup 2% plain Greek yogurt (1/2 Leaner)

- 1/2 cup reduced fat cheddar cheese, shredded (1/2 Lean)

- 5 tablespoon fresh cilantro, chopped (1/3 Condiment)

Preparation

- Brown the ground beef until it is completely done.

- In the slow cooker, add cream cheese, Rotel tomatoes, taco spice, and ranch seasoning while the meat cooks.

- Drain the oil from the meat and place it in the slow cooker.

- Combine the beef, cream cheese, and Rotel in a mixing bowl.

- Chicken broth should be poured over the meat mixture.

- Cook for 4 hours on LOW or 2 hours on HIGH.

- Stir in the Greek yogurt just before serving.

- Divide the Ingredients into 5 servings (about 2 generous cups per serving).

- Add the cheddar cheese (nearly 2 tablespoon per bowl) and, if preferred, garnish with cilantro (1 tablespoon per bowl).

14. Crock Pot Chicken Taco Soup

Preparation time: 120 Minutes

Cooking time: 550 minutes

Servings: 4

Calories (100 gr): 584

Nutritional information: carbs: 43 gr; proteins: 69 gr; fats: 54 gr

Ingredients

- 2 cups reduced sodium chicken broth (2 Condiments)

- 2 cups water

- 1 can (10 ounces) rotel diced tomatoes with green chilies (2 1/2 Greens)

- 1 tablespoon taco seasoning (2 Condiments)

- ½ tablespoon cumin (½ Condiment)

- ¼ tablespoon chili powder (½ Condiment)

- ½ tablespoon garlic powder (1 Condiment)

- 12 oz raw chicken breasts ~ yields 9 oz cooked (1 ½ lean)

- 1 ¾ cups cabbage, chopped (3 ½ greens)

Toppings:

- 2 oz Kraft 2% Mexican Cheese ~ ¼ cup per bowl (½ lean)

- 4 tablespoon sour cream ~ 2 tablespoon per bowl (2 Healthy Fats)

- Fresh cilantro ~ optional

Preparation

- In a crock pot, Mix diced tomatoes, chicken broth, cabbage, taco seasoning, water, chili powder, cumin, garlic powder, and chicken. Before serving, shred the chicken breasts in the crock cooker. Divide the soup into dishes and top with 14 cup cheese and 2 tablespoons sour cream. If desired, garnish with cilantro.

15. Chocolate And Raspberry Tartlets

Preparation time: 20 Minutes

Cooking time: 20 minutes

Servings: 2

Calories (100 gr): 103

Nutritional information: carbs: 5 gr; proteins: 16 gr; fats: 9 gr

Ingredients

For the pudding:

- 1 medium ripe avocado

- 1/2 medium banana {about 1/4 cup mashed}

- 10 teaspoons cocoa powder

- 1 tablespoon vanilla extract or coffee liquor

- 1 teaspoon honey or maple syrup, optional

- 1/4 teaspoon salt

For the tartlets:

- 30 mini phyllo shells

- 1 cup raspberries

- Mint leaves optional

Preparation

For the pudding:

- In a food processor, combine all of the Ingredients in the order given, beginning with the avocado and ending with the salt.

- Blend until the mixture is totally smooth. Refrigerate for for 10 minutes, covered.

For the tartlets:

- Arrange the phyllo shells on a plate when ready to serve. Fill one spoonful of pudding into each tiny shell. Finish with a raspberry on top of each. They are best served within an hour of being constructed.

16. Curry Roasted Cauliflower Soup

Preparation time: 50 Minutes

Cooking time: 25 minutes

Servings: 4

Calories (100 gr): 169

Nutritional information: carbs: 5 gr; proteins: 16 gr; fats: 9 gr

Ingredients

- 1 ½ cups (186 g) roasted cauliflower florets (3 Greens)
- ¼ teaspoon curry powder (½ Condiment)
- ¼ teaspoon cumin (¼ Condiment)
- ⅛ tablespoon garlic powder (¼ Condiment)
- ⅛ tablespoon onion powder (¼ Condiment)
- ⅛ tablespoon salt (½ Condiment)
- 1 cup vegetable broth (1 Condiment)
- ½ cup water
- ¼ cup lite coconut milk (1 Healthy Fat)
- Garnish: 1 tablespoon chopped cilantro (1/16 Condiment)

Preparation

- Preheat the oven to 450°F before roasting the cauliflower. Spray the cauliflower florets with cooking spray and place them on a baking pan. Bake in the center of the oven for 25-30 minutes, or until browned and tender, tossing the florets regularly to ensure uniform cooking.
- In a small saucepan, combine the broth, ½ cup water, and the roasted cauliflower. Combine the curry powder, cumin, garlic powder, onion powder, and salt in a mixing bowl.
- Bring to a boil, then reduce to a low heat and simmer for 15 minutes. Mix in the coconut milk.
- Blend until smooth with an immersion blender (or in batches with a normal blender). To get the required consistency, add more water. Garnish with cilantro.

17. Creamy Crockpot Tomato Soup

Preparation time: 8 Minutes

Cooking time: 365 minutes

Servings: 8

Calories (100 gr): 112

Nutritional information: carbs: 25 gr; proteins: 65 gr; fats: 44 gr

Ingredients

- 2 tablespoon Olive Oil
- 5 medium Garlic Cloves minced
- 3 (28oz.) Can Roma tomatoes
- 1 (32oz.) Qt Low Sodium Vegetable Broth
- 1/3 cup Basil finely chopped
- 2 medium Bay Leaf
- 1/4 tablespoon Salt (optional)
- 1/2 tablespoon Black Pepper
- 1/2 cup Fat Free Heavy Cream
- 1/3 cup Parmesan Cheese shredded

Preparation

- Preheat the crockpot on High.
- 2 tablespoon olive oil and minced garlic in a pan over medium-high heat, sauté 2 to 3 minutes until slightly golden.
- After sauteing, add the tomatoes, vegetable broth, basil, bay leaves, salt (optional), and black pepper to the crock pot. To combine all of the spices, stir them together.
- Cook for 3-31/2 hours on high in a covered crock pot (low 6-7 hours).
- After the soup has been cooked, remove the bay leaves and purée the contents in a food processor or blender. If the soup is too thick, add roughly 1/2 cup water.After pureeing, add the heavy cream. Parmesan cheese and basil are sprinkled on top of each dish.

18. Coconut Colada

Preparation time: 5 Minutes

Cooking time: 5 minutes

Servings: 1

Calories (100 gr): 466

Nutritional information: carbs: 53 gr; proteins: 68 gr; fats: 64 gr

Ingredients

- 1 sachet OPTAVIA Essential Creamy Vanilla Shake
- 6 oz Unsweetened Coconut Milk
- 6 oz Diet Ginger Ale
- 4 tablespoon Unsweetened Coconut Milk divided
- 1/4 tablespoon Rum Extract
- 1/2 cup Ice

Preparation

- Combine the OPTAVIA Essential Creamy Vanilla Shake, coconut milk, diet ginger ale, 2 tablespoons shredded unsweetened coconut, rum

- essence, and ice in a mixing bowl. Blend until smooth and frosty in a blender.

- Divide the mixture into two pina colada glasses and top with the remaining 2 tablespoons shredded coconut. Serve right away.

19. Coconut & Hemp Green Smoothie

Preparation time: 5 Minutes

Cooking time: 10 minutes

Servings: 1

Calories (100 gr): 86

Nutritional information: carbs: 9 gr; proteins: 7 gr; fats: 6 gr

Ingredients

- 1 sachet OPTAVIA Green Renewal Shake

- 1/2 cup Cucumber chopped

- 1 stalk Celery chopped

- 1 cup Raw Baby Spinach (optional)

- 1 stalk Kale (optional)

- 1 tablespoon Fresh Mint

- 1 tablespoon Hemp Seeds

- 1/2 cup Refrigerated Unsweetened Coconut Milk

- 1 small Ice (optional)

Preparation

- Blend all Ingredients in a blender for 1 to 2 minutes on high, or until desired consistency is attained.

20. Chocolate Mini Cheesecakes

Preparation time: 10 Minutes

Cooking time: 25 minutes

Servings: 3

Calories (100 gr): 370

Nutritional information: carbs: 30 gr; proteins: 5 gr; fats: 0 gr

Ingredients

Crust:

- 1 cup oreo cookie crumbs

- 2 tablespoons of melted butter

Cheesecake:

- 12 ounces cream cheese, at room temperature

- ½ cup sugar

- 2 tablespoons of unsweetened cocoa powder

- ¼ cup sour cream

- ½ tablespoon vanilla

- 2 eggs, at room temperature

- 4 ounces semisweet chocolate, melted

Ganache:

- 3 ounces semisweet chocolate

- ¼ cup heavy cream

- Whipped Cream:

- ¾ cup heavy cream

- 3 T. Powdered sugar

- 3 T. Unsweetened cocoa powder

- ½ tablespoon vanilla extract

- Mini Hershey bars to garnish

Preparation

- Preheat the oven to 325 degrees Fahrenheit. Paper cupcake liners should be used to line a cupcake pan.

- To make the crust, combine the cookie crumbs and butter and press into 12 cupcake cups.

- 5 minutes in the oven set aside.

- Reduce the oven temperature to 300°F.

- If you have a paddle attachment, combine the cream cheese, sugar, and chocolate on low speed.

- Mix in the sour cream and vanilla extract. One at a time, add the eggs. Then, just until combined, add the melted chocolate.

- Bake for 15 minutes, then turn off the heat and leave them in the oven for another 10 minutes. Then, crack the door open and let them stay for another 20 minutes.

- Place in the fridge to cool.

- Make the ganache while the cheesecakes are still cool. Chocolate and cream in a saucepan over medium-low heat. Whisk until the mixture is smooth.

- Ganache should be drizzled over each cheesecake. Chill.

- Make the chocolate whipped cream once the ganache has chilled. To firm peaks, whisk together the cream, powdered sugar, cocoa powder, and vanilla extract.

- Pipe on top and decorate with a small Hershey bar.Refrigerate, but allow it come to room temperature before serving for the creamiest results.

21. Cream Of Baked "Potato" Soup

Preparation time: 10 Minutes

Cooking time: 20 minutes

Servings: 4

Calories (100 gr): 177

Nutritional information: carbs: 19 gr; proteins: 32 gr; fats: 40 gr

Ingredients

- 1 1/2 cups cauliflower, fresh (3 Greens)

- 1 cup chicken broth (1 Condiment)

- 2 wedges light laughing cow cheese ~ I used garlic and herb (1 Healthy Fat)

- 1/8 tablespoon salt (1/2 Condiment)

- 1/8 tablespoon black pepper (1/4 Condiment)

- 1 tablespoon fresh chives, chopped (1/4 Condiment)

- 2 tablespoon reduced fat cheddar cheese (1/8 Lean)

- 1 tablespoon of Turkey Bacon bits (1 Condiment)

Preparation

- In a medium-sized saucepan, combine the cauliflower and broth. Bring the water to a boil. Reduce the heat to a low simmer, cover, and cook for 15 minutes, or until the cauliflower is very mushy and falling apart.Remove from the heat and purée until smooth using an immersion blender. Blend in the light laughing cow cheese, salt, and pepper until well mixed. Pour into a large mixing basin and stir in the cheddar cheese, bacon pieces, and chives. Keep heated in the oven until ready to serve.

22. Cheesy Spinach Souffle

Preparation time: 15 Minutes

Cooking time: 45 minutes

Servings: 8

Calories (100 gr): 545

Nutritional information: carbs: 9 gr; proteins: 18 gr; fats: 2 gr

Ingredients

- 6 eggs, beaten

- 2 tablespoons butter, cubed

- 8 ounces sharp cheddar cheese, cubed (I use Kraft sharp cheddar)

- 24 ounces cream style, small curd cottage cheese (or "old fashioned" cottage cheese)

- 2 10-ounce packages frozen, chopped spinach, thawed and squeezed dry

- 2 tablespoons flour

- 1 teaspoon salt

- **Directions**

- Preheat the oven to 350°F. Grease a 9 x 13 casserole dish or a similar size.

- Combine all of the Ingredients in a mixing bowl and pour into the prepared dish. Bake for 30-45 minutes, or until the center is set.

23. Cinnamon Bun Blondies

Preparation time: 5 Minutes

Cooking time: 20 minutes

Servings: 4

Calories (100 gr): 564

Nutritional information: carbs: 35 gr; proteins: 67 gr; fats: 29 gr

Ingredients

- 4 sachet OPTAVIA Cinnamon Cream Cheese Swirl Cake

- 1/2 tablespoon Cinnamon

- 1/2 tablespoon Baking Powder

- 2/3 cup Unsweetened Vanilla Almond Milk (optional)*

- 2/3 cup Cashew Milk (optional)*

- 2 tablespoon Unsalted Butter melted

- 3 tablespoon Liquid Egg Substitute divided

- 1 1/3 oz Pecans chopped

- 1 can Cooking spray

- 1/4 cup Light Cream Cheese

- 1 2 packet Zero-calorie sugar substitute

- 1/2 tablespoon Vanilla Extract

Preparation

- Preheat the oven to 350 degrees Fahrenheit.

- Combine Cinnamon Cream Cheese Swirl Cake, cinnamon, and baking powder in a large mixing basin. Stir in the milk, butter, and 2 tablespoons liquid egg whites until thoroughly mixed. Fold in the pecans.

- Pour batter into a bread loaf pan that has been gently oiled.

- In a small mixing bowl, add cream cheese, sugar substitute, vanilla extract, and the remaining 1 tablespoon egg white. Swirl the cream cheese mixture into the batter with a knife.Bake for 18–20 minutes, or until the batter is firm and gently browned.

24. Chocolate Velvet Pie

Preparation time: 30 Minutes

Cooking time: 60 minutes

Servings: 6

Calories (100 gr): 429

Nutritional information: carbs: 55 gr; proteins: 4 gr; fats: 10 gr

Ingredients

- Meringue crust:

- 3 egg whites, at room temperature

- 1/8 teaspoon cream of tartar

- Pinch of salt

- 1 cup superfine sugar (whiz in the food processor for about a minute)

- 1 teaspoon vanilla

- Chocolate velvet filling:

- 8 ounces semisweet chocolate, chopped

- 1/4 cup plus 2 tablespoons brewed coffee

- 2 teaspoons vanilla

- 2 cups heavy cream

- 1/3 cup sugar

- Grated chocolate, chocolate curls or chocolate shards to garnish, optional

Preparation

- Grease a 9-inch deep dish pie pan with cooking spray. Set aside.

- Preheat the oven to 350°F.

- White's egg should be frothy in the bowl of a stand mixer. Mix in the cream of tartar and the salt. Beat the mixture until soft peaks form. Add the sugar gently and continue to beat until stiff peaks form. Mix in the vanilla extract.

- Smooth the top of the meringue using an offset spatula. Bake for one hour, then turn off the oven and let the meringue to cool.

- Make the filling when the meringue shell has cooled.

- Microwave the chocolate and coffee in a microwave-safe dish for 30 seconds, then pause and mix. Repeat until the chocolate is melted and smooth. Allow to cool after adding the vanilla extract.

- Whip the cream and sugar together until firm peaks form. Add the cooled chocolate to the cream and carefully mix it in until no white streaks remain.

- Spread the topping on top of the meringue shell. If desired, garnish with chocolate. Allow to cool before serving.

25. Chocolate Peanut Butter Lava Cakes

Preparation time: 10 Minutes

Cooking time: 25 minutes

Servings: 2

Calories (100 gr): 175

Nutritional information: carbs: 40 gr; proteins: 42 gr; fats: 12 gr

Ingredients

- 4 Tablespoons butter or vegan butter

- 1/3 cup (2oz) Enjoy Life Semi-Sweet Mini Chips

- 1/2 cup powdered sugar

- 1 whole egg

- 1 egg yolk

- 1/2 teaspoon vanilla

- 1/4 cup gluten-free 1-to-1 baking flour blend with binder

- Pinch of salt

- 2 heaping teaspoons peanut butter

- Fresh berries for serving

Preparation

- Preheat the oven to 425°F. Set aside a quarter sheet pan or half sheet pan lined with foil. Set aside two 6oz ramekins or custard cups sprayed with nonstick spray. In a small bowl, whisk together the entire egg and the egg yolk, then put aside.

- In a medium-sized dish, combine the butter and tiny chips and microwave for 30 seconds. Stir, then microwave in 10-second intervals, stirring after each, until the chocolate is smooth and melted. Stir in the powdered sugar to mix. Stir in the whisked eggs and vanilla extract. Stir in the flour and salt to mix. Divide the batter evenly among the prepared cups (approximately 1/2 cup batter each), then pour 1 heaping spoonful peanut butter into the center of each. Help the peanut butter settle into the center of the batter with your finger.

- Place the cups on a baking sheet and bake for 12 minutes, or until the tops are soft but not jiggly. Allow the lava cakes to cool for 10 minutes before turning them out onto plates and serving with fresh berries. Just so you know, the longer the cakes rest, the more the "lava" hardens up. Before overturning, I prefer to take a 10-minute break.

26. Chewy Gluten-Free Chocolate Chip Cookies

Preparation time: 15 Minutes

Cooking time: 40 minutes

Servings: 3

Calories (100 gr): 244

Nutritional information: carbs: 35 gr; proteins: 54 gr; fats: 34 gr

Ingredients

- 4 Tablespoon butter

- 1/4 cup almond butter

- 1 large egg

- 1 tablespoon vanilla extract

- 1/4 cup almond flour

- 2/3 cup brown sugar

- 1 cup + 2 Tablespoon King Arther Measure for Measure Gluten-free Flour

- 1 tablespoon baking soda

- 1/3 cup chocolate chips

- Sea salt for sprinkling

Preparation

- Stir the butter and almond butter in a microwave-safe bowl. 1 minute in the microwave, or until the butter is melted

- Mix in the egg, brown sugar, almond flour, and vanilla extract.

- Spoon flour into a measuring cup, level over the top, and add to the bowl, along with 2 more teaspoons. If you scoop too much flour into the container, you'll end up with too much flour.

- Stir in the baking soda until well mixed. The dough may appear slightly dry, but you should be able to stir just enough to include all of the flour.

- Allow the dough to rest for 20 minutes after adding the chocolate chips.

- Scoop onto a prepared baking sheet, sprinkle with sea salt, and bake for 10 minutes at 375 degrees. You should be able to create between 16 and 18 cookies.Allow 5 minutes to cool before transferring to a cooling rack.

27. Cheesecake Peanut Butter Bars

Preparation time: 10 Minutes

Cooking time: 50 minutes

Servings: 3

Calories (100 gr): 426

Nutritional information: carbs: 43 gr; proteins: 6 gr; fats: 11 gr

Ingredients

For crust:

- 36 Oreos, processed to crumbs in food processor

- ½ cup salted butter, melted

For cheesecake:

- 24 oz cream cheese, softened

- 1 cup sugar

- ¼ cup sour cream

- 1 cup creamy peanut butter

- 1 teaspoon vanilla

- Pinch of salt

- 3 eggs

For chocolate topping:

- ½ cup butter

- 1 cup chocolate chips or 6 ounces chopped semisweet chocolate

Preparation

- Preheat the oven to 350 degrees Fahrenheit. Nonstick foil should be used to line a 9x13 pan.

- To prepare the crust, combine cookie crumbs and butter in a mixing bowl and press evenly into the bottom of the pan.

- 10 minutes in the oven

- To prepare the cheesecake, combine the cream cheese and sugar in a mixing bowl and beat until smooth. Sour cream is added first, followed by the peanut butter, vanilla extract, and salt.

- Add the eggs one at a time, mixing just until combined. Smooth the batter over the crust with an offset spatula.

- Bake for 30-35 minutes, or until the cheesecake seems to be largely set. In the very center, there may be a tiny wobble.

- Chill until cold after cooling to room temperature on a wire rack.

- Melt the butter and chocolate together in the microwave to produce the chocolate topping.

- Pour over cooled cheesecake and stir until smooth. Allow at least an hour to chill before slicing.

28. Chocolate Chip Gingerbread Chickpea Blondies With Maple Glaze

Preparation time: 15 Minutes

Cooking time: 25 minutes

Servings: 3

Calories (100 gr): 178

Nutritional information: carbs: 15 gr; proteins: 27 gr; fats: 55 gr

Ingredients

For the blondies:

- 1-15oz can chickpeas, drained and rinsed
- ½ cup cashew butter (or almond butter)
- 3 tablespoon pure maple syrup
- 2 tablespoon blackstrap molasses
- 2 tablespoon ground ginger
- 2 teaspoons vanilla extract
- 2 tablespoon ground flaxseed
- 2 tablespoon cinnamon
- ¼ tablespoon cloves
- ¼ tablespoon nutmeg
- ½ tablespoon salt
- ½ teaspoon baking powder
- ¼ teaspoon baking soda
- ⅓ cup chocolate chips

For the maple glaze:

- 1 tablespoon cashew butter
- 2 tablespoon pure maple syrup
- 1 tablespoon coconut oil
- ¼ tablespoon cinnamon
- ¼ tablespoon ground ginger

Preparation

- Preheat the oven to 350 degrees Fahrenheit. Coat an 8x8-inch baking dish with cooking spray or coconut oil.
- In a large food processor, combine all Ingredients except the glaze and process for two to three minutes, or until the batter is extremely smooth.
- In the preheated pan, spread the batter evenly. To uniformly press the mixture into the pan, use a spatula coated with cooking spray.
- Bake for about 25 minutes, or until a knife inserted into the center comes out clean.

- In the meantime, combine the glaze Ingredients in a small dish. Stir with a fork until everything is fully mixed. As you mix, the coconut oil should begin to melt somewhat. Set aside until the bars have completely cooled.
- Allow the bars to cool in the pan for 30 minutes on a wire rack before cutting into 9-12 bars.
- Snip off the corner of the glaze bag. Drizzle glaze across the bars.

29. Deep Dish Dark Chocolate Cake With Almond Butter Swirl

Preparation time: 30 Minutes

Cooking time: 35 minutes

Servings: 4

Calories (100 gr): 240

Nutritional information: carbs: 44 gr; proteins: 30 gr; fats: 15 gr

Ingredients

For the cake

- 6 Tablespoons coconut oil, or butter
- 1/2 cup dark chocolate chips
- 2 large eggs
- 1/2 teaspoon vanilla extract
- 1/2 cup no-sugar-added applesauce
- 3/4 cup blanched almond flour
- 1/2 cup cocoa powder, (Special Dark is recommended, natural is fine too)
- 2 Tablespoons granulated monk fruit sweetener, or granulated stevia
- 1/2 teaspoon baking soda
- 1/8 teaspoon fine sea salt

For the swirl

- 1/4 cup almond butter, (creamy, unsweetened) or other nut or seed butter of choice
- 1 teaspoon granulated monk fruit sweetener, or granulated stevia
- Pinch fine sea salt
- 1/4 cup dark chocolate chips

Preparation

- Preheat the oven to 350 degrees Fahrenheit. Set aside a 6" springform pan coated with nonstick spray.
- Melt the chocolate chips and butter/coconut oil together in a large microwave-safe mixing basin by microwaving on high for about 60 seconds, or

until nearly melted, and stirring until totally smooth.

- Stir in the remaining wet Ingredients (eggs, vanilla, and apple sauce).

- Whisk together the dry Ingredients (almond meal, cocoa powder, baking soda, sweetener, and salt) in a separate dish, then incorporate the dry mixture into the wet mixture.

- Smooth the mixture into an equal layer in the prepared cake pan.

- In a separate dish, combine the almond butter and granulated sugar to make the swirl. Spread spoonfuls of almond butter across the cake (or pour into a zip top bag, seal it, snip off the corner, and pipe thick lines of almond butter across the cake), then gently drag a butter knife or toothpick through to form the swirl pattern.

- Bake for 35-40 minutes, or until a toothpick inserted into the center comes out clean. Cool for 15 minutes in the pan before removing from the pan and cooling fully on a wire rack.

- Melt the remaining 1/4 cup chocolate chips and pour over the top of the cake while still warm. Allow to sit for a few minutes before serving.

30. Dark Chocolate Almond Oatmeal Cookies With Sea Salt

Preparation time: 8 Minutes

Cooking time: 30 minutes

Servings: 4

Calories (100 gr): 169

Nutritional information: carbs: 5 gr; proteins: 16 gr; fats: 9 gr

Ingredients

- 1/3 cup coconut oil, melted

- 3/4 cup maple syrup

- 2 eggs

- 1 cup unsalted, creamy almond butter

- 2 teaspoons vanilla

- 3 1/4 cups rolled oats

- 1/2 teaspoon cinnamon

- 1/2 teaspoon baking soda

- Cup chopped dark chocolate

- Maldon sea salt (or any coarse sea salt)

Preparation

- Preheat the oven to 350 degrees Fahrenheit. Line a baking sheet with parchment paper.

- In a medium mixing bowl, combine the coconut oil, maple syrup, eggs, almond butter, and vanilla extract. Separately, in a large mixing basin, combine the rolled oats, cinnamon, baking soda, and dark chocolate. In a large mixing bowl, combine the wet and dry **Ingredients** and whisk to incorporate until the dry mixture is uniformly covered.

- Sprinkle a few sea salt flakes on top of each cookie and place 1/4 cup of dough on a baking sheet, allowing a couple inches between them.

- 12 minutes in the oven, or until golden brown

31. Doughy Peach Pie Bars

Preparation time: 20 Minutes

Cooking time: 18 minutes

Servings: 3

Calories (100 gr): 164

Nutritional information: carbs: 32 gr; proteins: 46 gr; fats: 50 gr

Ingredients

- Bottom Crust Layer

- 2 cups oat flour, spooned into cup and leveled off

- 1/2 Teaspoon salt

- 1 large egg

- 1/4 cup honey

- 1/4 cup 2% greek yogurt

- 2 tablespoons butter, cold and cut into small cubes

- Middle Layer

- 3-4 ripe peaches, thinly sliced

- Streusel Topping

- 2/3 cup old-fashioned oats

- 1/2 cup walnuts, finely chopped

- 2 tablespoons butter, melted

- 2 tablespoons honey

- 1 teaspoon cinnamon

- 1/8 teaspoon salt

Preparation

- Preheat the oven to 375 degrees Fahrenheit.

- In a mixing basin, combine oat flour, salt, egg, honey, and Greek yogurt to make the bottom crust layer. Add the chilled butter and work it into the dough with your fingertips. The dough will not crumble like sand, but rather have the consistency of biscuit dough. Dough should be pressed into a greased 9 × 11 inch casserole dish.

- Arrange the cut peaches on top of the dough.Make the streusel topping now. Combine the oats, walnuts, butter, honey, cinnamon, and salt in a mixing dish. Sprinkle streusel on top of the peaches. 18 minutes in the oven Consume warm or keep in the refrigerator and consume cold

32. Dairy-Free Pumpkin Bars

Preparation time: 5 Minutes

Cooking time: 25 minutes

Servings: 6

Calories (100 gr): 250

Nutritional information: carbs: 32 gr; proteins: 16 gr; fats: 32 gr

Ingredients

- 2/3 cup oil (i use avocado oil)
- 2/3 cup brown sugar
- 1 cup pumpkin puree
- 1 egg (or a flax egg)
- 1 tablespoon vanilla
- 1 tablespoon cinnamon
- 1 & 1/3 cup flour (i use white whole wheat)
- 1 tablespoon baking soda
- Chocolate chips, to taste

Preparation

- In a mixing dish, combine the oil, brown sugar, pumpkin, egg, and vanilla extract.
- Combine the cinnamon, flour, baking soda, and chocolate chips in a mixing bowl.
- Stir until everything is fully mixed.
- Bake at 375°F for 20-25 minutes in a 9x9 pan coated with parchment paper.

33. Date Sweetened Chocolate Chip Cookies

Preparation time: 5 Minutes

Cooking time: 10 minutes

Servings: 2

Calories (100 gr): 121

Nutritional information: carbs: 14 gr; proteins: 26 gr; fats: 28 gr

Ingredients

- 3/4 cup chopped medjool dates (if yours aren't super soft, soak them in hot water for 5–10 min, then drain)

- 2 eggs
- 1/3 cup oil (i use avocado oil)
- 1 tablespoon vanilla extract
- 1 cup old fashioned rolled oats
- 1 tablespoon cinnamon
- 1/2 tablespoon baking soda
- 1/3 cup white whole wheat flour
- 1/3 cup chocolate chips (or dried fruit of choice)

Preparation

- In a food processor, combine the chopped dates and pulse until finely chopped.
- Process for 1 minute after adding the eggs, oil, and vanilla.
- Process the oats, cinnamon, and baking soda until the oats are chopped.
- Pulse a few times to incorporate the flour.
- Pulse a couple more times after adding the chocolate chunks.
- Bake for 10 minutes at 350°F.
- This recipe yields 12-14 tiny cookies.

34. Dairy-Free Dark Chocolate Mousse

Preparation time: 5 Minutes

Cooking time: 5 minutes

Servings: 3

Calories (100 gr): 186

Nutritional information: carbs: 10 gr; proteins: 3 gr; fats: 17 gr

Ingredients

- 2 medium ripe avocados
- 2 Tablespoon. Cocoa powder
- 3 Tablespoon. Full-fat canned coconut milk
- Pinch of sea salt (optional)
- 1–2 packets Stevia In The Raw®

Preparation

- Avocados should be cut in half lengthwise. Remove the pit from each avocado and use a big spoon to scoop the flesh into the container of a blender or food processor.
- Mix the remaining Ingredients. Blend until smooth. If desired, taste and adjust the sweetness.

35. Delicious Banana Cake

Preparation Time: 10 minutes
Cooking time: 30 Minutes
Servings: 4

Ingredients:

- 1 tbsp. Butter
- 1 egg
- 1 peeled banana
- 1 cup white flour
- 1 tbsp. Baking powder
- ½ Tbsp. Cinnamon powder
- 1/3 cup brown sugar
- 2 tbsp. Acacia honey
- Cooking spray

Preparation:

- Preheat oven at 350°F.
- In a bowl, blend and beat butter, acacia honey, brown sugar, peeled banana, cinnamon powder, egg, flour and baking powder.
- Spray the cake baking dish.
- Pour the flavored mixture into the baking dish.
- Cook for 30 minutes.

Nutritional information:

- Calories: 305 kcal
- Protein: 5.9 g
- Fat: 5.7 g
- Carbohydrates: 59.8 g

36. Simple Cheesecake

Preparation Time: 10 minutes
Cooking time: 15 Minutes
Servings: 15

Ingredients:

- 1 lb. Cream cheese
- ½ Tbsp. Vanilla extract
- 1 cup graham crackers
- 2 eggs
- 2 cups fresh strawberries
- 4 tbsp. Brown sugar
- 2 tbsp. Soft butter

Preparation:

- Crush the graham crackers.
- Melt the butter and blend well with the crackers.
- Transfer the composition to a cake pan and compress.
- Place pan in the air fryer and cook for about 4 minutes at 350°F.
- Meanwhile, take a bowl and beat cream cheese, brown sugar, vanilla extract and eggs.
- Pour evenly the delicious cream over the crackers crust.
- Cook the cheesecake in the air fryer at 310°F for 15 minutes.
- Let the cake cool down and place it in the fridge for about 3 hours.

Nutritional information:

Calories: 134 kcal, Protein: 3.4 g, Fat: 11.5 g, Carbohydrates: 4.1 g

37. Cherries Bread Pudding

Preparation Time: 10 minutes
Cooking time: 10 Minutes
Servings: 4

Ingredients:

- 6 glazed doughnuts
- 1 and ½ cup whipping cream
- 4 egg yolks
- ¼ Cup brown sugar
- 1 cup cherries
- ½ Cup raisins
- ½ Cup chocolate chips

Preparation:

- In a medium bowl, mix well cherries, egg yolks and whipping cream, until creamy.
- Take another bowl, blend and stir brown sugar, raisins, doughnuts and chocolate chips.
- In a big bowl, combine the 2 mixtures and transfer the new composition to the oiled pan.
- Place it into the air fryer and cook for 1 hour at 310°F.
- You can serve it with ice cream.

Nutritional information:

- Calories: 431 kcal, Protein: 6.8 g, Fat: 24.1 g, Carbohydrates: 47.3 g

38. Amaretto Bread Dessert

Preparation Time: 15 minutes
Cooking time: 8 Minutes
Servings: 12

Ingredients:

- 1 lb. Bread dough
- 1 cup brown sugar
- 12 oz. Chocolate chips
- 1 cup heavy cream
- 2 tbsp. Amaretto liqueur
- ½ Cup light butter

Preparation:

- Turn dough and cut into 20 pieces.
- Slice each piece in halves.
- Brush dough slices with light butter and brown sugar.
- Cook them for 5 min in the air fryer at 350°F.
- Turn them again and cook for 3 more minutes.
- Remove from the air fryer and serve on a platter.
- Meanwhile, melt the heavy cream and chocolate chips in a pan over medium heat.
- Put in the sauce the amaretto liqueur and turn.
- Pour the cream into a bowl.
- Serve the delicious bread dippers with the amaretto sauce.

Nutritional information:

- Calories: 386 kcal, Protein: 4.2 g, Fat: 19.0 g, Carbohydrates: 46.6 g

39. Vanilla & Cinnamon Wrapped Pears

Preparation Time: 10 minutes
Cooking time: 10 Minutes
Servings: 4

Ingredients:

- 4 puff pastry sheets
- ½ Tbsp. Cinnamon powder
- 1 fresh egg
- 2 juicy pears
- 2 tbsp. Brown sugar
- 14 oz. Vanilla custard

Preparation:

- Cut pear in halves.
- Slice pastry sheets and place them in a flat baking dish.
- Pour a spoon of vanilla custard in the middle of each sliced pastry sheet.
- Place pear halves and wrap them up.
- Brush pears with egg, cinnamon, and brown sugar.
- Cook in air fryer's at 320°F for 15 minutes.

Nutritional information:

- Calories: 410 kcal
- Protein: 7.4 g
- Fat: 20.9 g
- Carbohydrates: 51.2 g

40. Cinnamon-Spiced Bananas

Preparation Time: 5 minutes
Cooking time: 10 Minutes
Servings: 4

Ingredients:

- 3 tbsp. Light butter
- ½ Cup corn flour
- 8 bananas
- 3 tbsp. Cinnamon sugar
- 2 fresh eggs
- 1 cup panko breadcrumbs

Directions:

- Blend eggs in a small bowl.
- Place light butter in a pan and warm up over medium heat.
- Lay panko into the pan, cook for about 3-5 minutes and transfer it to a bowl.
- Enfold each banana piece in corn flour, panko and egg blend.
- Take them in the air fryer, sprinkle cinnamon sugar, and cook at 280°F for 10 minutes.
- Serve while still hot.

Nutritional information:

- Calories: 222 kcal
- Protein: 4.6 g
- Fat: 7.7 g
- Carbohydrates: 36.5 g

41. Cocoa Cake

Preparation Time: 5 minutes
Cooking time: 17 Minutes
Servings: 6

Ingredients:

- 1 oz. Light butter
- 1 tbsp. Cocoa powder
- 3 fresh eggs
- 3 oz. Flour
- ½ Tbsp. Lemon juice
- 3 oz. Brown sugar

Preparation:

- Squeeze juice from lemon.
- Combine and beat in a bowl 1 tbsp. Light butter with cocoa powder.
- Take another bowl and blend well the rest of the butter with flour, sugar, eggs and lemon juice.
- Transfer half of the mixture into a cake pan.
- Put half of the cocoa blend, spread, add the rest of the butter layer, and crest with remaining cocoa.
- Put into the air fryer and cook at 360°F for 17 minutes.
- Serve on a platter after it cooled down.

Nutritional information:

- Calories: 221 kcal
- Protein: 6.1 g
- Fat: 8.9 g
- Carbohydrates: 26.1 g

42. Simple Apple Bread

Preparation Time: 5 minutes
Cooking time: 40 Minutes
Servings: 6

Ingredients:

- 3 cup apples
- 1 cup sugar
- 1 tbsp. Baking powder
- 2 cup flour
- 1 tbsp. Vanilla extract
- 2 fresh eggs
- 1 butter stick
- 1 tbsp. Apple pie spice
- 1 cup natural freshwater

  Preparation:

- In a bowl, blend well with a mixer: eggs, vanilla, sugar, butter stick and apple pie spice.
- Place apples and turn.
- In another bowl, mix baking powder and flour.
- Combine the 2 mixtures, add water, turn and transfer them to a pan.
- Cook at 320°F for 40 minutes.

  Nutritional information:

- Calories: 304 kcal
- Protein: 7.5 g
- Fat: 4.2 g
- Carbohydrates: 58.3 g

43. Banana Bread

Preparation Time: 5 minutes
Cooking time: 40 Minutes
Servings: 6

Ingredients:

- ¾ Cup sugar
- 1/3 cup low-fat milk
- 1 fresh egg
- 1/3 cup butter
- 2 bananas
- 1 tbsp. Baking powder
- ½ Tbsp. Baking soda
- 1 tbsp. Vanilla extract
- 1 and ½ tbsp. Cream of tartar

Preparation:

- In a small bowl, blend flour, baking soda and baking powder.
- In a different bowl, mix the remaining Ingredients.
- Mingle the 2 mixtures, place in a pan and then in the air fryer.
- Cook at 320°F for 40 minutes.

Nutritional information:

- Calories: 289 kcal, Protein: 4.6 g, Fat: 12.5 g, Carbohydrates: 39.8 g

44. Petit Gateaux

Preparation Time: 5 minutes
Cooking time: 20 Minutes
Servings: 3
Ingredients:

- 1 fresh egg
- 4 tbsp. Sugar
- 4 tbsp. White flour
- 2 tbsp. Oil
- ½ Tbsp. Baking powder
- 4 tbsp. Low-fat milk
- ½ Tbsp. Orange zest
- 1 tbsp. Cocoa powder
- Salt

Directions:

- Mix all Ingredients in a bowl.
- Transfer mixture in oiled ramekins.
- Arrange ramekins in the air fryer and cook at 320°F for 20 minutes.

Nutritional information:

- Calories: 222 kcal, Protein: 5 g, Fat: 13.2 g, Carbohydrates: 22.3 g

45. Nutmeg Apples With Maple Syrup

Preparation Time: 10 minutes
Cooking time: 10 Minutes
Servings: 4
Ingredients:

- 1 tbsp. Maple syrup
- 2 tbsp. Cinnamon powder
- 4 tbsp. Light butter
- ½ Cup fresh water
- 5 fresh apples
- ¼ Cup white flour
- ½ Tbsp. Nutmeg powder
- ¾ Cup oats
- ¼ Cup brown sugar

Directions:

- Warm up apples in a pan over medium heat.
- Pour in maple syrup, nutmeg, cinnamon, and water.

- In a bowl, blend butter with flour, sugar, salt, and oat. Turn.
- Sprinkle the mixture over the apples.
- Place everything into the air fryer and cook at 350°F for 10 minutes.

Nutritional information:

- Calories: 371 kcal
- Protein: 4.7 g
- Fat: 13.5 g
- Carbohydrates: 69.4 g

46. Berries Cheesecake

Preparation Time: 20 minutes
Cooking time: 20 Minutes
Servings: 6
Ingredients:

- 2 tbsp. Light butter
- ½ Tbsp. Nutmeg powder
- 16 oz. Cream cheese
- 2 fresh eggs
- 1 tbsp. Rum extract
- ½ Cup ginger cookies
- ½ Tbsp. Vanilla extract
- ½ Cup sugar
- Berries

Directions:

- In a bowl, create ginger cookie crumbs.
- Brush the pan with the butter and scatter evenly cookie crumbs on the bottom. Put in the fridge.
- In a bowl, beat rum, vanilla, nutmeg, and eggs. In the end, sprinkle the cookie crumbs.
- Place the mixture in the air fryer and cook at 340°F for 20 minutes.
- Remove the pan from the fridge and pour over it the cream.
- Decorate with berries.
- Place the cheesecake in the fridge for about 2 hours.

Nutritional information:

- Calories: 347 kcal, Protein: 8.6 g, Fat: 28.9 g, Carbohydrates: 13.4 g

47. Vanilla Cookies

Preparation Time: 10 minutes
Cooking time: 14 Minutes
Servings: 12

Ingredients:

- 6 fresh eggs
- 4 oz. Cream cheese
- ½ Tbsp. Baking powder
- 3 oz. Cocoa powder
- 2 tbsp. Vanilla extract
- 6 oz. Coconut oil
- 6 tbsp. Brown sugar

Preparation:

- Mix all Ingredients in a blender.
- Line with foil a baking dish.
- Place the mixture into the baking dish.
- Bake it in the air fryer at 320°F for 14 minutes.
- Remove the baking dish from the fryer and cut the cookie sheet into rectangles.

Nutritional information:

- Calories: 261 kcal, Protein: 6.2 g, Fat: 21.9 g, Carbohydrates: 9.8 g

48. Hazelnut Brownies

Preparation Time: 10 minutes
Cooking time: 22 Minutes
Servings: 4

Ingredients:

- 1 fresh egg
- 1/3 cup cocoa powder
- 1 tbsp. Peanut butter
- 1/3 cup sugar
- ¼ Cup flour
- ¼ Cup hazelnuts
- ½ Tbsp. Vanilla extract
- 7 tbsp. Light butter
- ½ Tbsp. Baking powder
- Salt

Preparation:

- Warm pan with 6 tbsp. Butter and the sugar over medium heat. Turn and cook for 5 minutes.

- In a bowl, blend well cocoa powder, salt, eggs, vanilla extract, hazelnuts, baking powder, and flour.
- Pour the butter sauce over the above mixture. Mix well and place everything back in the pan.
- In a bowl, combine peanut butter with 1 tbsp. Light butter and heat in microwave for a few sec.
- Top with brownies blend.
- Bake at 320°F for 17 minutes.

Nutritional information:

- Calories: 338 kcal, Protein: 5.6 g, Fat: 27.5 g, Carbohydrates: 21.3 g

49. Blueberry Scones

Preparation time: 10 minutes
Cooking time: 10 minutes
Servings: 10

Ingredients:

- 1 cup flour
- ½ Cup heavy cream
- 1 cup blueberries
- 2 tbsp. Vanilla extract
- ½ Cup light butter
- 2 fresh eggs
- 6 tbsp. Brown sugar
- 2 tbsp. Baking powder
- Salt
- Vanilla ice cream

Preparation:

- In a medium bowl, mix well baking powder, blueberries, flour and salt.
- In a different bowl, blend heavy cream, sugar, eggs, vanilla extract and butter.
- Combine the 2 mixtures, until dough is created.
- Cut the dough into 10 triangles.
- Place them on a baking sheet.
- Cook them at 320°F for 10 minutes.
- Serve cold and decorate with ice cream.

Nutritional information:

- Calories: 222 kcal, Protein: 3.4 g, Fat: 13.5 g, Carbohydrates: 21.2 g

Conclusion

Throughout this book, we aimed at informing and guiding you effectively through every element of the Lean and green diet. We have provided recipes, tips and guidelines to help you make the most of your experience with the Lean and green diet. We want you to walk away from this book feeling satisfied and prepared for your journey with the Lean and green diet. However, After 13 chapters, some of the information may have become a little fuzzy, i've summarized all of it here for you.

The Lean and green diet aims to promote weight loss through a low-carb, high-protein diet in which sugar is not allowed. The diet has three different plans to choose from. All of these plans consist of eating six small meals a day. Depending on the diet plan you chose, a large portion of your meals will be provided by ways of prepackaged, ready meals or snacks called fuelings.

Each diet plan is focused on where you are in your life and what your desired outcome is. The first plan is the Optimal Weight 5 & 1 plan. This is the most common plan for people looking to lose weight quickly. In the 5 & 1 plan, you will eat five fuelings a day, and one meal which you will have to prepare at home. The second plan is the Optimal Weight 4 & 2 & 1 plan. This plan is almost the same as the 5 & 1 plan. However, it was designed to be a bit more flexible for people who have problems with sticking to diets, or a change in lifestyle. The plan consists of four fuelings a day, two homemade meals and one snack per day. The third plan is the Optimal Health 3 & 3 plan. This plan is for people who have finished their diet plan and are trying to maintain their weight and healthy lifestyle. The designated Optimal Health fuelings in this plan contain less nutrients than the others because you are supplementing with three Lean and Green meals; thus, you should be receiving enough nutrients from these meals.

The Lean and green diet is designed to help people lose weight fast and healthily through reducing calories and carbohydrates via portion controlled meals. In the Optimal Weight 5 & 1 plan, you will be limited to 800–1000 calories a day divided into six equal portions. Five of these portions are supplied by the Lean and green fueling products. These products have been designed to be high in fibre, low in sugar and contain probiotics and Garcinia Cambogia. While the research shows mixed results, it can be said that studies have shown greater results in weight loss with meal replacement plans compared to those with the traditional calorie-restricted diet schemes. Studies also suggest that reducing your overall calorie intake is as effective for weight and fat loss as low carb diets. This means that, in terms of ideal weight loss strategies, the Lean and green diet covers all three of these important factors in weight loss.

Following the Lean and green diet, itself, is relatively easy. All you really need to do is follow your routine of eating the necessary six meals a day, every two or three hours. In all of the three Lean and green diet plans, a large quantity of your meals will consist of fuelings. The choice of which fuelings you eat are dependent on you. All that is left that

you really have to do is follow your schedule. All that is left is your Lean and Green, homemade, meals.

When it comes to the Lean and Green meals, they have been designed specifically to give you the optimal amount of nutrients, each day, with every meal. They provide a healthy portion of fibre, vegetables, healthy fats and lean proteins. All of these elements are specifically measured and stated at the beginning of each recipe so you can control your intake on your own. Or if you do not feel confident to do it on your own, you can sit down with your couch and design meal plans.

While creating these meal plans, one of the most important elements is to ensure that you are receiving enough vitamins and minerals, fibre, plant compounds, healthy fats and proteins. Each of these work hard with your body, through various processes, to keep it running smoothly and comfortably. Without them functioning properly, you are at more risk for chronic diseases, such as kidney disease and type 2 Diabetes. You will also feel more lethargic and have a lower mood. This is all because the food we eat acts as our natural fuel to keep our body going. In this way, we should look at the food we eat as a type of medicine. Some food does have medicinal properties, such as cinnamon for blood pressure, pineapple which helps for indigestion, and turmeric helps for inflammation and swollen joints.

In the instance of the Lean and green diet, like any diet, there are some people who should not follow the diet for their own, various reasons. The first is anyone under the age of 13, as they are still in their development stages and stunted calories may negatively affect their growth. The second group is that of pregnant women or women who are breastfeeding. This is because it is important to eat as much nutrients and minerals as possible during this time, and not limit yourself. The third group necessary to mention, is anyone who exercises vigorously for more than 30 minutes a day. If you do, you will essentially be burning off more calories, through the exercise, than you are taking in through the diet. Needless to say, this could be detrimental to your health. Next, is anyone who has a health condition in which they take specific medication, such as high blood pressure medication. Or anyone that has an illness that may be thrown off by a change in diet. Finally, we focus on anyone who suffers from an eating disorder, as their main focus should be on receiving enough nutrition as possible, and keeping themselves healthy.

That being said, for those that can follow the Lean and green diet, there are things that you can and cannot eat. Alcohol is a big no-no. Not only for health reasons but for the way it promotes your appetite. Next, only healthy fats are allowed, so all those yummy products that we're so used to, like butter or coconut oil, are off the table. Lastly, anything containing high amounts of sugar is not allowed. This is because sugar promotes weight gain and is an unhealthy, quick filler to your meals. All this basically means that you will still be indulging, but in similar, healthier alternatives. What you will focus on eating while on the Lean and green diet is lean proteins, high fibre products, vegetables and various condiments, to keep the food from becoming bland.

We're hoping that throughout this book, with the introduction of the recipes, diet plans and fuelings, that you will now feel confident to take on the Lean and green diet. We have added around 100 recipes for your convenience sprinkled lightly throughout the book, as well. This is to ensure that you have no problems when it comes to having to make your own Lean and Green meals. There is no better satisfaction than working hard to create a well-rounded and healthy life. You will not only feel better, but you will look healthier and more energetic.

Meal Plan 5&1

	WEEK 1	WEEK 2
Monday	Chicken Nuggets Parmesan Zucchini Rounds Berry Mojito Brownie Cookies Delicious French Toast Sticks 90. Tuna Salad (L&G)	Flavorsome Waffles Cabbage and Radishes Mix Chocolate Donuts Berry Mojito Zucchini Spaghetti Grilled Split Lobster (L&G)
Tuesday	Maple Pancakes Little Fudge Balls Chocolate Donuts Mocha Cake Vanilla Shake 46. Bacon Frittata with Asparagus(L&G)	Brownie Pudding Cups Peanut Butter Cookies Maple Pancakes Green Bean Casserole Pumpkin Waffles Creamy Pork Belly Rolls (L&G)
Wednesday	Richly Tasty Crepe Tropical Smoothie Bowl Cabbage and Radishes Mix Shamrock Shake Flavorsome Waffles Pasta with Avocado and Cream (L&G)	Shamrock Shake Vanilla Shake Tiramisu Shake Little Fudge Balls Tropical Smoothie Bowl Chicken and Bok Choy (L&G)
Thursday	Green Bean Casserole Peanut Butter Cookies Pumpkin Waffles Vanilla Frappé Tiramisu Shake 98. Beef with Mushrooms (L&G)	Vanilla Frappé Parmesan Zucchini Rounds Delicious French Toast Sticks Richly Tasty Crepe Mint Cookies 37. Meatball Lasagna (L&G)
Friday	Mint Cookies Zucchini Spaghetti Brownie Pudding Cups Crunchy Cookies Potato Bagels Orange Chicken (L&G)	Mocha Cake Chicken Nuggets Brownie Cookies Crunchy Cookies Potato Bagels Pumpkin Smoothie (L&G)
Saturday	Green Bean Casserole Mocha Cake Zucchini Spaghetti Vanilla Shake	Potato Bagels Vanilla Shake Berry Mojito Maple Pancakes

	Brownie Pudding Cups	Mocha Cake
	Quinoa Porridge (L&G)	Grilled Salmon with Cucumber Dill Sauce (L&G)
	Cabbage and Radishes Mix	Parmesan Zucchini Rounds
	Pumpkin Waffles	Vanilla Frappé
Sunday	Shamrock Shake	Little Fudge Balls
	Maple Pancakes	Cabbage and Radishes Mix
	Peanut Butter Cookies	Richly Tasty Crepe
	Vinegar Chicken(L&G)	Risotto with Green Beans and Sweet Potatoes (L&G)

	WEEK 3	WEEK 4
	Peanut Butter Cookies	Peanut Butter Cookies
	Pumpkin Waffles	Brownie Cookies
Monday	Tropical Smoothie Bowl	Vanilla Shake
	Brownie Pudding Cups	Tropical Smoothie Bowl
	Brownie Cookies	Shamrock Shake
	34. Spaghetti Squash with Cheese and Pesto (L&G)	Chicken Enchilada Soup (L&G)
	Flavorsome Waffles	Crunchy Cookies
	Crunchy Cookies	Chocolate Donuts
Tuesday	Tiramisu Shake	Mocha Cake
	Green Bean Casserole	Flavorsome Waffles
	Shamrock Shake	Cabbage and Radishes Mix
	97. Veggies and Fish Bake (L&G)	48. Tuna Cobbler (L&G)
	Chocolate Donuts	Chicken Nuggets
	Chicken Nuggets	Zucchini Spaghetti
Wednesday	Zucchini Spaghetti	Richly Tasty Crepe
	Mint Cookies	Brownie Pudding Cups
	Delicious French Toast Sticks	Potato Bagels
	Plum and Avocado Smoothie (L&G)	Tilapia Tacos (L&G)
	Brownie Pudding Cups	Mint Cookies
	Pumpkin Waffles	Maple Pancakes
Thursday	Shamrock Shake	Vanilla Frappé
	Brownie Cookies	Green Bean Casserole
	Tropical Smoothie Bowl	Pumpkin Waffles
	Air Fryer Pork Chop & Broccoli (L&G)	Roasted Pepper Pork Prosciutto (L&G)

	Peanut Butter Cookies	Parmesan Zucchini Rounds
	Potato Bagels	Tiramisu Shake
Friday	Green Bean Casserole	Little Fudge Balls
	Vanilla Shake	Berry Mojito
	Delicious French Toast Sticks	Delicious French Toast Sticks
	Zucchini Omelet (L&G)	Beef with Broccoli or Cauliflower Rice (L&G)
	Chicken Nuggets	Zucchini Spaghetti
	Zucchini Spaghetti	Brownie Pudding Cups
Saturday	Flavorsome Waffles	Vanilla Frappé
	Tiramisu Shake	Crunchy Cookies
	Chocolate Donuts	Potato Bagels
	Green Apple Smoothie (L&G)	86. Turkey Meatballs with Herbs (L&G)
	Maple Pancakes	Maple Pancakes
	Mocha Cake	Delicious French Toast Sticks
Sunday	Little Fudge Balls	Green Bean Casserole
	Vanilla Frappé	Mocha Cake
	Cabbage and Radishes Mix	Shamrock Shake
	37. Meatball Lasagna (L&G)	25. Salmon Burgers (L&G)

Meal plan 4&2&1

	Week 1	Week 2
Monday	Brownie Cookies	Cabbage and Radishes Mix
	Crunchy Cookies	Mocha Cake
	Vanilla Frappé	Tiramisu Shake
	Potato Bagels	Green Bean Casserole
	29. Chicken Omelet (L&G)	Tilapia Tacos (L&G)
	Green Mango Smoothie (L&G)	Chicken & Zucchini Muffins (L&G)
	70. Taco Stuffed Portobellos (Snack)	53. Mint Chocolate Cheesecake Muffins (Snack)
Tuesday	Richly Tasty Crepe	Vanilla Frappé
	Mint Cookies	Delicious French Toast Sticks
	Shamrock Shake	Potato Bagels
	Chicken Nuggets	Zucchini Spaghetti
	28. Zucchini Frittata (L&g)	Baked Cheesy Eggplant with Marinara (L&G)
	Chicken & Strawberry Lettuce Wraps (L&G)	Mozzarella Pork Belly Cheese (L&G)
	71. Mini Pepper Nachos (Snack)	59. Personal Biscuit Pizza (Snack)
Wednesday	Tiramisu Shake	Berry Mojito
	Mocha Cake	Peanut Butter Cookies
	Pumpkin Waffles	Chocolate Donuts
	Flavorsome Waffles	Tropical Smoothie Bowl
	36. Fish Lettuce Tacos (L&G)	Green Pea Guacamole (L&G)
	Cheesy Cauliflower Soup (L&g)	Lean and Green Smoothie 1 (L&G)
	67. Pinto's & Cheese Fueling Hack (Snack)	49. Cauliflower Pizza with Chicken & Tzatziki (Snack)
Thursday	Tropical Smoothie Bowl	Richly Tasty Crepe
	Peanut Butter Cookies	Chicken Nuggets
	Vanilla Shake	Crunchy Cookies
	Berry Mojito	Pumpkin Waffles
	Coconut Pancakes (L&g)	43. Chicken & Zucchini Pancakes (L&G)
	80. Winter Salad (L&G)	Pork Dumplings with Sauce (L&G)
	69. Grilled Mahi with Jicama Slaw (Snack)	54. Neapolitan Froyo Popsicles (Snack)
Friday	Cabbage and Radishes Mix	Flavorsome Waffles
	Zucchini Spaghetti	Parmesan Zucchini Rounds
	Delicious French Toast Sticks	Brownie Cookies

	Parmesan Zucchini Rounds	Vanilla Shake
	30. Chicken Pesto Pasta (L&G)	Basil Duck Fillet (L&G)
	88. Pan Fried Salmon (L&g)	Zucchini Omelet (L&g)
	64. Buffalo Cauliflower Wings (Snack)	66. Very Veggie Dip (Snack)
	Chocolate Donuts	Mint Cookies
	Green Bean Casserole	Shamrock Shake
Saturday	Richly Tasty Crepe	Cabbage and Radishes Mix
	Mint Cookies	Mocha Cake
	31. Crab Cakes (L&g)	Plant-Powered Pancakes (L&G)
	Maple Lemon Tempeh Cubes (L&G)	Crispy Pork Cutlets (L&G)
	72. Curried Chicken Salad Wraps (Snack)	73. Cilantro Lime Fish (Snack)
	Brownie Cookies	Green Bean Casserole
	Crunchy Cookies	Vanilla Frappé
Sunday	Vanilla Frappé	Delicious French Toast Sticks
	Potato Bagels	Potato Bagels
	42. Chicken Cordon Bleu (L&G)	Pork Chop with Brussels Sprout (L&G)
	77. Cheesy Zucchini (L&G)	Carrot Cake Oatmeal (L&G)
	61. Caprese Pizza Bites (Snack)	70. Taco Stuffed Portobellos (Snack)

	Week 3	Week 4
	Chicken Nuggets	Vanilla Shake
	Mint Cookies	Peanut Butter Cookies
Monday	Flavorsome Waffles	Mocha Cake
	Vanilla Shake	Flavorsome Waffles
	Maple Lemon Tempeh Cubes (L&G)	27. Mini Mac in a Bowl (L&g)
	81. Energizing Mocha Smoothie (L&g)	Risotto with Green Beans and Sweet Potatoes (L&G)
	51. Thin Mint Cookies (Snack)	63. Smash Potato Grilled Cheese (Snack)
	Pumpkin Waffles	Delicious French Toast Sticks
	Potato Bagels	Vanilla Frappé
Tuesday	Vanilla Frappé	Green Bean Casserole
	Chocolate Donuts	Pumpkin Waffles
	41. Avocados Stuffed with Salmon (L&G)	95. Salmon with Pineapple (L&g)
	Chicken & Broccoli	Roasted Pepper Pork Prosciutto

	Bake (L&G)	(L&g)
	50. 2-Ingredient Peanut Butter Energy Bites (Snack)	58. Skinny Chicken Queso (Snack)
Wednesday	Parmesan Zucchini Rounds	Richly Tasty Crepe
	Berry Mojito	Zucchini Spaghetti
	Tiramisu Shake	Cabbage and Radishes Mix
	Tropical Smoothie Bowl	Chicken Nuggets
	47. Spaghetti Squash Casserole (L&g)	Basil 'n Lime-Chili Clams (L&g)
	78. Veggie Crusty Pizza (L&G)	Baked Potato Topped with Cream Cheese and Olives (L&G)
	63. Smash Potato Grilled Cheese (Snack)	65. Cheddar & Chive Savory Smashed Potato Waffles (Snack)
Thursday	Crunchy Cookies	Potato Bagels
	Brownie Cookies	Berry Mojito
	Delicious French Toast Sticks	Shamrock Shake
	Zucchini Spaghetti	Tiramisu Shake
	34. Spaghetti Squash with Cheese and Pesto (L&G)	Grilled Salmon with Cucumber Dill Sauce (L&G)
	Corner-Filling Soup (L&G)	84. Free Tofu (L&G)
	57. Mini Peanut Butter Cups (Snack)	51. Thin Mint Cookies (Snack)
Friday	Peanut Butter Cookies	Crunchy Cookies
	Shamrock Shake	Tropical Smoothie Bowl
	Green Bean Casserole	Brownie Cookies
	Mocha Cake	Chocolate Donuts
	Chicken & Asparagus Frittata (L&g)	48. Tuna Cobbler (L&g)
	Quinoa with Vegetables (L&G)	Chicken & Zucchini Muffins (L&g)
	56. Cranberry Sweet Potato Muffins (Snack)	60. Mini Cranberry Orange Spiced Cheesecake (Snack)
Saturday	Cabbage and Radishes Mix	Parmesan Zucchini Rounds
	Richly Tasty Crepe	Mint Cookies
	Flavorsome Waffles	Vanilla Frappé
	Tiramisu Shake	Crunchy Cookies
	33. Pasta with Avocado and Cream (L&G)	Curried Pumpkin Soup (L&g)
	82. Flavored Sandwich Filling (L&g)	Chicken & Bell Pepper Muffins (L&g)
	68. Personal Portobello Mushroom Pizzas (Snack)	72. Curried Chicken Salad Wraps (Snack)

	Maple Pancakes	Mocha Cake
	Mocha Cake	Flavorsome Waffles
Sunday	Little Fudge Balls	Delicious French Toast Sticks
	Vanilla Frappé	Vanilla Frappé
	44. Lemon Parmesan Salmon (L&g)	38. Lettuce Salad with Beef Strips (L&g)
	Watermelon Strawberry Smoothie (L&G)	Watermelon Kale Smoothie (L&g)
	61. Caprese Pizza Bites (Snack)	70. Taco Stuffed Portobellos (Snack)